"*The Integration of Psychology and Christianity* is an excellent and comprehensive overview of integration in the following areas or domains: worldview , theoretical, applied, role, and personal. I highly recommend it as essential reading for everyone interested in integration and as a required text in courses on the integration of psychology and Christianity."

Siang-Yang Tan, senior professor of clinical psychology at Fuller Theological Seminary and author of *Counseling and Psychotherapy: A Christian Perspective*

"By approaching the question of how to integrate Christianity and psychology in various levels and domains, Hathaway and Yarhouse have provided an immensely valuable resource for both newcomers and the well initiated. I appreciate the scholarly depth and personal care that energizes this excellent book."

Justin L. Barrett, author of *Thriving with Stone Age Minds: Evolutionary Psychology, Christian Faith, and the Quest for Human Flourishing*

"Hathaway and Yarhouse provide an articulate and cogent presentation supporting the integration of psychology and Christianity. Both are seasoned clinicians, teachers, and administrators with a wealth of knowledge and experience. They provide a comprehensive review of five domains of integration: worldview, theoretical, applied, role, and personal. While highly philosophical in the early worldview and theoretical domains, their discussion becomes much more clinical and personal in the later domains. They offer a compassionate and clear discussion of important issues in integrating psychology and Christianity while holding a high view of Scripture and valuing the science of psychology. One of the novel areas they discuss is role integration, in which they advocate for taking leadership positions and influencing the mental health professions in ways consistent with the historical roots of Christian faith. This book has broad relevance to the field and should be especially helpful to advanced undergraduate and graduate students."

Clark D. Campbell, senior associate provost and professor of psychology, Biola University

"Two seasoned and sophisticated Christian psychologists update the discussion of Christianity's relation to the science and practice of psychology, using a 'domain' framework that helps make clear and accessible sense of the whole field. I recommend it."

Robert C. Roberts, distinguished professor of ethics, emeritus, Baylor University

"In demonstrating the comprehensiveness of a domain-based approach, the authors draw on psychological theory, clinical theory and research, philosophy, Christian theology, social justice, and the psychology of religion and spirituality, at points justly illustrating their exposition with their own remarkable contributions to the field. A truly brilliant tour de force by two of the leading integrationists of our time, writing at the apex of their immensely productive careers, that aptly shows how much the Christian integration movement in psychology has accomplished and how far it has progressed since its founding in the 1970s."

Eric L. Johnson, professor of Christian psychology at the Gideon Institute of Christian Psychology and Counseling, Houston Baptist University

The Integration of
PSYCHOLOGY &
CHRISTIANITY

|

A Domain-Based Approach

|

William L. Hathaway and
Mark A. Yarhouse

Foreword by Stephen E. Parker

Academic
An imprint of InterVarsity Press
Downers Grove, Illinois

InterVarsity Press
P.O. Box 1400, Downers Grove, IL 60515-1426
ivpress.com
email@ivpress.com

*InterVarsity Press® is the book-publishing division of InterVarsity Christian Fellowship/USA®, a movement of
students and faculty active on campus at hundreds of universities, colleges, and schools of nursing in the United
States of America, and a member movement of the International Fellowship of Evangelical Students. For
information about local and regional activities, visit intervarsity.org.*

*All Scripture quotations, unless otherwise indicated, are taken from The Holy Bible, New International
Version®, NIV®. Copyright © 1973, 1978, 1984, 2011 by Biblica, Inc.™ Used by permission of Zondervan.
All rights reserved worldwide. www.zondervan.com. The "NIV" and "New International Version"
are trademarks registered in the United States Patent and Trademark Office by Biblica, Inc.™*

*While any stories in this book are true, some names and identifying information may have been changed
to protect the privacy of individuals.*

Figures 2 and 3 are in the public domain.

Cover design and image composite: Autumn Short
Interior design: Jeanna Wiggins
Image: Vector geometric pattern: © naqiewei / DigitalVision Vectors / Getty Images

ISBN 978-0-8308-4183-7 (print)
ISBN 978-0-8308-4184-4 (digital)

Printed in the United States of America ♾

*InterVarsity Press is committed to ecological stewardship and to the conservation of natural resources in all our
operations. This book was printed using sustainably sourced paper.*

Library of Congress Cataloging-in-Publication Data

*Names: Hathaway, William L. (William Lloyd), author. | Yarhouse, Mark A.,
    1968—author.*
*Title: The integration of psychology and Christianity: a domain-based
    approach / William L. Hathaway and Mark A. Yarhouse.*
*Description: Downers Grove, IL : InterVarsity Press, [2021] | Series:
    Christian association for psychological studies books | Includes
    bibliographical references and index.*
*Identifiers: LCCN 2021012983 (print) | LCCN 2021012984 (ebook) | ISBN
    9780830841837 (print) | ISBN 9780830841844 (digital)*
*Subjects: LCSH: Psychology—Religious aspects—Christianity. |
    Christianity—Psychology.*
*Classification: LCC BF51 .H385 2021 (print) | LCC BF51 (ebook) | DDC
    200.1/9—dc23*
LC record available at https://lccn.loc.gov/2021012983
LC ebook record available at https://lccn.loc.gov/2021012984

| P | 25 | 24 | 23 | 22 | 21 | 20 | 19 | 18 | 17 | 16 | 15 | 14 | 13 | 12 | 11 | 10 | 9 | 8 | 7 | 6 | 5 | 4 | 3 | 2 |
| Y | 37 | 36 | 35 | 34 | 33 | 32 | 31 | 30 | 29 | 28 | 27 | 26 | 25 | 24 | 23 | 22 | 21 |

To those colaborers
in the integration project who have
preceded us and to those who will follow.

CONTENTS

FOREWORD

Stephen E. Parker

IF YOU HAVE PICKED UP THIS BOOK, chances are good that you have an interest in the "integration" of psychology and Christianity. Perhaps like me your interest has spanned many years encompassing the many permutations of such endeavors. Or perhaps you are just beginning your exploration of this topic in a college or university course where this is an assigned text. Either way, you are in for a treat. I dare say this is one of those rare books where you will find yourself wishing the authors had written more.

There is much to like in this book. The novice and veteran alike will find their organizing paradigm (the domain approach) a helpful way to reflect on the various ways one might approach the integration of Christian faith and clinical theory and practice. In addition, the historical overview at the beginning of each chapter provides an excellent orientation not only to the larger integration project but to what has been done in each of the separate domains. The opening chapter reminded me of my own beginnings with the integration question and the bewildering variety of voices I encountered. I found their sorting and summarizing of decades of work a model of clarity that well prepares one for what follows.

Although both of the authors are clinical psychologists by training and direct this writing toward a primary audience of those in the clinical mental health professions (e.g., psychologists, counselors, social workers), the "domain" approach outlined here has applicability beyond clinical work. Not only do I think nonclinical psychologists (e.g., industrial-organizational or developmental ones, even those interested primarily in theoretical psychology) will find this approach of interest, I also see other professions such as clergy, nurses, educators, and human relations specialists benefiting from this approach.

In making this observation I speak from personal experience. My own training in the integration of psychology and theology began outside the discipline of clinical psychology. Having obtained master's degrees in both psychology and Christian ministry, I enrolled in a chaplaincy training program at a psychiatric hospital. There I was challenged to think about and practice integration in a variety of the domains identified in this book (e.g., theoretical, applied, role, and personal) although we didn't call them domains so much back then. The goal of that integration program was to move in the direction of becoming more whole (psychologically and spiritually) within one's own personhood (this is one of the models of integration the authors discuss). This work as a clinically trained chaplain spurred me to pursue further integrative work, which resulted in a doctoral degree in "theology and personality studies."

As you might guess, this program was weighted heavily on theoretical integration (e.g., of various theologies and personality theories). It was exciting to pursue this work under the tutelage of people like James Fowler, whose work in faith development provided one way of looking at the intersection of theology and psychology, while others exposed me to object relations psychology and its potential for understanding religious development. This latter study lead to a special interest in the work of D. W. Winnicott, while my theological training was deepened with courses in the theology of people like Kierkegaard and Moltmann. I found myself stimulated by these various theoretical intersections and remember thinking, while writing a doctoral exam that invited a comparison and contrast of the nature of the self in Kierkegaard and object relations theory, *What a great question!* Since then, much of my own work has been in the area of theory integration. For instance, I have explored how one's developmental history influences the way one thinks about God (I even wrote about this in Winnicott's life). On the other hand, I have written about various ways the Holy Spirit is at work in human development. As I read this book as one not trained in clinical psychology, I found myself repeatedly resonating with what I read. You too will find yourself interacting with what you encounter here, whether you're formally trained as a clinician or not.

There are other things to like in this book as well. The main audience of Christian clinicians will value their metaphor of "mining" Christianity for psychological insights. One often hears the complaint that the integration traffic between Christianity and clinical thought and practice seems heavily traveled in the direction of psychology to Christianity (e.g., adapting various REBT models for use with Christians), but not so well traveled in the direction from Christianity to psychological thought and practice. In an explicit articulation of how

Christianity has informed clinical practice, the authors explore some of the exciting work on the inclusion of things such as forgiveness, gratitude, and graciousness in clinical protocols. In a more implicit way, the authors also mine Christian theology for an anthropology (basic view of the human) that might inform the way clinicians think about their work (e.g., a contrast between Augustine's and Irenaeus's anthropology—more on this later). This is one of the areas where I found myself wishing they had written more!

In addition, I think the chapter on role integration will help young professionals in particular to think about the issues involved when one takes on a professional role regulated by the state and tries to line this up with living faithfully to one's Christian values when these seem to come into conflict. The authors are good role models in this regard as they share something of their own experiences with this.

Finally, the reader will appreciate the irenic spirit in which this book is written. Although helping the reader understand that the relationship between Christianity and science involves a complex history, they also point out how various Christian theologies have influenced how the integration question is approached (e.g., Roman Catholic vs. Reformed Protestant Christianity). For instance, I found their connection between how Augustine's theology compared to Irenaeus's theology might help one understand how differing clinical models think about their primary task as either repairing something that is broken or developing something toward maturity to be not only insightful but a breath of fresh air. This irenic spirit is also present as they describe some of the ways that evangelical Christians differ in approaching these questions. Where they differ from others or have a clearly articulated preference, they treat alternative approaches with fairness and appreciation.

It has been my privilege to have worked with the authors of this book and to have observed and benefited from the development of the approach offered here as well as from their examples as Christian professionals. I think you too will profit from them and commend this book to you without reservation.

ACKNOWLEDGMENTS

INTEGRATION, IF IT FULFILLS ITS POTENTIAL, incorporates all of life. So this list is no way exhaustive and feels incomplete. Early on, a vision for integration arose through the books and mentors I (Bill) encountered in the InterVarsity fellowships I attended. My professors in my undergraduate psychology and philosophy programs at Taylor University, such as Mark Cosgrove and Win Corduan, provided key foundations for me. In my graduate training at Bowling Green State, I am indebted to the Christian faculty who provided an integrative oasis, such as Bruce Edwards and James Taylor. Ken Pargament's mentoring was deeply formative in my thinking about how spiritual functioning is a vitally relevant and normal area for study in the psychology-related disciplines. I would have little reason to be concerned about integration if it were not for those spiritual leaders who modeled a desire to live out the lordship of Jesus in all of life: Enoch and the wonderful staff at Spring Hill Camps, Pastors Miller and Smith, and those faithful disciples with whom I had the privilege to serve in the military.

The Regent faculty, staff, and students have been sources of wonderful insight, feedback, and encouragement over these last twenty years and are too numerous to call out by name here, but I am indebted to you all. The wonderful network of Christian scholars at our small family of sister faith-based institutions have been integrative role models and trailblazers. There is a lifetime of brief but generous encounters with many who have contributed to the integration project, such as a lunch mentoring conversation with Donald MacKay after my first attempt at a scientific conference presentation as a grad student. For Mark's friendship, collaboration, and persistence in seeing this project to completion. To my wife Viva and family who have endured my pursuit of the integration project throughout our family history, I cannot express enough my gratitude for your love and support. Finally, may anything of value from these integrative musings be attributed to the Author and Perfecter of the integrated life that awaits all of us who pass through Calvary's way.

• • •

In any attempt to acknowledge people who have shaped my thinking on integration, I (Mark) run the risk of leaving out important contributions from those who have influence me through the years. Some of them I have not had the chance to meet or have only met as an acquaintance (James K. A. Smith, Alvin Plantinga), while others I had as professors at some point in my education (Nicholas Wolterstorff, Mary Stewart Van Leeuwen), while others were mentors and colleagues (Stanton Jones, Richard Butman, Mark Talbot). I would also like to thank Bill, in particular, for his friendship and for the countless conversations over many years, often extended informal discussions about Christianity and psychology, particularly in the areas of role integration, but in every domain we cover in this book. Former colleagues Jen Ripley, Cassandra Page, James Sells, and Olya Zaporozhets have been a part of ongoing integration conversations for many years, as were many colleagues at the university.

I want to thank colleagues at Wheaton College who sat in on monthly integration forums the year before publication and provided helpful feedback on drafts of the book chapters, including Terri Watson, Ben Pyykkonen, David Van Dyke, Raymond Phinney, Sandra Rueger, and Ted Kahn. I would also like to thank colleagues Sally Canning, Ward Davis, Tao Lui, John McConnell, and Barrett McRay for their ongoing encouragement and support. As I direct the Sexual & Gender Identity Institute, I am also grateful for current and former students and staff who have been a part of SGI in recent years, including Micaela Hardyman, Chuck Cruise, Ashley Lewis, Anne Seibert, Ethan Martin, Kevin Biondolillo, Daniel Thomas, Matt McRay, and Kelly Arensen. Former students and now colleagues Julia Sadusky, Heather Brooke, Charity Lane, and Emma Bucher have also shaped my thinking on clinical integration discussions in important ways. My wife, Lori, is a constant source of support and encouragement in my own faith journey. There are many others, I am certain, who have influenced my thinking and helped me work out some difficult topic or find a way forward on a subject that was difficult for me to work out. I am grateful for those friends and colleagues who have been such an important part of these integration discussions.

1

INTEGRATION

The Very Idea

I

FOR SEVERAL DECADES NOW, students and professionals have been investing their time, talents, and resources in pursuit of the "integration" of the profession and science of the contemporary psychology-related fields and Christianity. This book provides an overview of this *integration project*, focusing on psychology but also touching on its development in related fields such as professional counseling, marriage and family therapy, and social work. We will focus on work done in the clinical and professional areas of these fields, which is where most of the integrative writing has been done; it is also the specialization area for both of the authors. Yet we believe the approach we take in this book has relevance to integration in the nonclinical areas of psychology as well and will illustrate that with examples in each chapter.

In the context of psychology and Christianity, the term "integration" has been used to refer to the integration of different sorts of things: the integration of Christian theology and psychological theory, Christian spiritual disciplines and psychological practice, Christian and professional values, replacing select worldview assumptions of contemporary psychology with Christian ones, and even the revision of approaches to psychological "knowing" that allow for theologically informed psychology. Also, it is important to note, while not framed explicitly as an integration project, Catholic efforts to formulate a Christian approach to a scientific psychology were present since psychology's earliest decades or perhaps even before. Recently, attention has been given to Ferdinand Überwasser of the Old University of Münster. As an eighteenth-century Catholic scholar holding the title of professor of empirical psychology and logic (Schwarz & Pfister, 2016), Überwasser conceptualized an empirical psychology a century before Wilhelm Wundt, whose laboratory psychology is frequently presented as the start of psychological science.

Efforts at the integration of faith and academic disciplines are of course not unique to psychology and Christianity. There have been formal efforts to integrate Christianity with law, medicine, and various natural sciences. The fashionable rendering of the phrase "integration of faith and learning" has been credited to Art Holmes (1975) in his *The Idea of a Christian College*, although the notion was evident in earlier works (i.e., Gaebelein, 1954).

There are several possible starting points that could be identified for this contemporary psychology-related integration project in the evangelical world. In 1952, Taylor University's Hildreth Cross published *An Introduction to Psychology: An Evangelical Approach*. In 1954, Clyde Narramore, together with his wife, Ruth, launched the successful *Psychology for Living* radio program and other ministries. The Christian Association for Psychological Studies (CAPS) was founded in 1956 with an integrative mission. Fuller Theological Seminary launched its doctoral programs in clinical psychology in 1965 with a stated desire to "put the cross at the center of psychology." Out of the work done by the Narramores, the similarly pioneering Rosemead School of Professional Psychology was birthed in 1968. Professional integrative journals, such as the *Journal of Psychology and Theology* and the *Journal of Psychology and Christianity*, have now published regular volumes of integrative work for decades. The establishment of rigorous, peer-reviewed venues of this sort to disseminate scholarly work in an academic enterprise is necessary for a scholarly project to be taken seriously. It also functions as a marker that the project has to some degree become a meaningful niche within a discipline.

In addition to the growth of integrative doctoral programs in professional psychology, the latter part of the twentieth century witnessed an explosion of integrative masters and undergraduate psychology and counseling programs at Christian schools. Many of these programs have tailored themselves to prepare their students for careers in related mental health professions outside of psychology, such as licensed professional counseling or marriage and family therapy. There have also been organized efforts to integrate Christianity and social work. For instance, the North American Association of Christians in Social Work grew out of a series of conferences held at Wheaton College in the early 1950s. Its mission is to ". . . equip its members to integrate Christian faith and professional social work practice" (NACSW, 2020).

This book will be most directly focused on the integration project in psychology, but we believe it will be directly applicable to frame integration efforts in the related mental health fields as well. While we are both psychologists, we also have relevant experience with these related fields. Bill is dean of a school that includes CACREP-accredited professional counseling and an APA-accredited doctoral program in clinical psychology. Mark is credentialed as a marriage and family therapist and also teaches in an integrative psychology department that also has dual APA and CACREP accreditation. Both have supervised trainees and instructed courses for students in a range of these mental health professions.

Beyond these North American efforts, the academic integrationist movement has gone international, spawning programs such as the Moscow Christian School of Psychology in 1995 and other collaborations such as The European Movement for Christian Anthropology, Psychology and Psychotherapy. Outside of academic settings, explicitly integrative Christian practice contexts have grown to represent the spectrum of practice contexts (i.e., group practices, psychiatric inpatient and residential facilities, interdisciplinary one-stop shops, consultation centers, etc.). In addition, applied integration contributions have also occurred at a semi-popular level drawing from Christians in a variety of mental health professions and counseling ministry vocations. On the counseling front, Collins's (1980) influential *Christian Counseling* text provided a wide-ranging guide offering practical guidance on how to counsel from a faithfully Christian approach informed by the mental health fields. Collins expanded on this resource by serving as the general editor for dozens of volumes of a series of professional Christian counseling texts covering a wide range of counseling problems during the 1980s and 1990s.

The American Association of Christian Counselors started in the 1980s and grew rapidly in the following decades. It has emerged as the largest professional trade association in Christian counseling with nearly 50,000 members and holding large conferences of Christian caregivers from diverse professional backgrounds. The conferences feature the most popularly influential contributors in Christian counseling, such as Mark McMinn, Gary Smalley, and Larry Crabb. As Christian life and leadership coaching has emerged as a distinct niche for integrative mental health professionals, the AACC conferences have also showcased high impact Christian professionals in this niche. For instance, Henry Cloud and

John Townsend (1992) are frequent presenters, known both for their bestselling self-help books on boundaries as well as their highly successful training and consulting enterprise impacting millions within the church and corporate world.

Given the sheer growth of its academic, institutional, and applied forms, the integration project seems well on its way to realization. Integrationists typically believe they bring a value-added contribution to both their psychology-related disciplines and their Christian communities. Our assessment is indeed that progress has been made and the project has become more sophisticated. Still, there remain foundational issues to be worked out and many aspects of the project into which the integration community is just now venturing. For instance, what scientific methodology should characterize an integrative approach to the psychology-related fields? To what extent can biblical revelation and Christian thought be an explicit source of ideas for psychological theory development? How do professional ethics relate to biblical morality? How are we to navigate professional/disciplinary role conflicts with Christian norms? How can the church be effectively engaged in a manner well-aligned with the mission of God's kingdom to help resolve the world's critical mental health crisis?

The purpose of this text is to take stock of the project to date, to provide an introduction for individuals who wish to come on board, to highlight work yet to be done, and to offer a framework we think may strategically organize and focus this work. We presume both the value of contemporary psychological science *and* the truth of Christianity. While some of our reasons for believing these starting points are warranted will be evident, we will not attempt to offer a full apologetic for them in this text.

Some have claimed the integration project is inherently flawed and needs reformation or possibly even reformulation under a different label and vision— although none have emerged as a widely accepted alternative among those Christians who enter the academic and applied discipline of psychology. Such integration project detractors have made their cases on varied grounds, which we will engage throughout this book. We remain open to the idea of shifting to a new label for the integration project should a compelling one emerge. However, we are not aware of any proposed alternative that more accurately summarizes what Christians have been attempting to achieve under the integration banner.

Proposals by Christians who find value in the psychology-related fields have included an emphasis on ideas such as transformation, conversation, or *thinking Christianly* about our disciplines, which still seem to us—at their core—an integrative endeavor. Some dissenters from the integration project are discontent with what they perceive as an anemic presence of Christian thought and life or the professional/scientific weakness of its product. From our perspective, to the extent these concerns are founded, this represents inadequate realization of the integration project, not an inadequacy integrative vision itself.

The term "integration" has been put to sundry tasks in contemporary discourse beyond this specifically Christian endeavor. The *Oxford Learner Dictionary* defines integration as "the act or process of combining two or more things so that they work together." The Latin origin for the term conveys the notion of "renewal, restoration to wholeness." So virtually anything that is not already whole can be considered grist for the integration mill. As a fruit of the civil rights movement, many settings were *integrated*, bringing previously segregated racial groups within the same schools or public venues. In chemical engineering, *process integration* attempts to design its product more efficiently by considering the interaction of the various component processes from the outset.

Integration projects have been seen in purely secular contexts. The interdisciplinary movement in academia has attempted to build models, degree programs, and garner institutional support for integrating across disciplines. In some cases, these efforts have even spawned their own interdisciplinary study areas and degrees. One way of thinking about contemporary psychology is that it emerged from the interdisciplinary study of natural science, anthropometrics, medicine, and philosophy. It can be understood as arising from attempts to use investigative methods inspired by the experimental sciences of the nineteenth century to answer questions in what might today be called *philosophy of mind* and *ethics*. In that sense, it was an *integrative* discipline from its inception.

More recently, the American Psychological Association's *Standards of Accreditation for Health Service Psychology* (2015) have formally identified the discipline-specific knowledge areas requires to be covered in an accredited psychology program. These include topics familiar to psychology majors like cognitive, biological, or social aspects of behavior. But with the 2015 standards came an added requirement for programs to cover "advanced integrative knowledge" in psychology, (abbreviated "AIK" in accreditation shorthand). AIK is defined as ". . . graduate-level scientific knowledge that entails integration of multiple basic discipline-specific content areas" (APA IR C-7 D). The advanced integrative knowledge requirement came about in recognition that work in psychology routinely cuts across disciplinary subfields like social, cognitive, or biopsychology.

Research projects are now common in areas such as social cognition and cognitive neuroscience. APA does not delineate what specific topics or methods may constitute an AIK area, only that it involves the integration of multiple foundational areas at a graduate level.

Regardless of the specifics of what one is attempting to integrate, the integrative project assumes there are components to be brought together that are currently not united. But synthesis is not automatically a good thing. If we integrate spoiled milk with our cereal, it does not result in an improved breakfast. Such is the concern of integration project critics. These critics can be roughly placed into two camps. The first camp includes several proponents for a psychology or counseling approach derived from explicit Christian sources—either entirely or to a much larger degree than is evident among most integrationists. The nouthetic biblical counseling movement, associated initially with Jay Adams, argues that psychology operates from unbiblical beliefs that are detrimental to a biblically faithful approach to human functioning or to counseling. The very idea of integrating psychology and Christianity has been taken by some to imply some insufficiency in the Christian faith. If Jesus has provided us with abundant life, then why should we need to turn to this odd, Darwinian modern enterprise of psychology to fix our broken marriages, bind-up the demoralized, or "find ourselves"? Such ways of stating the issue seem to cast a shadow over the entire project. But this is only because the appropriation of psychology is somehow considered a divergent tangent from the redemptive and life-giving work of the Spirit. While not *antipsychology*, the Christian psychology movement has also criticized integration efforts in psychology for being insufficiently informed by Christian revelation and theology. Conversely, a second camp consists of some in the secular mental health professions and psychological disciplines who view the integrative project as an attempt to subvert the science and profession of psychology with religious bias and nonscientific beliefs.

Both camps feel their "breakfasts" would be ruined by the integration project, but they could not disagree more about what is the "spoiled milk." We will return to such perspectives throughout the text and find insight in their criticisms. Suffice it to say for now, we do not fit in either camp. Our view is that the integrative project in psychology, however it might be labeled, is a vitally important way to advance related concerns in both psychology and Christianity. Done properly, such a synthesis is enriching, holding the promise of a better psychology and further realization of essential Christian ideals in human lives.

Two Books—One Author

Another related discussion is central to locating our integration project: the issue of the unity of truth and the scope of Scripture. Consistent with others who approach this matter from an evangelical position, we hold to a high view of the authority of Scripture, seeing the Bible as true in all that it affirms. What is the range of truth God reveals to us in the Bible? Should Christians expect psychological science to be able to yield productive insights for our understanding of the human condition and how to intervene in it? Unlike the secular psychologist who rejects Christian faith, we believe Scripture provides psychological truths about humanity. Yet within at least some portions of the Christian world, differences may exist about *how much* truth one would expect psychological science to offer about human functioning relevant to Christians.

The idea that God reveals truth in two books has been implicit since ancient times in Christian thought and was explicitly stated in 1605 by Francis Bacon (McGrath, 2000). The two books are the books of nature and Scripture. By stating God is the author of both books, Christians typically mean that God has created the world and our knowing faculties in a way that reveal truths he intends for us to know from nature, and likewise has so inspired the writers of Scripture to convey the truths he intends for us to know from special revelation (i.e., Scripture). The idea is not that the Bible was literally *dictated* by God. Nor does this concept of the Bible as *God's Word* deny that the human authors God used to write Scripture reflected their own personalities, languages, and historical situations in their writings. But since the same perfect God reveals truth in these two books of world and Word, it does imply that the truth revealed therein will not conflict.

The most common view on this matter by Christians who have held to a high view of biblical authority is that God has revealed what is needed for our salvation and his kingdom purposes during this age in between the resurrection and the return of Christ. Scripture provides a sufficient revelation that perfectly provides what God intends us to know through it (Vanhoozer, 2016). What is it that God intends for us to know from special revelation? Christianity has not typically presumed God revealed all truths about creation through Scripture. God did not intend the Bible as a standalone textbook on what can be known about all matters. Instead, it more commonly asserted that God has revealed in Scripture all that is needed for Scripture to serve as a yardstick against which Christian belief and practice is to be measured. Through the design of our senses and other providentially created natural faculties, God also made possible the discovery of other truths about creation that help us navigate our lives and world. Because both sources of truth are divinely provided, they will always be ultimately reconcilable since the same Creator speaks through both the book of Scripture and "book" of nature. This notion, that God is the author of all truth and that any truth that is discoverable from any source *is* God's truth (Holmes, 1977) has been a core inspiration for the integration project.

Still, this does not mean, that any particular Christian or group of Christians will be able to reconcile all data—either from Scripture, nature, or both—at any particular moment this side of the return of Christ. God's knowledge is absolutely true, but we are not God: "we have this treasure in jars of clay to show that this all-surpassing power is from God and not from us" (2 Cor 4:7). How is one to interpret Scripture, and what role should any biblical theology we derive from it play in any systematic theology that would be implicit or explicit in an integrated psychology? The answer one might give to these questions will be impacted by specific theological traditions and approaches that one brings to the text and the data.

Such discussions are the preoccupations of theologians, and we can at best give a cursory opinion here. Our integrative approach holds that Scripture is inspired in such a way that it has sufficient clarity to serve the functions God desires, which minimally include being a standard for Christian belief and practice. But *we will not* place a boundary around what God may reveal through Scripture in advance of actually looking to see what God appears to be saying through the text. To put the matter a bit more technically: we accept no *a priori limiting principle for the scope of Scripture.* Something is *a priori* if it is held prior to examining the evidence. While an *a priori* limiting principle may help prevent conflicts by rendering Scripture mute on any topic outside of the predetermined boundaries, one needs to have sufficient biblical and theological warrant to accept such a principle if one is to respect the authority of God, who is the source of all truth. We have not been convinced there is biblical or theological warrant for such a limiting principle and remain open to Scripture functioning as a source of truth on knowledge areas more commonly informed by science in our era. Of course, this would not mean we know in advance that God intends to reveal truth about such things in the Bible. We simply strive to remain open as we engage the Scriptures. For example, if the teaching of Scripture is clearly that there is a continuation of the person in a disembodied state, then we would reject physicalist monism, the idea that we consist only of our bodies and its properties.

Physicalist monism is a metaphysical view, a belief about the nature of reality but not a finding of science. However, it is widely assumed in contemporary neuroscience—at least about humans. The vitally important question for us is not what helps us to easily assimilate or correlate our Christian understandings within contemporary psychology, but rather what God does, in fact, reveal through his Word.

Christian understandings of health and our ability to help others contend with illness or injury are dramatically enhanced through the advances of modern medicine. Similarly, we believe psychological science has much to offer in the way of a Christian understanding of the human flourishing and languishing. Neither medicine nor psychology is infallible. When Scripture, rightly interpreted, conflicts with contingent findings of any human science, we hold Scripture to be the higher standard. Yet, just as when one carefully struggles to harmonize passages of Scripture that may on the surface appear at odds without rejecting any portion of Scripture, (such as James's and Paul's teaching on works and salvation), so too one should not quickly gloss over tensions that exist between a robust psychological finding and a prior Christian understanding. To be sure, psychological findings are derived from empirical observations which may not have even been replicated. Such findings are prone to human observational, methodological, and interpretative errors. But still, while the Word of God is completely true, our understanding of it is not infallible.

When a well-supported and robust psychological finding that has survived critical review creates tension within a Christian understanding, we would recommend holding such tension in mind in a prayerful state, seeking God's wisdom. The hermeneutical philosopher Paul Ricoeur (1981) argued that interpretative insight is fostered when a reader does not too quickly foreclose on a possible understanding of the text by failing to attend to those parts which do not fit well into that hasty interpretation. One engages in this overly hasty *assimilation* or foreclosure if, based on one's prior understandings, one jumps to a conclusion that does not well make sense of all the text before us. In such cases, readers ignore or discount the very parts of the text that could have corrected their misreading and led to new understandings.

Remaining in the *productive moment of tension* caused by attending to the alien (i.e., that which we do not understand and that does not easily assimilate) prompts creative new insights and possibilities. To the extent any contingent scientific finding leads us to an accurate rethinking of Scripture in a way that results in a new or expanded understanding of that text, we would, in fact, be aligning our understanding more, not less, with the authority of God's Word. We would be forming a *more biblical* understanding.

Let us consider examples of how persistent reflection or discovery have enhanced our ability to understand and correctly hear Scripture as Christians. We can see such a development in theology in the early Christian understanding of the diverse Old Testament prophetic streams Christians now have widely understood as messianic. These prophecies reflected figures often thought distinct from one another in the mind of Jews living in the Second Temple period (e.g., the promised Davidic ruler, the great high priest, the suffering servant), but the New Testament writers understood them as all being fulfilled in the person of Jesus (Bird, 2009). We can also see such productive novel Christian interpretation in the formulation of a trinitarian theology. Nicene Christians understand the doctrine of the Trinity as clarifying what one must say about God the Father, God the Son, and God the Holy Spirit to correctly convey what Scripture teaches (Sanders, 2016). We also see it in shifting understandings of biblical language that construed some biblical phrases as phenomenological or metaphorical rather than literal in the wake of changing understandings of the world from natural science. For instance, the verse, "He shakes the earth from its place and makes its pillars tremble" (Job 9:6) is understood now by Christians as metaphor, not a literal description of a stationary earth (Lennox, 2011). But such productive development is unlikely if the truth seeker glosses over the tension by too quickly reading their own prior prejudices about the text into their interpretation. If we either ignore the empirical realities to preserve a preexisting pet Christian understanding or contort Scripture to have it align with psychological claims, we will have likely missed God's truth. The resolution of such tension can only be truth productive if it faithfully represents both Word and world with the clear teaching of the Word never being compromised.

But to be attentive to such tensions, we need to believe that knowledge of the respective truths on an intersecting topic is possible both from Scripture *and* psychological science. This brings us back to the issue of the scope of Scripture. Some have rejected the need for psychological science for Christian counseling. Some biblical counselors have argued that regarding counseling, Scripture is sufficient for all we need to know in that area (Lambert, 2016). The sufficiency of Scripture proponents do not merely claim we can get all we need for counseling from the Bible; typically, they also assert there is something inherently flawed with psychological science when it addresses issues that inform counseling and clinical practice, making it an improper source for Christian caregiving. From a quite different direction, others understand the scope of Scripture to refer to such a truncated set of spiritual concerns, that the Bible rarely, if ever, is expected to impinge on the claims of psychological science. What the Bible appears to say about the nature of an immaterial soul, agency, human motivation, marriage and family life, sexuality, or any other topic is irrelevant to what our psychological science might address on such a view. The Enlightenment fact-value dichotomy common in theological liberalism may be reflected in this latter viewpoint: Scripture is seen, at best, as only a font of values, never a source of authoritatively revealed psychological facts (Rashkover, 2016).

Perhaps an illustration is in order of how Christians in the mental health fields may disagree with one another. Not too long ago, I (Mark) was invited, along with Mark McMinn, to a special convening of leaders in the Association of Certified Biblical Counselors (ACBC). After making presentations in areas of ethics and gender, Mark was asked during the Q&A session what biblical counselors get wrong about Christian integrationists. Mark shared that the attendees at the ACBC event appear to think integrationists have a low view of Scripture, when in fact integrationists view themselves as having a high view of Scripture precisely because they see themselves as carefully engaging themes and principles derived from Scripture but not demanding more from Scripture than what Scripture itself promises. Put differently, when Mark teaches on sexuality and sex therapy, he does not look to specific passages from Scripture for a protocol for therapy to treat a woman presenting with symptoms of what today is referred to as genito pelvic pain and penetration disorder. It is not that Scripture fails to address pain or sexuality; rather, it does not promise to deliver the level of details often looked for in developing intervention strategies for various concerns clinicians might address in their work.

We can see there are differences between how integrationists and biblical counselors view the scope of Scripture. At the same time, integrationists do not hold one position on the scope of Scripture. For our part, we do not believe in so narrow an understanding of that scope as to make scriptural claims irrelevant to our psychological theories and conjectures. Whenever Scripture speaks on a topic, affirming truths about it, we believe the Scripture assertion true and thus do not assume any *a priori* range of topics on which Scripture is silent. However, we also believe there are many aspects of the human condition that psychological science can inform us about that are not deducible from Scripture. We believe this to be the case even in areas that are the focus of psychological well-being and counseling. As with the discoveries of archeology, some of these psychological findings can elucidate the truths of Scripture in ways previously unknown to us but never in contradiction of the Scripture itself.

Two Ancient Christian Rationales for Integration

While the integration of psychology and Christianity may be a relatively new project, there are two ancient strands of Christian thought that resonate well with this integration project, each with a distinct focus. We might engage in integration in order to help repair what has been broken from the fall. We also might engage in integration to further grow into the mature bearers of God's image we were created to be. The former notion resonates with Augustine's theology of the fall, while the latter echoes Eastern Christian themes. Augustine conceptualized humanity's original state before the fall of Adam and Eve as perfect and complete. Sin brought with it a fracturing of perfection. Redemption is now, under this framework, a work of repair. As fallible, fallen human beings, we meander about the shattered pieces of our formerly paradisiacal world. We can only, in this present age, move forward by incremental degrees through divine providence and the sanctifying power of the Spirit toward a more unified, integral state of being that restores the damaged image of God humans were created to display. A vital part of that restorative providence is the special revelation God has provided to us through Scripture. The intellectual project for Christian believers in this fallen state is a *faith seeking understanding* (*fides quaerens intellectum*, Anselm's often cited phrase) that strives to reassemble from shards of our broken world something of the original that was shattered.

Rather than seeing our original state as pristine and complete, Irenaeus saw humanity as created innocent but immature. For Irenaeus, Adam and Eve were like children. Their moral failures were not a fracturing of the creative intent of God but rather predictable steps in human development. God allowed death to put an outer limit on human suffering and made the world in such a way that humans could begin a journey that would allow the image of God to be realized in a more mature and deeper way. For both Augustine and Irenaeus, the fall requires the redemptive work of Christ for our salvation. But for Irenaeus, a fuller image of God is to be realized by humanity through the postfall journey through redemption than was present before the fall.

Such perspectives have impacted psychology in ways that may be under-appreciated by many in the field. Martin Seligman is a pioneer for the contemporary positive psychology movement with its emphasis on cultivating strengths and positive emotion rather than focusing on mental illness. Dr. Seligman (2006) conducted a workshop on positive psychology at the university where both authors were employed at the time (i.e., Regent University). He provided a surprising example of how ancient Christian perspectives might be still impacting the psychological disciplines, and by extension, integration. Although not a Christian, he was aware of the faith foundations at Regent. During the workshop, he quipped that Western psychology has been too *Augustinian* and needs to be more *Pelagian.* By that he meant we have too heavily focused on repairing what is broken and fixing pathology rather than on promoting growth and health. While not convinced to move toward the heresy of Pelagianism from his comment, we appreciated his point about the Augustinian legacy in the psychological professions. It was noteworthy that such an influential leader in psychology readily acknowledged the large footprint left by Augustinian theological tradition on the secular discipline of psychology.

The two ancient orthodox theological understandings we have explored in this section both provide impetus for an integration project. They construe our journey to wholeness as a harkening back and restoration, in Augustine's case, and a developmental progression that benefits from even our failings, in the case of Irenaeus. Thus, on both of these theological perspectives, integration can be construed as serving a productive role. The Augustinian perspective might call for an integration project attempting to repair our brokenness from the vantage point of a creation paradigm that is the blueprint for well-being. The Irenaean view sees in our current state opportunities for discovery and transformative growth that moves further on the telos God has intended for us from the outset of creation. Both would not be surprised to see our lives, academic disciplines, and professions somewhat fragmented or in need of Christian alignment in this present age. Both would call us to a more holistic engagement of God's Word and world for fostering our development. Thus, we find ancient Christian rationales reinforce the contemporary motivation of those who labor with the integration project to press ahead.

A Metatheoretical Classification of Integrative Domains

In the first portion of this chapter, we described the concept of integration and briefly recounted some of the recent history around the integration of faith and learning construct in psychology. The integration project can be thought of crudely as a set of efforts to put together Christian faith and contemporary psychology. There have been many varied approaches to how integration is fleshed out, and there is no uniform strategy that has won the day. This has led some to argue for abandoning the integration moniker for the project and for pursuing some other term to serve as our clarion call. In this text, we will take a different strategy. We will continue to use the integration term but will try to capture some of the complexity in this project by using a *domain* framework. We are using domain here to mean an area of life which has perceptible demarcations, soft boundaries, responsibilities, and activities that characterize its area of life. The domains are different historically situated spheres of life for integration for all those who follow Christ and thus who are called to submit every area of life to the lordship of Christ.

An emphasis on, and/or taxonomy of, domains is present in multiple fields. The World Health Organization's (2001) *International Classification of Functioning* (ICF) delimits, defines, and codifies the adaptive life domains that can be impacted by illness. According to the ICF, "*Domains* are a practical, meaningful set of related physiological functions, anatomical structures, actions, tasks, or areas of life" (p. 216). It recognizes—but only briefly addresses—religion and spirituality as one of those adaptive life domains in which humans often function. Still, the ICF framework means an authoritative world body in health care recognizes that humans function in distinct, but often overlapping, life domains in ways that can reflect flourishing or impairment depending on the impact of diseases and other factors.

We would also assert that the Neo-Calvinist notion of *sphere sovereignty* advanced by Abraham Kuyper is relevant to our domain approach. Kuyper held there were different areas of life, each with their own distinct authority and responsibilities, with none subservient to the others (e.g., state, church, family, etc.). These spheres are all to be lived out *coram Deo*—"before the face of God" (Mouw, 2011). Kuyper's sphere sovereignty might be thought to imply an integration approach something like what Carter and Narramore (1979) referred to as one form of parallelism. A parallelist Christian of this type who is also a psychologist by vocation likely considers the explicit forms of the Christian life as distinct from one's conduct as a psychologist. Such a Christian would likely act indistinguishably from non-Christian psychologists during their practice hours or in their lab, apart from perhaps an added incentive to do excellent, ethical work "for the Lord" (Col 3:23). At church, they may be a typical Christian, fulfilling their Christian roles in that setting as well, perhaps as an elder or a faithful attender. Such a parallelism is a model for how to coexist as a psychologist and Christian, which may make sense only given certain approaches to role integration that we will return to in a later chapter.

We do not intend to imply anything like this sort of understanding by our use of the notion of integrative domains. We would argue that a default compartmentalization of professional life and one's Christian faith would rarely represent an integrative form of life. In addition, such compartmentalization overlooks the boundary diffusion within contemporary psychological science itself. Psychology is a highly diverse set of theoretical, methodological, and praxis habits, many of which naturally converge on areas of Christian understanding and praxis. We use the notion of domains to refer to some of the natural areas of recognizable effort, activity, and content in psychology within which Christians have been striving to live in biblically faithful ways before the face of God. Further, as we will see in later chapters, Christians have also been increasingly working to not only respond with biblical fidelity to the playing field delimited by these secular psychological domains but have been working to shape the domains and even to foster new ones.

Figure 1 presents our integrative domains model. Many of these are familiar labels or concepts in the integration literature. *Worldview integration* refers to the attempt to reposition contemporary psychology on a coherent biblical worldview. This typically involves the identification of the alternative worldviews informing and shaping psychology and a rethinking of how psychology is altered or informed when grounded on a biblical worldview. *Theoretical integration* attempts to modify psychological theories, especially personality theories, to fit with a Christian theological understanding, to cultivate psychological theories from the soil of Christian thought in a way that enhances psychological theory building, or to use psychological understandings to inform theology. *Applied integration* is the attempt to either culturally adapt or accommodate secular interventions or helping approaches for use with a

Christian population or to develop explicitly Christian interventions and helping approaches derived from Christian thought and practice. Most explicit discussion of applied integration has occurred in clinical or counseling practice, but a small number of integrative programs in other applied areas (e.g., the doctoral program in Industrial-Organizational Psychology at Seattle Pacific University) now exist. Tan (1996) noted that clinical integration may occur either explicitly or implicitly. *Explicit* integration involves a treatment that declares itself to be Christian or that utilizes a recognizable technique shaped by Christian thought or practice. *Implicit* integration occurs when standard practice approaches are used in a way that is guided by Christian beliefs or values despite there being no explicit Christian identification. *Role integration* refers to living out in integrity role expectations and patterns arising from a psychological vocation in a particular context in a way that is simultaneously faithful to one's Christian identity. Finally, we use *personal integration* to refer to the personal discipleship journey of the Christian who is a psychologist (or by extension any similar profession). Personal integration is illustrated by what Farnsworth (1985) called "wholehearted integration." Where much of the early work in the integration project was conceptual, focusing on theoretical integration, for instance, personal integration recognizes the central role of our spiritual formation of cultivation of Christian passions for the fully developed integration project.

Integration domains are not watertight compartments. They intersect each other and have mutual impact. However, we believe they represent distinguishable areas of thought, activity, and socialization in the profession of psychology. Each has at least some soft boundaries and distinctive enough concerns to make their being treated as separate spheres productive. We also believe this focus on worldview, theory, applied considerations, roles, and personal formation helps us understand the emphasis and impact of much of the integration effort to date and affords strategic opportunities for the integration project moving forward. There are missional and other reasons for Christians to not waste the opportunity to enter these domains in Spirit-filled and biblically faithful ways. We organize the chapters in our text around these domains as a result.

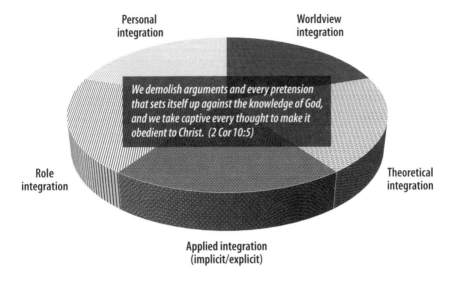

Personal integration

Worldview integration

We demolish arguments and every pretension that sets itself up against the knowledge of God, and we take captive every thought to make it obedient to Christ. (2 Cor 10:5)

Role integration

Theoretical integration

Applied integration (implicit/explicit)

Figure 1. Integration domains

Much of the early work in the integration of psychology and Christianity has been described by Worthington (1994) as "unsystematic and rudimentary" (p. 79). Worthington identified a "second wave" starting in the mid-1970s and declining by the early 1980s. The second wave was dominated by efforts at formulating integrative models that might be described as fitting largely into our theoretical and worldview integration domains. By the 1990s, Worthington saw a "third wave" emerging, characterized by greater effort at detailed intradisciplinary integration and empirical engagement, developments which he welcomed and invited. The last few decades have been marked by a greater emphasis on clinical integration and the emergence of evidence-based Christian treatment approaches and techniques (Worthington et al., 2013). A growing concern for navigating the demands of professional ethics and regulatory standards with Christian integration has been present in recent years reflecting the challenges of role integration (Sanders, 2013). Finally, scattered contributions on the importance and relevance of personal Christian formation for the Christian psychologist has been present during the integration project and has gained momentum with the spiritual direction trend in evangelicalism (Crisp et al., 2019). Before launching into our domain-focused survey, we will first consider the complex and foundational topic of method in psychological science.

Summary

The contemporary *integration project* represents an effort by Christians to, in some way, unify or integrate the contemporary psychological sciences and professions with Christianity. This project has precursors predating contemporary psychology but has gained most momentum over the last half-century by evangelical contributors. Integration efforts have been associated with a motivation to learn from God's two sources of revelation: Word and world. A parallel commitment is maintaining personal fidelity to the Christian faith and professional and scientific integrity in one's discipline. While some noteworthy evidences of progress exist, some integration project detractors have opposed the project or called for its reformulation. We find good reason to continue to explicitly pursue the integration project. A domain-based approach is offered to position existing integration work in a more organized fashion and to facilitate intentional progress on various aspects of the integration task. This framework will be used as an organizing framework for our presentation of the project in this text.

References

Bird, M. F. (2009). *Are you the One who is to come? The historical Jesus and the messianic question*. Baker Books.

Carter, J. D., & Narramore, B. (1979). *The integration of psychology & theology: An introduction*. Zondervan.

Cloud, H., & Townsend, J. (1992). *Boundaries: When to Say Yes, How to Say No to Take Control of Your Life*. Strand Publishing.

Collins, G. R. (1977). *The rebuilding of psychology: An integration of psychology and Christianity*. Tyndale House.

Collins, G. R. (1980). *Christian counseling: A comprehensive guide*. Word.

Commission on Accreditation. (2017). *Implementing Regulation C-7: Discipline-specific knowledge*. Author. Retrieved from www.apa.org/ed/accreditation/section-c-soa.pdf.

Crisp, T. M., Porter, S. L., & Ten Elshof, G. A. (Eds.). (2019). *Psychology and spiritual formation in dialogue: Moral and spiritual change in Christian perspective*. InterVarsity Press.

Farnsworth, K. E. (1985). *Wholehearted integration: Harmonizing psychology and Christianity through word and deed*. Baker Books.

Gaebelein, E. (1954). *The pattern of God's truth: Problems of integration in Christian education*. Oxford.

Holmes, A. (1975). *The idea of a Christian college*. Eerdmans.

Holmes, A. (1977). *All truth is God's truth*. InterVarsity Press.

Lambert, H. (2016). Counseling the sufficient Word. In H. Lambert, W. Mack, D. Bookman, D. Powlison (Eds.), *Sufficiency: Historic essays on the sufficiency of Scripture* (pp. 121-48). Association of Certified Biblical Counselors.

Lennox, J. (2011). *Seven days that divide the world: The beginning according to Genesis and science.* Zondervan.

McGrath, A. (2000). *Science and religion.* Blackwell.

McRay, B., Yarhouse, M. A., & Butman, R. E. (2016). *Modern psychopathologies: A comprehensive Christian appraisal* (2nd ed.). IVP Academic.

Mouw, R. (2011). *Abraham Kuyper: A short and personal introduction.* Wm. B. Eerdmans.

North American Association of Christians in Social Work. (2020). Mission & Christian Identity. www.nacsw.org/about-nacsw/mission/

Rashkover, R. (2016). Liberalism, post-liberalism and the fact-value divide. *Modern Theology, 33*(1), 140-62.

Ricoeur, P. (1981). *Hermeneutics and human sciences.* (J. B. Thompson, Ed. & Trans.). Cambridge University.

Sanders, F. (2016). *The Triune God.* Zondervan.

Sanders, R. (2013). *Christian counseling ethics.* InterVarsity Press.

Schwarz, K. A., & Pfister, R. (2016). Scientific psychology in the 18th century: a historical rediscovery. *Perspectives on Psychological Science, 11*(3), 399-407.

Seligman, M. E. P. (April 2006). *Positive psychology: Current developments and future directions.* Lecture conducted at Regent University.

Tan, S.-Y. (1996). Religion in clinical practice: Implicit and explicit integration. In E. P. Shafranske (Ed.), *Religion and the clinical practice of psychology* (pp. 365-87). American Psychological Association.

Vanhoozer, K. J. (2016). *Biblical authority after Babel: Retrieving the Solas in the spirit of mere Protestant Christianity.* Brazos.

World Health Organization. (2001). *International classification of functioning, disability, and health.* Author.

Worthington, E. L. (1994). A Blueprint for intradisciplinary integration. *Journal of Psychology & Theology, 22*(2), 79-86.

Worthington, E. L., Johnson, E. L., Hook, J. N., & Aten, J. D. (Eds.). (2013). *Evidence-based practices for Christian counseling and psychotherapy.* InterVarsity Press.

Yarhouse, M. A. (2015). *Understanding gender dysphoria: Navigating transgender issues in a changing culture.* IVP Academic.

Yarhouse, M. A. (2019). *Sexual identity and faith: Helping clients achieve congruence.* The Templeton Foundation.

Yarhouse, M. A., & Sells, J. (2017). *Family therapies: A comprehensive Christian appraisal* (2nd ed.). IVP Academic.

Yarhouse, M. A., & Tan, E. S. N. (2014). *Sexuality & sex therapy: A comprehensive Christian Appraisal.* IVP Academic.

PSYCHOLOGICAL SCIENCE

Christian Truth and Method

Figure 2. Duck-rabbit illusion (reprinted from Jastrow, 1899)

IN 1892, A GERMAN MAGAZINE published an ambiguous drawing asking whether it was a duck or rabbit. A version of this "duck-rabbit" illusion (fig. 2) has been reprinted by psychologists and philosophers since illustrating how perception is shaped, at least in part, by aspects of the perceiver's prior cognition rather than merely determined by the raw sensory input itself (Jastrow, 1899; Wittgenstein, 1953). In the early twentieth century, the Danish doctoral student Edgar Rubin (1915) wrote a doctoral thesis about optical illusions including the now famous Rubin vase (fig. 3), an image either seen as a vase or twin faces depending whether one is focusing on the figure or the background (Pind, 2012; Schooler, 2015).

These two images are examples of "bistable" images. These and many other perception studies have been undertaken by twentieth-century Gestalt psychologists and more recently by cognitive neuroscientists (Wiseman et al., 2011). The ambiguous images are ubiquitous in intro psychology textbooks as examples of how our perception of wholes (*gestalts*) is never simply a bottom-up assembly of the sensory features but rather a mental interpretation of the data filling in the gaps (Myers & DeWall, 2017). Just how much of what we *see* when we look at the world is a product of our prior mental habits, beliefs, contextual priming, or other mental characteristics we bring to experience?

Is Integration for Real? Knowledge, Reality, and Subjectivity in Constructivist Epistemology

It is likely no surprise that many social scientists believe human self and social understandings are heavily influenced by cultural beliefs and presuppositions. What many may not realize, however, is that a substantial stream of contemporary thought also holds that perceptions of the physical world are also a biased output of human subjectivity. Constructivist epistemology, a term popularized in psychology by Jean Piaget (1967), emphasizes that all mental perceptions we have of the world are "constructed" by the perceiver. There are nuances to this model and a spectrum of positions ranging from those that view humans as living in an entirely subjective world created from our mental life to those that see the external world as playing a substantially determinative role in what we perceive. Piaget's studies of cognitive development attempted to identify how and to what degree *a priori* cognition and incoming information from the senses interacted to shape our thinking. He saw his project in *genetic epistemology* as a scientific attempt to flesh out Kant's influential philosophical understanding of human knowledge from the Enlightenment.

Kant began his eighteenth-century philosophical explorations about the nature of knowledge as a rationalist, believing knowledge came from reason and innate ideas. After encountering Hume's account of empiricism arguing knowledge

Figure 3. Rubin Vase (reprinted from Schooler, 2015)

comes from the senses, Kant reports being awoken from his dogmatic slumber. He set about developing a model of epistemology that has since been understood as an attempted synthesis of rationalism and empiricism. On Kant's model, our perceptions of the sensible world are shaped and made possible by patterns of organizing sensory information that exist prior to sensory input—in an *a priori* manner. He believed we never directly perceive the world as it is in itself (i.e., the *noumenal reality*). Our perceptions are always of the *phenomenal* world, the world as it appears to us. The phenomenal world is synthesis of our *a priori* conditions of mind and the sensory input. As Kant (1987/1790) explained:

> If the human mind is nonetheless to be able even to think the given infinite without contradiction, it must have within itself a power that is supersensible, whose idea of the noumenon cannot be intuited but can yet be regarded as the substrate underlying what is mere appearance, namely, our intuition of the world [Weltan-schauung]. For only by means of this power and its idea do we, in a pure intellectual estimation of magnitude, comprehend the infinite in the world of sense entirely under a concept . . . (Kant, 1790, n.p.)

Critical Realism

Kant's position has been summarized in divergent ways by philosophers depending on what aspects of his thought they emphasize and how they have construed some of his claims. Kant referred to his own theory as *transcendental idealism* but understanding the nuances of what he meant by this label is one of the more contested points about Kant's philosophy (Stang, 2018). Regardless, his philosophy emphasized what has been called the *Kantian wall*: the assertion that we can only know things as they appear to us, not things as they are in themselves. This notion is core to *critical realism*, which holds something like the idea that we can know the world but only indirectly as reflected in our constructed mental pictures of it (Losch, 2009). This emphasis on indirect or mediated knowledge of the world has led some critical realists to think of truth in a manner similar to naive realists (i.e., those who think we can just see the world directly in an unmediated way). Truth is, on such accounts, a *correspondence*: an idea is true if it accurately represents (i.e., matches) the way the world is. Critical realists, unlike naive realists, however, do not claim to ever be able to determine when such an idea corresponds to the world with certainty.

Integrationists have taken a variety of positions on psychological epistemology and have frequently argued for varieties of realism (e.g., that there is a human mind–independent reality). Critical realism has tempered this longstanding evangelical emphasis on objective truth with an admission of our human fallibility as knowers. Christians believe in an all-knowing God who never errs in his knowledge. God's truth is *truth* about the way things really are. But God's perfect, absolute knowledge, even when revealed to us through inerrant Scripture, does not imply infallible human understanding of that truth. The Christian philosopher Corduan (1986) put it aptly: the Christian posture toward our Christian knowledge claims should be one of commitment with humility. We believe our Christian beliefs are true and God's truth a sure anchor. While we believe God has perfect knowledge, Scripture and history make it clear that *we* do not.

If perfect objective knowledge of truth is thought by Christians to only be present in the mind of God, then what role is left for objectivity in human knowledge? One possible answer often espoused by those influenced by postmodern thought is that objectivity is something we should move "beyond." Postmodern constructivists believe all knowledge is socially constructed. Thinking of our earlier discussion of Kant, they adopt a constructivism on steroids. They embrace the idea that all we know directly is the phenomenal world, and we believe that world is generated from our linguistic and cultural backgrounds. Some Christians have seen in this postmodern framework a leveling between scientific and theological claims making a way for theological perspectives to again have voice after a scientifically dominated age (Grenz, 1996; Watson, 2004). We will discuss this postmodern perspective more below but for now, suffice it to say, this view would see the demise of objectivity in accounts of knowledge, including those in psychology, as not entirely unwelcome.

A common alternative approach among integrationists who value psychological science involves attempts to preserve a belief in a mind-independent reality and knowledge that to some extent reflects that reality. Critical realism has been perhaps the most prevalent framework adopted for this goal among integrationists (Jones, 1994; Van Leeuwen, 1985). If a real world exists that God has made, if knowledge of truths about at least some aspects of that world are important for us in God's divine plan, and if God has made provision for us to achieve such knowledge, then the pursuit of objective knowledge becomes a Christian duty. To borrow the motto of Kepler that became a banner for key architects of modern science: We study psychological science to "think God's thoughts after Him." Such devotional insight is only nonidolatrous if we are at least glimpsing to some degree the mind of the Creator in our human knowledge of the creation.

Objectivism of a Sort

Christian varieties of realism found inspiration in the critical realism of the chemist-turned-philosopher Michael Polanyi (Meek, 2017; Polanyi, 1958). Polanyi's work influenced evangelical theology, especially through the theological writings of Thomas F. Torrance (1982). Independently, the Catholic theologian Bernard Lonergan (1997/1957, 1971) argued for an influential Catholic version of critical realism with convergent features. For Lonergan, the fact that humans can understand the universe at all, that it is intelligible, is best explained by the Christian view that there exists a real world independent of the human mind and a God who has designed us to afford at least some knowledge of that world (Fitzpatrick, 1982).

During my (i.e., Bill) graduate studies in philosophy, I attended a lecture by a renown philosopher of science, Marjorie Grene, who had worked with Polanyi. Grene, herself not a theist, gave a talk on the Catholic early-modern philosopher Descartes. She was struck at how God served as a *bridge principle* between human mental representations of the world and the external world for Descartes. If God is the sort of God Christians believe in, then he would not allow responsible truth seekers to be capriciously deceived about truth. While not convinced by Descartes's answer, she recognized it at least provided some reason to think knowledge was possible, and she confided that she did not have a clear basis for such confidence in her own thinking yet. A few years later in my doctoral psychology studies, a methodology professor was promoting evolutionary epistemology as such a bridge principle for psychology. Evolutionary epistemology argues that evolutionary forces exert selective pressures, over time, on our belief states such that truth-approximating beliefs persist longer than less true beliefs and thus yield progress in human knowledge (Campbell, 1974). I asked the professor why evolution would select for true beliefs as opposed to merely situationally useful beliefs that could even be false: research on protective illusions provide examples of beliefs that are demonstrably untrue but still functionally beneficial (Taylor & Brown, 1988). The professor could only offer the vague suggestion, against psychological counter-evidence, that true beliefs may be more psychologically adaptive over time.

Neither Polanyi nor Lonergan were unaware of the challenges to naive realism in contemporary thought and sought to show how objectivity still served a valuable role in our understanding of the knowing processes, even when accounting for the subjective aspects of knowledge highlighted by the constructivists. For Polanyi, objectivity is not about a detached perfect knowledge of the external world free of human subjectivity. Instead, objectivity is a participatory commitment of a knower to the object of study. Objective knowledge is "personal knowledge." Even with a full awareness of the fallibility of human knowing, the widespread Christian belief that there is a truth "out there" to be known, and a truth-giver to whom we are accountable, can foster a regulative ideal. This potent idea that real objective truth exists can motivate both our knowledge seeking aspirations and humility in our knowledge claims about that truth.

Common-Sense Realism

Both of us have been drawn to Christian forms of critical realism in light of these types of considerations. One of us (Bill) has also been increasingly drawn to another form of realism, known as *common-sense realism*. Common-sense realism, inspired by the eighteenth-century Christian philosopher Thomas Reid, rejects the *representational theory of mind*. Representationalism understands true beliefs in terms of a mental picture of the world perfectly copying the way the world is. In contrast, common-sense realism has been described as a *thermometer theory of mind*: we have true knowledge when our mental states accurately detect those aspects of the world they are designed to perceive. Mercury in a thermometer moves in proportional response to changes in temperature, but the changing mean kinetic energy in a room that humans perceive as a change in temperature bears little resemblance to this changing mercury line. The reality may be accurately tracked but is hardly *represented* by this instrument.

God has designed us to know things about the universe. Yet human knowing is, like that thermometer, a sensing of a subset of aspects of the world, not a God's eye view that perceives all reality exhaustively and without error *as it is in itself.* When a human has a visual image of the world that accurately tracks an object's movement or other visible features, true—but limited—knowledge is present. The visual picture in our heads is far from a complete and perfect image of the world. Just think of two examples: We do not perceive any electromagnetic energy radiating from an object that may be outside the narrow spectrum of light visible to humans. Nor do we perceive the microscopic space that exists within the object or its subatomic structure.

Common-sense realism, like critical realism, recognizes that God has designed humans to know truly but in limited ways (Wolterstorff, 2000). One difference between the two views arises over the issue of constructivism. The critical realist is more likely to embrace the language of construction. Our perceptions of all reality are mental constructs for the critical realist—a kind of limited sketch of the world drawn from the paper and ink of our prior mental contents. We can only ever know the sketch on a critical realist account.

In contrast to this global constructivism, common-sense realism does not see our mental contents as consisting entirely of constructions. The presence of some constructed mental content is not necessarily denied, but at least some perceptions are held to be direct readouts of the world. In *The Social Construction of What?*, Hacking (2000) has offered a cogent rejection of the idea that all knowledge is socially constructed. On the common-sense view, some aspects of reality can be known directly because those aspects cause our faculties sensitive to them to produce perceptions that accurately track the aspects being encountered. J. J. Gibson's (1966) work on optical ambient light shows that patterns of light in any given setting impact the eyes in ways that accurately convey perceptions of distance. This bottom-up process led him to argue that the senses should be considered a perceptual system in direct contrast to the dominant cognitive-constructivist view that sensation was a distinct process from perception.

Common-sense realism accounts for an aspect of experience that is not well explained by critical realism. If we only ever *know* the world as it appears to us, and if such appearances are always shaped by our prior sociocognitive or other features, how do we explain the robust transferable knowledge of the psychological world found and utilized by psychologists operating in different worldviews? Whether it is Miller's discovery of the "magic number seven" regarding short-term memory capacity, the demonstrable process of priming in cognitive psychology, or repression expounded by Freudian thought, such findings are often taken up and redeployed in very different theoretical frameworks. These are effects that can be re-demonstrated by others who interpret them in divergent ways from the original theorists that first identified them. This is not surprising for the common-sense realist, but it is unclear how constructivism can account for transferable, demonstrable knowledge clusters allowing us to reliably produce predictable effects in the world.

An important caveat is in order here. Common-sense realism was very influential in the nineteenth-century American academy and created a rich soil for the "new psychology" to launch its quickly secularized forms (Spilka, 1987). Yet some have charged that common-sense realism underappreciated the role of human fallenness in our cognitive capacities and presented too optimistic a view of human knowing even if devoid of explicit Christian starting points (Maier, 2004, Noll, 1985). Common-sense realism set the stage for Christians to be too optimistic about the potential of new social sciences to find agreement through scientific method regardless of the worldviews the scientists brought to their investigations. This, in fact, may be a fair criticism of nineteenth-century common-sense realism, but it is not an inherent flaw in the epistemology itself.

Common-sense realism looks to inductive examination of instances of reliable knowledge production to determine when investigations should be trusted and when they should not. A consequence of this is that what will count as a reliable knowledge pathway will be dependent upon what is actually attempted by a knowing community. Maier (2004) claimed that, following McCosh's common-sense realism, there were three themes that came to characterize the new discipline of psychology, which excluded the possibility of a psychological science that would include God as part of its explanatory approaches thus preventing any opportunity for a serious theistic psychological science to be explored. These included:

- a sharp division of intellectual labor between science and theology with scholars from both disciplines staying on their own turf

- a compartmentalization of science and faith as *separate spheres* for Christian scientists; such scholars should not let their faith influence their science

- the idea that as separate spheres, there would be no biblical or theological tests that would properly apply to science

From a Christian perspective, the quick degeneration in the latter part of the 1800s from a Christian moral psychology to a religion emancipated psychology characterized by a truncated naturalism may be seen as evidence that psychological methods are flawed when it comes to accurately sorting out spiritual realities. We do not find this surprising. Attempts to study matters of the soul primarily through laboratory methods inspired from experimental natural science would have little competency in tracking truth about nature transcendent realities. In recent years, reformed epistemologists have resuscitated common-sense realism with the qualification that on such matters as the belief in God, disagreement would be expected. This qualification arises from the view that the unregenerate mind has a compromised ability to detect the truth in that area due to the noetic effects of the fall (Plantinga, 2015; Wolterstorff, 2000). Thus, a common-sense realist does not necessarily assume that consensus on theological or spiritual aspects of reality would be forthcoming through scientific exploration, even if an otherwise productive scientific method is followed.

Before moving on to discussion of psychological methods, we will make a comment about another paradigm that has heavily impacted the psychological sciences. Pragmaticism is a distinctively American contribution to modern thought that sought to bypass perennial philosophical debates over topics about the ultimate nature of reality or objective truth in favor of what was of practical consequence to organisms contending with adaptive challenges they faced in the world (Robinson, 1996). The proponents of American pragmatism included influential contributors to the rise of the new psychology, such as William James and John Dewey. For the purposes of our discussion here, we would note that pragmatism asserted that human knowing, and even truth itself, are merely tools bequeathed us through evolution to adapt to the concrete realities of life. In one sense, pragmatic perspectives can be thought of as "antirealist" since they are not concerned about what is objectively true. Yet they also represent their own attempt to define truth, not on objective, mind-independent terms, but rather in terms of the practical consequences of *fruits* of an idea. While there are things to be learned from this paradigm, the integrationist movement has not widely embraced pragmatism for various reasons such as its instrumental view of truth (i.e., truth is merely just what is practically useful for the human knower). Still, pragmatism has impacted how psychology frequently approaches religion, as evidenced by James's (1997/1902) *The Varieties of Religious Experience,* or the early work of psychologists such as E. S. Ames. Despite his Christian background, Ames's acceptance of pragmatism led him to hold "that traditional interpretations of religion—interpretations marked by an adherence to metaphysical realism and the view that religious propositions correspond to reality—are unjustified and therefore should be rejected" (Clanton & Gunter, 2014, p. 379).

Psychological Science(s) and Method

Wolterstorff (1988) argued that Christian scholarship should take some foundational Christian ideas as axioms or truth claims that are taken as sufficiently established in order to function as starting points for further investigation. He referred to these as Christian *control beliefs.* Rather than first expending substantial energy on proving these beliefs to a non-Christian mind, we do what naturalists do. We simply go about our scholarship treating the control beliefs as axioms and then see what we can develop relying on them as starting points. Christian control beliefs are important for psychology to reach its full potential as a "science of the soul." Some of these have been at least partially inherited in psychology likely because of the deep Christian roots in the academy. That heritage is not typically appreciated or consciously realized by psychologists. Confidence in the view that reality is the sort of thing whose truths can be mined by science sprang up on theistic soil of the Christian vision of the academy. While some late nineteenth-century scholars advanced a notion that science and religion have always been at odds (i.e., the Draper-White warfare thesis), historians of sciences now more generally support a complexity thesis (Numbers, 2010). Religion has been the fertile soil and direct sponsor of much scientific activity and development, with occasional conflicts arising more from situational or contextual factors than any tension endemic to the science-religion interrelationship.

Contemporary psychology emerged from several converging influences in the mid-nineteenth century, which precipitated the "new psychology," as it was then called. Exploration of psychological topics had long been part of moral philosophy and theology. The nineteenth century's contribution was the attempt to frame psychological inquiry in light of things that could be explored as an objective science. Students in history and systems courses review the multiple psychological schools—psychophysics, structuralism, and functionalism—that gave rise to this new psychology. Behaviorism and psychoanalysis offered important new influences during the early twentieth century as the discipline differentiated further and grew into a global force. The third wave—humanistic psychology, the cognitive revolution, and behavioral neuroscience camps—were some of the other developments impacting psychology during the century and beyond. In addition to these scientific paradigms, the rise of professionally regulated psychology, especially after the Boulder Conference that created an early scientist-practitioner training model for clinical psychology, would have a transformative impact on the field moving many of its community from roles as academic-researchers to practitioners. This resulting trend led to tensions over the relative role of science and practice in contemporary psychology and the eventual factional separation of many psychological scientists from APA to form what is now the Association for Psychological Science.

Given this rapid and heterogenous development that occurred in this young discipline and even younger profession of psychology, it should not be surprising that psychology is currently a methodologically pluralistic discipline that, by some accounts, has resulted in a fractured disciplinary identity (Sternberg, 2005). Various "unity of psychology" proposals have been offered in response to this fragmentation. Given that the discipline of psychology itself has debated whether it is a coherent unified discipline, what sense does it make to talk about the integration of *psychology* with Christianity? That will remain a live question for any integration project. Similar "unity of science" debates are present in science as a whole and are not unique to psychology (Ruphy, 2017).

Two Methodological Camps

There are two broad methodological camps that have shaped psychology as a discipline with many forms of specific research method and investigatory cultures within those camps. The first camp is the natural science-inspired quantitative approaches that try to reliably and validly measure aspects of psychological functioning so that scientific psychological models can be evaluated considering this data. Experimental methods attempt to create controlled studies that allow for strong evidence about causes of observable psychological phenomena. Non-experimental quantitative methods attempt to demonstrate measurable relationships, group differences, attitudes, or other patterns that then can be used to test or build various psychological theories or models. Quantifiable methods are by their nature always at some level reductive and limited to what is measurable. This has at times led to the notion that psychological science must be totally reducible to the measurable and quantifiable (McFall, 1991).

A second disciplinary camp in psychology utilizes approaches to understanding human functioning more inspired by the humanities. Wundt, who is credited with founding modern psychological science with the opening of his experimental psychology lab in Leipzig, himself argued there needed to be two psychologies: one that studies the objective, measurable, and lawful features of human experience patterned after the natural sciences and a folk psychology more akin to scholarship in the humanities. In a related discipline of nineteenth-century historiography, Dilthey (1991/1893) talked about the dual scholarly goals of *explanation* versus *understanding* for his human science discipline. The natural science-inspired areas of psychology—such as studies of sensation and perception—were better positioned to develop explanatory models, while more literary aligned folk explorations were better suited for "data-thick" understandings that did not so much explain as elucidate or give context to phenomena. Methodological developments in both the quantitative and qualitative camps have continued to shape psychology-related investigations to this day. Yet in addition, a key current trend is to utilize *mixed method* approaches drawing from them both.

As psychologists who have been reading and contributing to psychological research articles for many years, we regularly find information that helps us better understand and better explain real-world psychological experiences of people. Furthermore, as clinical psychologists, we have both drawn from the tools of applied clinical science to understand and assist in intervening with the concrete difficulties facing our clients. Bill, for instance, during a two-year period, had the job of interpreting a Minnesota Multiphasic Personality Inventory administered to every inpatient that came on to an alcohol inpatient unit at a military hospital. The patients were admitted in twenty-person cohorts every two weeks. He wrote up the test results as a blind-screening, meaning they were scored and interpreted following the empirically informed approach developed for the MMPI without benefit of interview. The inpatients then met with Bill for testing feedback about halfway through the thirty-day program. The consistent experience of these feedback sessions is that testing had accurately identified and distinguished some major contributing factors to their alcohol abuse patterns. We could both offer many other examples but suffice it to say, despite the relatively early state of psychology as a scientific discipline, we have found it to be a treasure trove of information that is directly relevant to a wide swath of the human condition.

Should Christians have a particular approach to psychological science or methodology? One line of integrative thought is that Christians should be "humanizers of science" (Evans, 1977). This perspective argues that Christians should move away from the reductive, quantitative traditions that tend to disregard the rich world of human experience in favor of "human science methods" that are typically qualitative, phenomenological, or hermeneutic. Others argue against methodological naturalism seeing it as inherently biased against theism (Slife & Reber, 2009). A longstanding proposal in contemporary psychology is to limit psychological theories to what can be studied in natural terms. While on the surface this may be a nonstarter for a theistic worldview, proponents of methodological naturalism argue it is only an investigatory strategy intended to buttress the development of psychology as a science. Even if there are extra-naturalistic features to human existence, such as a supernatural dimension to persons, such features cannot be studied scientifically and are therefore outside the scope of psychological science. Slife and Reber (2009) are not persuaded and counter that there is no proper basis on which psychology should adopt a methodology that is implicitly biased against a potential theoretical/explanatory option.

We would argue that Christian-integrated psychology should indeed be humanized. A rigorous Christian-integrated psychology must understand the experiential and "soulish" world of humanity. But it would be question begging to see this as justification for the adoption of *qualitative-only* methods over quantitative ones unless one knows in advance that quantitative investigation of the person would be uninformative on a Christian view. If the experimentalists would have Christian psychologists function as humanity engineers, the qualitative-only proponents would limit us to being soul poets. We would take issue with any *a priori* limitation in our methods. God made us as embodied creatures whose physicality is governed by principles of the natural world. God made the universe in a way that can be enumerated both in number and kind. This is also true about at least a substantial range of the features of our embodied existence as humans. Material-biologic features of our existence have been profitably studied using natural science informed methods that continue to yield much fruit. But we are also living souls made in the image of God. Because the Christian belief in the Trinity holds that a perfect God exists eternally as a tripersonal being, this also implies that eternal state of being is relational (Hasker, 2013). Based on such a Christian view of persons and our role in creation, a careful analysis of meanings and our being-in-the-world is also needed for a Christian-integrated psychology. Thus, something like nonreductive, interpretative, phenomenological, and other qualitative approaches will be needed to supplement the quantitative approaches that focus on studying living things only in terms of what others can observe. A Christian psychological scientist, it would seem, should see the value and importance of understanding humans both as *objects* and *subjects* of study. Methods conducive to both investigation goals are needed.

While some general integrative approaches may be relevant to psychology in its varied forms, it is becoming increasingly evident that greater sophistication in integration will require integration at a more differentiated level. So, for example, there is a Christian integrative cognitive-behavioral psychology (viz., Pearce, 2016) or Christian integrative psychodynamic works (viz., Sorenson, 2004). Christian psychologists doing developmental cognition study in the cognitive science of religion have also explored ways to engage their field informed by a Christian perspective (viz., Barrett, 2012). This growth in Christians engaging in specialized, niche areas of psychological research and practice may suggest we have moved now to a form of engagement that would make any general models of integrating Christianity and psychology unproductive. Perhaps what we need is a vast number of integration projects tied to each focal area of psychological work. But we believe the domain approach we present through this book is compatible with an appreciation that the full form any integration project may take would likely be heavily shaped by the specific features of each area of research or practice in which one is engaged. The domain approach notes the areas of psychology in which these more local projects live and thus provides a meta-framework to call attention to shared integrative forms and concerns that may be frequent features in each domain.

While we are not prepared to offer a prescription for the specific forms of investigative activity that should universally characterize Christian integrative psychology, we can say something about the metacriteria for such methods in light of our epistemological discussions in this chapter. To the extent psychology is a science, it is one that asks research questions that can be answered with investigatory methods that have some potential to generate converging inter-subjective judgments in a community of scholars. To accomplish this, one must be competent in well-developed research approaches that can be understood and compellingly embraced by one's research peers. This means the research must be done in a manner that is open to peer review and reported in a manner that allows for replication, when possible, given the area of work.

A Christian recognition that humans are not reducible to mere matter or subject to purely reductive explanations does not mean Christians in the psychology-related fields are warranted in a pendulum-swing to viewing the psychological as having no observable public footprint. Gnosticism was an ancient heresy with which the church had to contend. The Gnostics viewed the material world as evil but believed we could be delivered from it by achieving an elite, esoteric spiritual knowledge. Once achieved, it would not matter what happened in our body because the body was not the *real us*. Some Gnostics justified living sinful lives because of this disregard for the body. It did not matter what happens with our embodied states as long as our spirit was enlightened. Against this type of understanding, John wrote:

> This is the message we have heard from him and declare to you: God is light; in him there is no darkness at all. If we claim to have fellowship with him and yet walk in the darkness, we lie and do not live out the truth. (1 Jn 1:5-6)

Humans made in the image of God are part of a reality that transcends the material. This does not mean the spiritual and physical are irrelevant to each other. Our spiritual state is reflected in visible fruits manifested in how we "walk" in the world. That which can be seen with the senses can be measured. Accordingly, we caution against an overreaction to the truncated naturalism present in psychology by going to the other extreme and acting as though the public, observable life of humans is irrelevant to what is important about them. Such an approach would be analogous to the errors of the Gnostics.

Christians should be aware of the truth-adducing potential of various psychological research methods as well as their limitations and wield them as effective tools to help the researcher glimpse the truth about psychological realities that are the focus of interest. Christians should well master any tool that helps us better understand God's creation. But we should also model the creativity of that Creator by developing inventive investigatory strategies that help psychology study human persons in a way well calibrated to the reality being studied. As with remarkable Christian scientists of the past, like Michael Faraday who developed ingenious laboratory tests demonstrating an underlying unity to two phenomena scientists of his day perceived as distinct (i.e., electricity and magnetism),

Christian integrative psychologists should be busy about developing new investigative methods capable of capturing the full range of reality we are trying to study when no available method is enough for the task.

The recent trend toward mixed methods, especially when looking at the religious dimensions of life, may be one way this could occur (Sisemore, 2016). For example, Mark has been utilizing mixed methods in his study of sexual minorities at Christian colleges and universities (Yarhouse et al., 2018). The quantitative measures provide helpful information on campus climate, psychological distress, and emotional well-being, while the qualitative interviews provide the humanizing aspects that enrich the overall account of the experiences of sexual minorities of faith.

Another way to approach research as a Christian could be a more creative application of standard research approaches but in a way that leaves open the full possibility of a view of the person that well accords with a Christian view. For instance, Barrett (2012) observes that the research in the cognitive science of religion shows children are naturally disposed in the course of development to believe in supernatural beings even if raised in an unbelieving context. But the choice of what to study about persons, and how to go about studying it, will be heavily impacted by what one thinks about an area before engaging in the research. This brings us back to the topic of worldviews, which will be the focus of our first integrative domain.

Summary

Contemporary psychology emerged from older philosophical, theological, and ethical approaches to its subject matter largely due to its demarcation from these fields as a new *scientific* approach. The rise of this *new psychology* emerged at a time when philosophical challenges to the idea of science as a way to learn about objective reality were being debated in the academy. Kant's critical realism suggested humans might be able to know things about reality but only in a mediated and indirect way. In the twentieth century, Kant's perspective was taken up by Swiss psychologist Jean Piaget in his constructivist approach to the development of cognition. Constructivism holds that mental perceptions of the world are constructed or built up by the perceiver from prior mental content. Some variety of constructivism is now widely held in the cognitive sciences.

Integrationists have widely embraced critical realism in their approaches to integration. It provides an account for how one can claim to be discovering things about reality through science while at the same time recognizing that our perceptions of reality are shaped by our prior beliefs. Thus, scholars should not be surprised if other psychological scientists with different starting points arrive at different conclusions when studying the same data. Common-sense realism is another approach that recognizes we can know true things about the real world but without seeing the world from an all-knowing *God's eye* perspective. This perspective contributed heavily to the rise of contemporary psychology as a distinct field. It may be a useful view for moving the integration project forward now as well, but some qualification is needed.

Two broadly distinct approaches to psychological scholarship exist. Quantitative methodologies modeled after the way natural sciences study the world in a measurement-based science have been widely utilized in psychology. Yet a second approach more aligned with scholarship in the humanities has also been present. These can be generally summarized under the qualitative tradition. Integrationists have sometimes argued that an integrative approach should prefer one or the other of these methodological traditions. The current authors find reason to embrace both scholarly traditions in attempting to do psychological science in a faithfully Christian way. Humans are both objects in nature and creatures who have idiosyncratic perspectives and linguistically shaped experiences. The Christian integrationist should embrace all truth-productive tools providentially made available to us by our Creator for studying the full reality, objective and subjective, of the human condition.

References

Barrett, J. L. (2012). *Born believers: The science of children's religious belief.* Free Press.

Campbell, D. T. (1974). Evolutionary epistemology. In P. A. Schilpp (Ed.), *The philosophy of Karl R. Popper* (pp. 412-63). Open Court.

Clanton, J. C., & Gunter, J. (2014). Edward Scribner Ames, pragmatism, and religious naturalism: A critical assessment. *The Heythrop Journal, 55*(3), 375-90.

Corduan, W. (1986). Humility and commitment: An approach to modern hermeneutics, *Themelios, (11)*3, 83-88.

Dilthey, W. (1991). *Introduction to the human sciences, Vol 1.* Princeton University. (Original work published 1893)

Evans, C. S. (1977). *Preserving the person: A look at the human sciences.* InterVarsity Press.

Fitzpatrick, J. (1982). Subjectivity and objectivity: Polanyi and Lonergan. *Higher Education Quarterly, 36*(2), 183-95.

Gibson, J. J. (1966). *The senses considered as perceptual systems.* Houghton Mifflin.

Grenz, S. J. (1996). *A primer on postmodernism.* Wm. B. Eerdmans.

Hacking, I. (2000). *The social construction of what?* Harvard University.

Hasker, W. (2013). *Meta-physics and the tri-personal God.* Oxford University.

James, W. (1997). *The varieties of religious experience.* Simon & Schuster. (Original work published 1902)

Jastrow, J. (1899). The mind's eye. *Popular Science Monthly, 54,* 299-312.

Jones, S. L. (1994). A constructive relationship for religion with the science and profession of psychology: Perhaps the boldest model yet. *American Psychologist, 49*(3), 184-99.

Kant, I. (1987). *Critique of judgment.* (W. S. Pluhar, Trans.). Hackett. (Original work published 1790)

Lonergan, B. (1971). *Method in theology.* Herder & Herder.

Lonergan, B. (1997). Insight: A study of human understanding. *The Collected Works of Bernard Lonergan, Vol 3.* University of Toronto Press. (Original work published 1957)

Losch, A. (2009). On the origins of critical realism. *Theology and Science, 7*(1), 85-106, doi:10.1080/14746700802617105

Maier, B. N. (2004). The role of James McCosh in God's exile from psychology. *History of Psychology, 7*(4), 323-39.

McFall, R. M. (1991). Manifesto for a science of clinical psychology. *The Clinical Psychologist, 44*(6), 75-88.

Meek, E. L. (2017). *Contact with reality: Michael Polanyi's realism and why it matters.* Cascade.

Myers, D., & DeWall, G. N. (2017). *Psychology* (12th ed.). Worth.

Noll, M. (1985). Common sense traditions and American Evangelical thought. *American Quarterly, 37*(2), 216-38.

Numbers, R. L. (2010). *Galileo goes to jail and other myths about science and religion.* Harvard University.

Pearce, M. (2016). *Cognitive behavioral therapy for Christians with depression: A practical tool-based primer.* Templeton.

Piaget, J. (1967). Logique et connaissance scientifique. *Encyclopédie de la Pléiade, 22.* Gallimard.

Pind, J. L. (2012). Figure and ground at 100. *The Psychologist, 25*(1), 90-91.

Plantinga, A. (2015). *Knowledge and christian belief.* Eerdmans.

Polanyi, M. (1958). *Personal knowledge: Towards a post-critical philosophy.* University of Chicago Press.

Robinson, D. N. (1996). *An intellectual history of psychology* (3rd ed.). University of Wisconsin Press.

Rubin, E. (1915). *Synsoplevede Figurer: Studier i psykologisk Analyse. Første Del* [Visually experienced figures: Studies in psychological analysis. Part one]. Copenhagen and Christiania: Gyldendalske Boghandel, Nordisk Forlag.

Ruphy, S. (2017). *Scientific pluralism reconsidered: A new approach to the (dis)unity of science.* University of Pittsburgh.

Schooler, J. (2015). Bridging the objective/subjective divide: Towards a meta-perspective of science and experience. In T. Metzinger & J. M. Windt (Eds.), *Open MIND, 34*(T). MIND Group. doi:10.15502/9783958570405

Sisemore, T. (2016). *The psychology of religion and spirituality.* New Work: Wiley & Sons. E-Text.

Slife, B. D., & Reber, J. S. (2009). Is there a pervasive implicit bias against theism in psychology? *Journal of Theoretical and Philosophical Psychology, 29*(2), 63-79.

Sorenson, R. L. (2004). *Minding spirituality.* Routledge.

Spilka, B. (1987). Religion and science in early American psychology. *Journal of Psychology & Theology, 15*(1), 3-9.

Stang, N. F. (2018). Kant's transcendental idealism. In E. N. Zalta (Ed.), *The Stanford Encyclopedia of Philosophy.* Retrieved from https://plato.stanford.edu/archives/win2018/entries/kant-transcendental-idealism

Sternberg, R. (Ed.). (2005). *Unity in psychology: Possibility or pipedream?* American Psychological Association.

Taylor, S. E., & Brown, J. (1988). Illusion and well-being: A social psychological perspective on mental health. *Psychological Bulletin, 103*(2), 193-200.

Torrance, T. F. (1982). *Reality and evangelical theology: The realism of Christian revelation.* InterVarsity Press.

Van Leeuwen, M. S. (1985). *Studies in a Christian world view, Vol. 3. The person in psychology: A contemporary Christian appraisal.* Wm. B. Eerdmans.

Watson, P. J. (2004). After postmodernism: Perspectivism, a Christian epistemology of love, and the ideological surround. *Journal of Psychology and Theology, 32*(3), 248-61.

Wiseman, R., Watt, C., Gilhooly, K., & George, G. (2011). Creativity and ease of ambiguous figural reversal. *British Journal of Psychology, 102*(3), 615-22. doi:10.1111/j.2044-8295.2011.02031.x

Wittgenstein, L. (1953). *Philosophical investigations.* (G. E. Anscombe, Trans.). Macmillan.

Wolterstorff, N. (1988). *Reason with the bounds of religion.* Wm. B. Eerdmans.

Wolterstorff, N. (2000). *Thomas Reid and the story of epistemology.* Cambridge University Press.

Yarhouse, M. A., Stratton, S. P., Dean, J., & Lastoria, M. (2018). *Listening to sexual minorities.* IVP Academic.

3

WORLDVIEW
INTEGRATION

‖

WE NOW TURN TO DISCUSSION of the first of the integrative domains we will consider, that of worldview integration. We define integration in this domain as *an attempt to reposition psychology with a cognitive frame that is coherently embedded within Christian thought and premised on Christian assumptions.* This project did not arise in a vacuum. The notion of a *worldview* has been a frequently mentioned idea in a variety of disciplines and popular contexts, especially over the last century. But to understand the rationale for worldview integration, we believe some important intellectual history about the idea and its origins in the theory of knowledge (i.e., epistemology) need to be first examined. After that review, we will shift to an exploration of some of the most common worldviews encountered in contemporary psychology and point to the contours a worldview integrated psychology might take.

Kant (1790) coined the German term *weltanschauung* that would be translated later into English as "worldview" in his *Critique of Judgment.* Kant used the term to convey a *perception of the sensible world* (Naugle, 2002). The late Christian scholar and worldview apologist James Sire (2020) offers this definition:

> A worldview is a commitment, a fundamental orientation of the heart, that can be expressed as a story or in a set of presuppositions (assumptions which may be true, partially true or entirely false) which we hold (consciously or subconsciously, consistently or inconsistently) about the basic constitution of reality, and that provides the foundation on which we live and move and have our being. (p. 6)

While it has not typically been the major focus of the integration project for most integrationists, worldview integration has been a recurrent theme in the integration literature. Collins (1977) asserted the need to reposition psychology on a biblical worldview.[1] Van Leeuwen (1985) offered a cogent defense of a Christian view of persons as part of a book series on Christian worldviews in various disciplines. More recently, Entwistle (2015) has devoted explicit attention to worldview topics in his text on integration. Perhaps the most focused worldview integrationist in psychology has been Mark Cosgrove. Cosgrove became a Christian while completing his doctorate in experimental psychology at Purdue University. After graduation he spent some years traveling to dozens of universities for Probe Ministries in Dallas, making a case for how Christian theism provides a better foundation for psychology than the alternative worldviews common in the discipline. He then served a distinguished career as an integrative psychology professor at Taylor University mentoring generations into the project.

Cosgrove's (2006) work seriously and broadly engages this topic of worldviews in integration. He takes head on the problem of arbitrating between worldviews. Since each worldview has its own internal logic, how does one make a rational case between multiple worldviews? Despite the problem of arbitrating across worldviews, Cosgrove (2006) offers the following claim: "The worldview we hold should not be a matter of personal preference. We must test our beliefs with evidence and logic" (p. 64). Cosgrove does not mean by this notion of testing any simplistic strategy of testing each belief that makes up a worldview in isolation. A holistic evaluation strategy is needed to do something like a worldview apologetic. Cosgrove (2006) advances the following metacriteria for worldview evaluation: *logical consistency, existential repugnance,* and *human nature.* Similar evaluative criteria have been advanced by others who engage in worldview apologetics (viz., Harris, 2004; Poplin, 2014). Because our project presupposes a Christian worldview, we will not explicitly pursue this apologetic task in our current

---

[1]The phrase "biblical worldview" has been used most often in evangelical literature (viz., Bufford, 1981). While formal attempts to operationalize it have been offered (i.e., Erdvig, 2020), we use it here as a placeholder for a Christian faith perspective that shares a minimal Christian orthodoxy and is committed to a fidelity to biblical revelation on any truth claim to which Scripture speaks. Thus, we believe two Christians who differ quite dramatically on some aspects of doctrine, such as a Wesleyan versus a Reformed view of predestination, may both represent a "biblical worldview" if they responsibly and plausibly ground such belief in biblical teaching. We are not asserting by this that both perspectives are ultimately correct readings of Scripture, but rather they both share a common commitment to biblical authority as the norm for their theologies and also share a minimal set of orthodox beliefs core to the Christian faith such as the existence of God, that God exists as a Trinity, or that salvation occurs through the work of Christ.

discussion. But we will briefly mention a key challenge that arises in the attempt to use evidence to arbitrate between worldviews.

The Quine-Duhem thesis in philosophy of science points to a challenge facing attempts to formally test theories. Complex theoretical assertions are not refuted by simple tests or crucial experiments. Theories are advanced embedded in a set of corollary beliefs that impact how empirical data bears on the perceived veracity of the theory. For instance, even if an observation results in data counter to a theory-derived hypothesis, one may view the testing apparatus that yielded the results as unreliable, or one may think of alternative explanations for the inconsistent finding rather than concluding the theory false. Thus, when counterevidence arises, a proponent can retain the theoretical belief by revising some corollary belief in a way that weakens the force of the counterevidence.

Cosgrove's work is a clear exemplar of the early Christian worldview integration project in psychology. By developing a faithfully Christian view of psychology, Christians can highlight the contributions to the discipline of an integrated approach. Such a project also makes it easier to identify where Christians would likely disagree with the alternative worldviews. Yet as with all worldview apologetics, we suspect worldview analysis will be unlikely, by itself, to move an adherent of a non-Christian worldview to a Christian theistic perspective. Still, such analysis is also important for the Christian to ensure a faithful approach to psychology in their own integrative efforts.

Begging the Worldview

Some years ago, Bill reviewed the many *amicus curiae* briefs the American Psychological Association filed in various court cases. The APA has had substantial impact, through such filings, on legal cases pertaining to vitally important areas of human functioning. Bill was privileged, while serving on APA governance, to be present when APA gave an award to Kenneth Clark, the pioneering psychologist whose research contributed to the court's rationale to end segregated schooling in *Brown v. Board of Education* (1954). Yet, despite such obvious value, it is also clear that in many of the briefs on topics like abortion or end-of-life matters, APA presented testimony only on a narrow range of psychological outcomes or correlates.

APA's legal briefs and policy statements are typically silent about many other factors that might have been considered a relevant consideration for public policy formation from the perspective of many Christians or those of other conventional faith perspectives. For instance, what are the spiritual or religious correlates, if any, of abortion choices? To be fair, it is often the case that little or no psychological research was conducted that would address such matters. Yet the decision by commission or omission to not research topics (e.g., whether spiritual struggles result from certain choices) that have often been points of tension for large segments of religious communities can be seen as evidence of researcher and disciplinary bias about what is culturally pertinent. For whatever reason, it is the case that the briefs and policy statements generated by APA and other mental health organizations rarely call attention to such unexplored, potentially relevant outcomes. This could, as we suspect has, resulted in giving the misleading impression to policymakers or courts that the psychological patterns on which they present data offers the whole story psychologically speaking.[2]

Worldviews impact what we see as relevant and what we investigate. They also set the standards of value for what we use as criteria and thus either explicitly or implicitly impact our moral reasoning and thinking. A person commits the logical fallacy of begging the question when they make an argument that somehow smuggles in part of the conclusion they are trying to prove as an assumption in the evidence used to argue for the conclusion. We suggest that contemporary psychology is sometimes guilty of an extended version of this fallacy. Let us call it by analogy *begging the worldview*. When a discipline's investigations are too limited by method or focus to consider other possibilities than those that naturally occur given the predominant worldview of those who conduct it, it can result in an erroneous inferential leap that the discipline provides good warrant for only worldview congruent perspectives. To put this in terms more common in the field of psychology, such worldview factors introduce *systematic biases* in the investigations and their inferred implications or applications.

Despite multiple invitations for APA to weigh in on end-of-life issue cases involving matters like assisted suicide, APA was reluctant to do so because it had not issued any policy statements in this regard. A working group was launched to generate a report and resolutions were considered by the dawn of

---

[2]This example is not intended to imply a uniformity of perspective among those who identify as Christians on any particular issue, such as abortion or assisted suicide, although it is the case that evangelicals continue to be strongly pro-life (Legaspi & Glahn, 2017). Regardless of one's position on these matters, it does not alter our larger point: psychology frequently weighs in on major social issues with data on only a subset of potentially relevant psychological variables that could be studied. In its contribution to public policy discussions, especially in recent decades, it routinely looks at psychological outcomes that are pertinent only to conceptions of personal well-being or adjustment that fit within a naturalistic, secular paradigm.

the new millennium. At that time, Christian psychologist Stan Jones was on the governing council of the association. The association moved to support client choice in pursuing assisted suicide in some circumstances, rather than a person's desire to end their own life as a mental health problem in its own right, as had traditionally been held to be the case in psychology. Jones took the unpopular step of speaking from the floor of council, first to object to the procedural method used by the governance structure to place the resolution on the agenda in such a way as to prevent any debate and approve the motion without a formal vote, and then to object to the content of the resolution itself (S. Jones, November 2, 2020, personal communication). The opposition to APA's 2001 *Resolution on Assisted Suicide* by Jones and others was narrowly defeated in an unusually close vote for APA policy actions (Faberman & Martin, 2001). While APA still has not formally adopted a position of support or opposition for assisted suicide, it has expressed support for an *end-of-life counseling* role in psychology for clients who are considering *hastened death* (Farberman, 1997; Faberman & Martin, 2001; Werth, 2017). Still, Jones gave voice to the perspective that such a role is in conflict with that of the intrinsic commitment to the value of life that he and others believed should characterize a mental health professional. The supporters of such policies have focused on the hedonic outcomes associated with such decisions.

We are quite importantly taught as psychologists or members of related fields to guard against biases that arise from factors like gender, race, or sexual orientation differences. Yet, caution about bias arising from the frequently opaque influence of our worldviews is much less common. Psychologists such as Jonathan Haidt, and scholars from other disciplines, have formed the Heterodox Academy to respond to what they see as a constricted range of ideological perspectives in the academy. They note the virtual "orthodoxy" of left-of-center political perspectives in academia. While many of them share these political leanings, they see this ideological homogeneity as an enemy of the robust freedom of thought necessary for a vibrant scholarly community. In contrast, the Heterodox Academic advocates for *viewpoint* diversity:

> Viewpoint diversity exists when members of a group or community approach problems or questions from a range of perspectives. When a community is marked by intellectual humility, empathy, trust, and curiosity, viewpoint diversity gives rise to engaged and respectful debate, constructive disagreement, and shared progress towards truth. (Heterodox Academy, 2020)

The Integration Project as a Diversity Contribution

We affirm the Heterodox Academy's concern about viewpoint diversity and also extend it formally to a concern about worldview diversity in psychology. But how would this advocacy for worldview diversity in the academy fit with the integration project we have described? Remember that Christian colleges, universities, publications, and professional forums have been among the most common contexts in which the integration project has been pursued. Many of these settings require some alignment with statements of faith and/or Christian conduct codes for scholars to be formally affiliated. This has sometimes led to charges that such explicitly Christian faith-based settings must operate inconsistently with the academic freedom valued in the contemporary scholarly disciplines including psychology.

We believe such concerns are misguided for at least two major reasons. First, despite the historical founding of Western universities as predominantly faith-based institutions until recent centuries, faith-based universities operate now as a private subset of colleges and universities in existence. Since traditional Christian perspectives or other nonsecular worldviews tend to be significantly underrepresented on most campuses today in many countries, private Christian institutions offering a venue for the exploration of the integrative vision add to the diversity of the modern academy. Second, despite the common core to the perspectives shared by orthodox Christians, Christianity is a vast religious tradition with a culturally and theoretically diverse set of theological instantiations. Consequently, robust Christian perspectives have been fonts for integrative work across the range of theoretical orientations and paradigms that have made up the contemporary social sciences. There simply is no good empirical reason to think that integration work would lead to an ideologically truncated approach to psychology or other academic disciplines.

One of the prominent arguments offered in support of academic freedom arose in the nineteenth century from a pivotal text by John Stuart Mill (1859) called *On Liberty.* Drawing on utilitarian ethical theory, Mill argued that cultures should be accepting of diverse *experiments in living* because, given human fallibility, we may be missing opportunities for happier lives if we do not allow people to try out new things. Applied to the academy, if we impose a narrow orthodoxy then we fail to see whether alternative perspectives might fare better. Would not Mill's argument then mitigate against required faith alignment among faculty, for instance, at Christian colleges? We do not think so. If the integration project were imposed on all academic communities, or even most of them in our current pluralistic world, it would be a fair concern. But it is only a relatively small subset of modern institutions where serious integrative work is being done by scholars who have voluntarily affiliated with institutions on the basis of their preexisting shared Christian worldview. Mill was concerned to allow more individualism and less cultural conformity than he perceived present in Victorian England. Yet while promotion of individualism may help us see new possibilities overlooked by the conformists, it is also true that some forms of life can only be tested in community. They require communal efforts aimed at shared goals. The existence of faith-based scholarly venues committed to the integration project is necessary for this *experiment* to be seriously conducted and evaluated. As APA's (2016) *Standards of Accreditation* notes: "Because of the United States' rich diverse higher education landscape, training can take place in both secular and faith-based settings" (from Standard IB2).

In the founding centuries of the first Western universities, worldview integration would have likely been a strange idea, even if the formal notion of a *worldview* had been already articulated. This is because most of these institutions shared a common Christian theism and would have just assumed that as their starting point (Glanzer et al., 2017). In these settings, scholarship itself was even conceptualized as a spiritual discipline (Pieper, 1952/1998). Perhaps for many contemporary psychologists, something like a default secular worldview is pervasively instilled in a manner analogous to how faith-based perspectives were a default worldview at the dawn of the first universities. We believe this is often the case and have observed many psychologists giving little or no thought to the worldview they presuppose in their work.

What are the varieties of worldviews? A common feature of worldview analysis is the generation of *worldview taxonomies* by identifying and comparing worldviews. There is no consensus taxonomy of worldviews. For the reader unfamiliar with worldview literature, the following comments may seem a bewildering list of "isms" that serve to cloud rather than clarify the intellectual landscape. Worldviews can be demarcated differently depending on what is being focused on. For instance, Entwistle (2015) has differentiated worldviews based on their religious or theological leanings (e.g., animism, polytheism, pantheism, monotheism). In the highly influential Christian primer on worldview analysis, Sire (1976) offered chapter-length treatments of worldviews that were influential philosophical alternatives to Christian theism when his first edition was published in 1976:

naturalism, existentialism, nihilism, deism, Eastern pantheistic monism, and New Age thought. His more recent editions have added chapters on postmodernism and Islamic theism (Sire, 2020). One's focus can zoom out and find fewer, very broadly defined worldview families as in Poplin's (2014) comparison of four "global" worldviews: Judeo-Christianity, material naturalism, secular humanism, and pantheism. But one can also zoom in and find important distinctions and subgroups within an already far more delimited set of perspectives. For instance, the atheistic philosopher John Gray (2018) provides a nuanced and revealing comparison of seven different forms of contemporary atheism.

The reader is referred to book-length treatments of worldviews such as Sire (2020) for a more complete introduction. For the purposes of our current discussion, we will briefly sample from worldview families that have most impacted the contemporary psychology-related fields. Sensitive and critical awareness of worldview issues is important to identify erroneous assumptive foundations that may undergird contemporary psychological work, thereby introducing systematic biases at odds with a faithfully Christian view of the world. Whatever else successful integration may mean in psychology, it would minimally imply an understanding of psychological functioning that is consistent with the basic contours of a Christian view of reality.

An important caveat bears repeating as suggested in an earlier chapter. Just as Gray (2018) has shown important distinctions can be made among the subfamilies of atheism, so one could distinguish between varieties of Christian worldview. We could contrast Wesleyan and Thomistic psychology, for instance. Such considerations are important for detailed and advanced work on the integration project. Yet much of psychology was developed based on secular and even post-Christian thought. Consequently, there is value in contrasting these alternative worldviews with the sort of generic or *mere* Christianity shared by many Christian traditions.

When talking about worldview families, we are talking about constellations of beliefs that reflect the common family traits that members of a worldview family tend to share. As with physical features that convey a *family resemblance*, no two people in a family may share all the same traits and there may be no traits that are shared by all members in a family. Yet a family resemblance is present when some set of features common in a family are shared in different subgroups across members of the family. So, family member one has features one, three, and seven. Family member two has features two, three, and six. Family member three has features one, four, and seven, or so on. In our account below, we will be attempting only to describe the set of commonly held features that characterize these worldview families. We are not claiming that any adherent of a worldview will have all of the family traits.[3]

Major Psychology Worldview Families

Naturalism. Perhaps the most influential worldview family impacting contemporary psychology is naturalism. Much contemporary psychology is steeped in naturalistic assumptions. Naturalism in psychology arises from a commitment to understand and explain psychological functioning only in terms of natural entities and processes. We will consider two alternative forms of naturalism in psychology: materialistic naturalism and secular humanism.

Materialistic naturalism. Naturalism, in its paradigmatic form, embraces a materialistic ontology. This is the view that all that exists is the material world and its properties. Materialistic naturalism denies the supernatural. It also usually embraces a corollary idea of mechanistic uniformity, which holds that everything in the universe is subject to regulating laws. Another principle inherent to naturalism is reductionism; that is, the assertion that higher-level things can be explained in terms of lower level, more basic physical entities, laws, and processes. Persons are *nothing but* a type of complex mechanism. Naturalism asserts that there is nothing beyond death. In other words, all of life is bounded by temporal existence between the womb and tomb. Life can be given meaning by those who are alive and imbue it with significance, but ultimately this meaning is only transient and subjective. History is nonteleological; it is not going anywhere *on purpose*. History is a linear chain of causes and effects determined by bottom-up natural processes.

Because humans are completely a part of the natural order and the natural world operates as a closed system conforming to natural laws, then our commonsense folk wisdom about persons, such as the idea that persons are agents with significant free will, is frequently seen as illusory. In his provocative text, *Beyond Freedom and Dignity*, the renown twentieth-century behaviorist B. F. Skinner (1971) presented a technocratic understanding of the human condition that

---

[3]We are indebted here to Wittgenstein's use of the concept of family resemblance as an alternative to the idea of an essence. However, we do not mean to imply a commitment to Wittgenstein's philosophy *per se* or to deny that there is a common set of beliefs all Christians will share upon our resurrection that would constitute *the essential* Christian worldview. As we will describe below, we think such a perspective can be approximated even in our current fallen state to some degree.

explicitly rejected ideas such as agency, freedom, or personal responsibility in favor of a picture of humans as merely environmentally determined animals mistakenly committed to the illusion of such personal qualities.

More recently, a special issue of the *American Journal of Bioethics* was devoted to the topic of whether neuroscience undermines personhood. The target article by Farah and Heberlein (2007) contrasts a cognitive neuroscience informed conception of the person with predominant prior views. Farah and Heberlein (2007) comment that " . . . personhood is a concept that everyone feels they understand but no one can satisfactorily define" (p. 39). They conclude further that "personhood is a kind of illusion" (p. 45). What difference does it make if personhood is an illusion? Farah and Heberlein (2007) themselves note that many of the most challenging controversies in bioethics stem from issues of whether the beings involved are fully persons. For instance, the morality of abortion, justifications for euthanizing patients in persistent vegetative states, or the moral status of those with substantially impaired cognitive functioning have most commonly hinged on considerations of whether the impacted parties are moral or legal "persons."

Given the eclipse of any transcendent, objective source for what is good, naturalists have most frequently resorted to some form of hedonism as a basis for moral value. Hedonism is a philosophy that holds right action is that which produces optimal pleasure and minimizes pain for the greatest number of sentient beings. This is a perennial position among naturalists. It is one many contemporary naturalists share with ancient materialists such as the Epicurean philosophers in Greece and the Charvaka school in India. The sexual revolutions in the 1920s and 1960s both grounded the apologetic for their radical cultural project in hedonic naturalism. This was clearly evident in the self-fulfillment gospel of the 1920s equating hedonistic naturalism with a scientific view of life, pitting itself against religion and traditional morality that were caricatured as nonscientific:

> One problem and only one troubles the minds of the younger generation: the problem of freedom in matters sexual. . . . We may sum up the quintessence of the sexual revolution by saying that the center of gravity has shifted from procreation to recreation. . . . To sum up: marriage as conventional coercion is on the verge of bankruptcy. Marital love as ritual and routine is no longer honored as either sacred or sweet . . . The sexual revolution is the most recent and the most profound phase of the scientific revolution: the drastic application of the principle of experimentalism to life. (Schmalhausen, 1928, pp. 14-19)

Yet hedonistic naturalism is not itself a finding of science but rather represents a metaphysical and ethical philosophy superimposed on science by its adherents. Christians responded to this regnant naturalism in twentieth-century psychological sciences in a variety of ways. Some Christian psychological scientists struck a *détente* with naturalism through a philosophical strategy known as complementarianism (MacKay, 1981; Myers, 2010). This approach to integration argues that a materialistic explanation of persons constitutes a valid but not exhaustive explanation. Other "levels" of explanation are possible and necessary to adequately account for the richness of what is being explained. It is important to note that proponents of this "levels of explanation" or "complementarian" approach are not stating that additional natural causes need to be included in the chain of natural explanations to account for something like human perception or consciousness. They are content to allow a typical neuroscientific explanation of the visual perception to fully account for the neuroscientific phenomenon of vision. Yet they also hold that another, different level of explanation is needed in terms of human intentionality, subjective experience, and agency to fully and adequately capture the qualitatively different ways of engaging the phenomenon.

This perspective is frequently illustrated with an analogy. Imagine you are driving home at night and see an electric sign displaying the words "Breakfast all day." We might be able, in principle, to provide a complete account of why the light is arranged in the pattern of those letters and those words, but nothing in this account will explain the meaning of the words. The semantic-linguistic level of analysis is needed in addition to the electro-photic-physical one to account for both the meaning of the illumination and its precise physical properties. In the same way, a description of human functioning at both a personal-agentic and physical-deterministic level are argued to be complementary aspects of a complete description of the person by those adopting this strategy.

This complementarian or *levels of analysis* view fostered serious Christian engagement in the cognitive and related human sciences. Christians could retain their traditional way of talking about the human condition and then shift in their scientific contexts to a thoroughgoing naturalistic study of psychological processes. This approach to integration was showcased in a fascinating exchange in 1971 between the eminent materialistic naturalist, B. F. Skinner, and the respected British physicist/information theorist, Donald MacKay, on William F. Buckley's popular public affairs show *Firing Line* (Steibel, 1971). Skinner repeatedly attempted to assert that his behavioral scientific account removed any need for talk of human choice, responsibility, or spiritual accounts of human life. MacKay fully accepted a deterministic account of human functioning but saw this as in no way exhausting the need for a complementary description of persons at the level of intentions, choices, or meanings. MacKay was a Christian who modeled serious science and Christian conviction for many scientists.

The complementarian strategy often rests on a philosophical belief that some types of properties or ways of talking about reality cannot be eliminated without a remainder by appealing to a lower level of physical reality. Some Christians and others accordingly have accepted physicalism about human persons but argued that this physicalism is nonreductive (Brown, Murphy, & Malony, 1998). Under certain sufficiently complex arrangements of matter, the nonreductionists argue that properties can emerge in which the whole is greater than the sum of the parts. Consequently, they believe physicalism is compatible with robust views of the human person as agents (Jeeves, 2004; Sperry, 1966). The integration project owes much to the complementarian strategy. Contributors like Malcolm Jeeves and Donald MacKay have done much to advance serious work in behavioral neuroscience as Christians.

Yet we would suggest such a strategy can promote a compartmentalization of two books of revelation. Explicitly Christian accounts of the person might be seen as irrelevant to the working out of a robust neuroscience. But what if that is not the case? As we noted earlier in the text, we do not find justification for any approach that rules out *a priori* the possibility that Scripture may provide truth claims about at least some aspects of our scientific formulations.

Consider, for instance, issues in the study of consciousness. The search for an adequate physicalist account of consciousness has been called the "Holy Grail" of neuroscience. Yet the research in this area has led to increasing concerns about the inability of materialism to account for the hard problems of consciousness. Rather than return to an older folk dualism, a growing number of consciousness scholars are turning to postmaterialistic options. For instance, Christopher Koch (2012) has reluctantly embraced a view of consciousness that sees it as a nonreducible property of certain types of information systems. He conceptualizes the material world not in classically physicalistic terms but rather as the sort of reality that just is conscious when arranged certain ways. This perspective has been labeled *panpsychism*—the notion that all matter is potentially minded—and it is a view classically associated with pantheistic worldviews rather than physicalism. Koch himself rejected this option earlier in his career and still describes himself as a "romantic reductionist" despite now reluctantly conceding something like a panpsychist view. Why should the Christians relinquish their modal past reading of biblical anthropology as implying a dualist view of the person merely to accept an alternative metaphysical view that is not itself a demonstration of science? Further, there are growing theological critiques arising about the potential of nonreductive physicalism to offer a faithfully biblical and theologically adequate view of the person (Loftin & Farris, 2018).

But we do not need to just look to Christian engagements with materialistic naturalism to find criticisms of the worldview. The eclipse of the person arising from radical scientific naturalism led to a reactionary movement in psychology itself that attempted to reassert our humanity without returning to explicitly Christian soil. This took the form of humanistic psychology.

Humanistic naturalism. Christian texts on worldviews frequently contrast a Christian view of the world with *secular humanism.* Cosgrove (2006) calls secular humanism a "street version of naturalism" (p. 98). Secular humanists find value, significance, and meaning in human persons. They may even defend notions of human agency, moral responsibility, and freedom but appeal to only humans themselves as the source of these elevated aspects of existence. They are secular in the sense that there is no transcendent or divine basis for human value or meaning. Not all humanists are naturalists, but secular humanists are most commonly naturalists.

John Dewey was a key architect of the twentieth-century secular humanism that broadly influenced contemporary psychology. Over the course of his career, this early psychologist, philosopher, and educational reformer, moved from nineteenth-century Christian progressive ideas to explicit advocacy of increasingly secular humanistic worldview. In a pivotal series of lectures at Yale later published under the title *Common Faith*, Dewey (1934/1991) advocated a nonsupernatural view of religious faith as a commitment to human ideals. His influence was substantial in the founding of the American Humanist Association less than a decade later (Poplin, 2014).

Maslow (1968) described humanistic psychology as a *third force* in psychology following psychodynamic psychology and behaviorism. These earlier two forces emphasized a deterministic and reductive view of human persons. In contrast, humanistic psychology saw humans as unique beings capable of freely reinventing themselves through their constructive ability to meaningfully interpret and thereby alter their experiences. Humanistic psychologists, such as Carl Rogers, saw humans as inherently good and human problems as arising from blocked human potential. While human relationships could impair our healthy growth, fracture our self-concepts, and instill anxiety when problematic, so they could also provide a necessary and sufficient condition for positive growth (Rogers, 1957).

The pioneering cognitive therapist Albert Ellis (1992) contributed an article to the *Humanistic Psychologist* advocating for a secular humanistic psychology and distinguishing it from other forms of humanistic psychology more aligned with an alternative worldview (viz., transpersonal psychology below). He noted: "Secular humanists are, almost by definition, relativists, skeptics, and non-dogmatists" (p. 351). Ellis described his Rational Emotive Therapy (RET) as "quite humanistic" but adjuring "spiritual, religious, and mystical overtones and implications" (p. 352). For Ellis, RET is characterized by secular humanistic features such as an emphasis on human choice, self-constructed values and meanings, long-range hedonism, unconditional self-acceptance, and the embrace of the 1960s human potential movement.

How should a biblically faithful Christian respond to humanistic naturalism? Cosgrove (2006) states: "For Christians the problem with secular humanism should not be in the word *humanism* but in the word *secular*. *Secular* means that the basis for everything we see and experience in the universe is atheistic, there is no God. . . . *Humanism*, on the other hand, is a perfectly acceptable word for Christians and their worldview" (p. 100). As Cosgrove also acknowledges, Christian humanism sees innate value in human beings as persons made in the image of God. But does this mean humans are *inherently* good? Christian teachings that humans are made in the image of God and yet ubiquitously marked by sin due to the fall create a problem for any unqualified acceptance of the third force's assertation that humans are inherently good by nature (Ramm, 1985).[4]

Christian critiques of the "self-psychology" movement, including those arising from humanistic psychology, soon emerged. Paul Vitz (1977) polemized against the "cult of self-worship" that had gained momentum since the 1960s in psychology. William Coulson was a Catholic psychologist who worked with Rogers and

---

[4]We recognize that this perspective is the clear predominant view of Western Christianity following Augustine but also that there are dissenting perspectives. There are heterodox views that deny that humans are fallen by nature. See Blackwell and Hatchett's (2019) theology text for an introductory review of these issues. We proceed on the broadly Augustinian-Calvinistic view that has been predominant in the evangelical integration project.

eventually served as chief of staff at Roger's institute. He explained the attraction of the Rogerian approach to persons:

> We Catholics who got involved in it thought this third force would take account of Catholic things. It would take account of the fact that every person is precious, that we are not just corrupted as Freud would have it, or a tabula rasa (clean slate), which is available to be conditioned in whatever way the behaviorist chooses; but rather we have human potential, and it's glorious because we are the children of a loving Creator who has something marvelous in mind for every one of us. (Matzat, 2020, n.p.)

Yet Coulson would later regret his uncritical acceptance of this perspective noting that " . . . we didn't have a doctrine of evil. . . . When we implied to people that they could trust their impulses, they also understood us to mean that they could trust their evil impulses, that they weren't really evil. But they were evil" (Matzat, 2020, n.p.).

The focus here is on the worldview considerations of humanistic naturalism, not on a Rogerian counseling theory. Watson et al.'s (2011) helpful summary and Christian assessment of Roger's person-centered therapy is recommended for more in-depth treatment of the counseling theory. They positively assess the humanistic valuing of persons over the reductionism of behaviorism. Christians can and have appreciated that aspect to this form of naturalism. Yet, they also acknowledge other aspects of the perspective appear less congruent with biblical views, such as the underappreciation of the impact of human sin or the reality of the divine. There was some indication that in his later years, Rogers recognized he had given inadequate attention to spirituality and religious development in his approach (Watson et al., 2011). Another humanistic psychology luminary, Abraham Maslow, early on came to believe that the naturalistic presumptions of even the third force provided an inadequate basis for the robust view of human worth, meaning, and personhood the movement desired to defend. This led Maslow and others on to a *fourth force* typically referred to as transpersonal psychology. Transpersonal psychology is frequently influenced by yet another worldview: *pantheistic monism.*

Pantheistic monism. Pantheism means all is god. On this view, all being, the universe itself, is *the* divine. The challenge with this shorthand definition is that many pantheistic worldviews do not conceptualize the divine in traditionally theistic terms. Often Eastern religions such as Buddhism and Hinduism are described as pantheistic systems; however, this is not always strictly correct as some varieties of these faiths may properly be considered atheistic, polytheistic, or even mono-theistic. To avoid this confusion, we use the more specific phrase *pantheistic monism*, to emphasize those perspectives that view being as one undivided divine whole—a worldview holding that ultimate reality is a single mental *whole* rather than a material composite. Our conscious awareness or perception of our existence as distinct selves is thought to be an illusory state of consciousness; yet, pantheistic monists typically argue that we can escape this illusory separateness and return to a unified consciousness in the divine mind through a process of realization.

Pantheistic monism usually propounds a moral perspective informed by kar-mic principles. Nothing is objectively good or bad on such a view, rather good and bad are the result of false consciousness that generates attachments to tran-sient illusory aspects of experience which inevitably result in suffering. Like ripples in a pond creating an illusion of a differentiated existence between the waves and the rest of the pond, so our perceptions of individual existence are impermanent perceptions that betray our fundamental identity and unity with the whole of the universe. Such karmic patterns may have an impact longer than just what an individual experiences during one human lifetime. They can rever-berate beyond our perceived mortal boundaries and into subsequent life experi-ences. This is the notion of *reincarnation* or *death-rebirth cycles.* Just as seasons follow repetitive sequences, so the karmic patterns evident in individual human lives continue beyond death until dissipated. But it is not so much "me" (that is myself in my current individual self-understanding) that returns anew in rein-carnation; rather, the manifestation of the eternal consciousness that has taken the form of this or that particular individual continues on through another cycle.

Now such accounts, of course, gloss over many subtle differences and the richness of specific worldviews such as the varieties of Vedic Hinduism, Theravadin Buddhism, or any of the wide range of New Age ideologies that exist. But they capture some of the common themes. Pantheistic monism is attractive to many contemporaries because it asserts our essential divinity and does not assert our inherent sinfulness. There is no transcendent reality separate from us but rather a transcendent "within" that we all share. Our own individual existence, plagued as it is with impermanence and suffering, is ultimately denied reality. The key thing is for us to cultivate transformations of consciousness that help us overcome our current illusions, often through meditative practices.

Pantheistic monism has been present within contemporary psychology since the discipline developed. Some of its key features have been embraced as early as Jung and James (Ryan, 2008). Jung's notion that we all share a "collective unconscious" has pantheistic connotations. James also described forms of consciousness he called *transpersonal* as early as 1905, coining the term in the English language (Ryan, 2008). Yet it is widely thought that the transpersonal movement gained most momentum in psychology in the 1960s.

Recall that the humanistic movement called psychology back to a serious appreciation of the distinctive aspects of humans *as persons*. A growing sense of materialistic naturalism's inability to undergird such appreciation led to what Maslow would call the *fourth force in psychology*. Maslow proposed a psychology that would explore the furthest reaches of human consciousness. Transpersonalists have often been drawn to a range of Eastern spiritual practices and perspectives, such as yoga and various forms of meditation, as well as to dream interpretation, drug use, or other approaches to promote consciousness-altering states (Hastings, 1999). Proponents such as Ken Wilbur, Stanislav Grof, Charles Tart, and others have explored various theoretical and clinical approaches consistent with this perspective. In 1968, the *Journal of Transpersonal Psychology* was launched, and in 1971, the Association for Transpersonal Psychology was formed. Formal venues have emerged committed to training students from a transpersonal perspective such as the Institute for Transpersonal Psychology (now Sofia University) or Columbia University's master's concentration in spirituality and mind-body practice.

It would be a mistake to equate transpersonal psychology with pantheistic monism despite the heavy presence of this worldview in the transpersonal movement. While the dominant characteristics of pantheistic monism pervade work done in transpersonal psychology, the movement itself is averse to formal doctrinal stances and is highly eclectic. A common theme among transpersonalists is the outworking of a psychology informed by what has been called the *perennial philosophy*. The notion of perennial philosophy is not limited to Eastern spiritual perspectives, yet it has been a common meme among those who wish to appropriate Eastern spiritualities in the West. Proponents of perennial philosophy believe there is a universal wisdom underlying all world religions that converges across various esoteric mystical systems. While it is an idea common in some mystical societies (i.e., theosophy) and movements (American Transcendentalism, New Age thought), it is also a belief shared among some prominent religious studies scholars (e.g., Houston Smith). Writer Ken Wilber's work has been particularly influential in this regard among transpersonalists, although he himself prefers to now call his approach integral psychology.

Despite this long and often prestigious lineage, transpersonal psychology has not been widely embraced in academic psychology. In the 1980s, attempts to create a division of transpersonal psychology in the APA were defeated on multiple occasions. In the same article where RET founder Albert Ellis defended his own model as truly humanistic, he offered a polemic against transpersonal trends in humanistic psychology, finding them too unscientific and too indebted to religion. It is not uncommon to find accounts of transpersonal psychology as a fringe movement by its critics. Yet despite tepid (or even hostile) reception in mainstream psychology, transpersonalists often point to the enormous impact of meditative practices, mindfulness-based interventions, and even the growing appreciation of religious beliefs and practices—regardless of their source—for client health and well-being as evidence of the vitality of their approach.

Indeed, such developments have had a major impact on contemporary psychological and cultural practice, especially in the West. Jon Kabat-Zinn's popularized form of mindfulness meditation is akin to Vipassanā meditation, a Buddhist practice. Schlieter (2017) notes that in its religious context, Vipassanā serves a salvific function liberating us from the false illusion of our individual existence and attachments to it. Kabat-Zinn retasked the technique in mindfulness-based stress reduction (MBSR) to function as a biomedical healing practice. Yet, Schlieter (2017) raises questions about whether the technique is as devoid of religion as Kabat-Zinn or others suggest. Still, some integrationists have found ways to advance Christian-integrated parallels or accommodations of mindfulness-based approaches.

How is a Christian to respond to transpersonal psychology or other attempts to build a psychology in pantheistic perspective? At a foundational level, pantheism's assessment of the nature of the divine, the nature of humanity, the nature of our spiritual state is fundamentally contrary to a biblical worldview. Additionally, any worldview that places subjective, precognitive content above revealed biblical teaching as a source of truth would be problematic for those who hold to a high view of Scripture. The penchant for the lust for the esoteric common in transpersonal circles reflected in practices such as mediumship, fascination with paranormal experiences, and the pursuit of trance states, all seem to run afoul of biblical warnings and prohibitions regarding occult involvement. Still Christians can and should appreciate the polemic offered by transpersonalists against the reductive materialism regnant in much of psychology. Christians can welcome this critique of materialism and the valuing of the spiritual common among transpersonalists.

Christian theism. One of the earliest projects in Christian worldview apologetics was James Orr's (1883) *The Christian View of God and the World as Centering in the Incarnation.* In that text, Orr recognizes the origin of explicit worldview thinking in Kant and then proceeds to lay out a compelling, and in many ways still relevant, description of a Christian worldview in contrast to a variety of alternative perspectives in his time. He notes:

> If God is a reality, the whole universe rests on a supernatural basis. A supernatural presence pervades it; a supernatural power sustains it; a supernatural will operates in its forces; a supernatural wisdom appoints its ends. The whole visible order of things rests on another—an unseen, spiritual, supernatural order—and is the symbol, the manifestation, the revelation of it. (Orr, 1883/1908, p. 76)

This vitally important starting point applied to our project would distinguish a theistic psychology from the alternatives we have thus far considered. Naturalistic psychology has often gained the most traction among those drawn to its scientific credibility. But what explains the success and credibility of science? Recall our earlier discussion about evolutionary epistemology in chapter two. The idea that the universe is a creation of a benign, omniscient, and omnipotent God provides a natural reason to suspect the universe will follow an orderly, lawful, and rational design. Thus, the scientific enterprise could be expected to yield fruit because it stems from humanity's use of the rational and other cognitive capacities bequeathed by our Creator to in some small way *reverse engineer* creation (i.e., to "think God's thoughts after Him").

What of our object and subject of study in psychological science? As with the humanistic movement in psychology, a consistent Christian psychological worldview will constitute a variety of *personalism*. Personalism reflects a varied group of proposals, some consistent with orthodox Christian worldviews and others not. A common set of themes are present across the varieties of personalism that concord well with a biblical worldview:

> These include an insistence on the radical difference between persons and nonpersons and on the irreducibility of the person to impersonal spiritual or material factors, an affirmation of the dignity of persons, a concern for the person's subjectivity and self-determination, and particular emphasis on the intersubjective (relational) nature of the person. (Williams & Bengtsson, 2020, n.p.)

Personalist philosophies have frequently taken as inspiration Christian theological explorations about the nature of persons in the Trinity. This is no accident. A profound implication for the integrative projects arises from the character of a trinitarian God: " . . . the objective existence of the trinitarian God whose essential character establishes the moral order of the universe and whose word, wisdom, and law define and govern all aspects of created existence" (Naugle, 2002, p. 260). Despite the complex developments in trinitarian thought over the centuries, orthodox accounts of the Trinity make it clear that reality must be ultimately understood in personal rather than impersonal terms. Yet his recognition is not a denial that for human persons neuroscientific and other physical processes constitute key features of how those persons exist in the world. It is an assertion that personhood is not merely an illusory artifact of brain processes but something that is nonreductively present in each human. It should also be noted that the objective, eternal relational, and multipersonal nature of the Trinity means that Christians must reject the diffusion of individual persons in pantheistic monism as much the eliminative reduction of persons in physicalism. The biblical picture of persons as substantial egos or moral agents who exist as individuals in relationships, is as much undercut by the pantheistic idea that such persons are illusions as it is by reductive physicalist accounts.

On a Christian view, we live in a universe that was intentionally created and we are persons who collectively were made to image the tripersonal God who intended us. As Marshall (2011) states: "In the Christian tradition creation is usually conceived of in such a way that it definitely requires a 'personal' God. In the Christian view the world must be understood to have its origin in a free and intelligent act of creation. God has made all things through his intellect and by a free decision of his will" (p. 401).

We have value because we exist as persons who were created to be image bearers of God.[5] That value is not an achievement dependent upon some human realization or developmental attainment but an endowment bestowed by our

---

[5]We believe that the concept of being made in God's image is the most robust and historically influential source for a commitment to human equity and dignity of all people. But sometimes those who espouse this doctrine have understood it in a way that denies all humans equality as divine image bearers. See Kilner's (2015) opening chapter for a compelling review of how understandings of the divine image, which suggest it can be *diminished* in some people served as justification for slavery and other forms of oppressive injustice. His thesis is that theologies of the divine image which associate it with some attribute of God that can be shared by humans to a variable degree, set the stage for discriminatory judgments about humans. Like Kilner, we reject any attributive or capacity-based idea of the image of God. We believe the most accurate reading of Scripture is that all humanity is made to share in the divine image in manner that grants them immediate and present equity of worth and dignity. While we do not claim that Scripture is clear about the details of how the *imago Dei* accomplishes this, we do believe the Scripture is clear about equal dignity of the *least* among us because of our joint creation in the divine image (Mt 25:45). So, any theology of the divine image must be consistent with the equal dignity of all of humanity regardless of any human distinction.

Creator. While secular psychology extols the universal worth and dignity of people, it has no robust basis for that equality. We are clearly not equal in capacity as individuals empirically. Some of us win gold medals; most of us do not. For some, calculus comes easy, but for most, not. In contrast to the naturalistic reduction of persons to experiential illusions, a trinitarian view sees persons in relation to the "divine persons" and their interrelationship as an eternal and principal aspect of existence. The Christian understanding is also *telic*: history has a providentially controlled flow and direction. Once the kingdom of God is fully realized, all in God's kingdom will reflect the image of God as divinely intended. "What we must do then is to understand our being as persons as grounded in God's constant creative purposes. There are certain capacities people have as people, even when empirically they seem to lack those capacities" (Evans, 1993, p. 111).

Ironically, by looking away from God to find ourselves in non-Christian worldviews, psychology loses both God and ourselves. Medieval theology debated whether concepts of divine persons must mean something different from our ordinary human understanding of persons (Friedman, 2011; Nielsen, 2011). But as we have seen, it is not clear that even in thoroughly inspecting human corporeal reality through modern science, that we can achieve a univocal and positive notion of personhood with an objective, empirical referent of the sort by humanists.

It may well be that we can only find a viable basis for our intuitions that humans are real persons, made for relationship, with dignity and inherent value regardless of any relative cognitive or psychological capacity, in the context of our redeemed communion with the tripersonal God who made us. While the *imago Dei* may provide a key to help us partially glimpse at least some of the divine mysteries of the Trinity, its probative function will likely be obscured if humanity understands itself apart from God (viz., Rom 1).

In contrast to secular psychology's underappreciation of sin, the Christian worldview holds that our current human predicament is inextricably bound to the effects of sin on the created order, including humanity:

> The catastrophic effects of sin on the human heart and mind, resulting in the fabrication of idolatrous belief systems in place of God and the engagement of the human race in cosmic spiritual warfare in which the truth about reality and the meaning of life is at stake. (Naugle, 2002, p. 274)

A Christian worldview further asserts that not only is the created order fallen, but that it is also being redeemed as the kingdom of God is present today through an event in history:

The gracious inbreaking of the kingdom of God into human history in the person and work of Jesus Christ, who atones for sin, defeats the principalities and powers, and enables those who believe in him to obtain a knowledge of the true God and a proper understanding of the world as his creation. (Naugle, 2002, p. 284)

A Comment on Two Distinct Christian Worldview Integration Strategies

We have considered some different Christian integrative efforts related to worldview integration in this chapter. We believe two different types of strategies are differentiated in these efforts. In his early primer on integration, Evans (1977) characterized the levels of analysis approach described above as an example of *perspectivalism*. Perspectivalists believe that different ways of looking at, or perhaps more accurately, *describing* the world may be equally valid at the same time. In regard to at least some phenomena, multiple accounts constructed at different, nonreducible levels, may be needed to give a full account. In contrast, *worldview repositioners* typically believe there is something incomplete or biased in a psychologically related field that operates on non-Christian starting points. They usually argue for a transformational repositioning of the field on explicitly Christian foundations.

We believe both approaches represent Christian worldview integration, but they may lead to different ways of living out one's professional or scientific life. Adopters of both strategies may espouse the same Christian doctrines and live out indistinguishable Christian lives in their religious practices or moral conduct. They may share similar Christian experiences and passions.

Yet we also suspect that the perspectivalist strategy will typically result in a professional or scientific conduct that has less discernable difference in content or method from that seen by equally well-trained members of the field who are not Christians. One possible caveat is the tendency for perspectivalists to report a motivation to excellence *as a professional* because of their Christian life. In contrast, we would expect there to be at least some distinctively Christian impact on the professional or scientific content and praxis of someone who is a worldview repositioner. But of course, such contrasts between the two strategies presupposes that they are fixed types that are consistently exemplified by the ones who adopt them. We will discuss an alternative suggestion in our next chapter that some approaches may be appropriate in specific psychological areas but not others.

An Overlooked Aspect of Worldviews: Implicit Cognition

As we bring this chapter to a close, we want to briefly note an important qualification on worldview thinking. Our explicitly articulated worldviews shape and direct our lives in many ways. Yet there is an implicit or *tacit* dimension to our approach to our worldviews that also heavily shapes our perceptions, intuitions, and thinking patterns (Polanyi, 1958/2015). Work in both psychology and theology highlight this. In his text *Thinking Fast and Slow*, Nobel laureate psychologist Daniel Kahneman (2013) contrasted the extensive body of knowledge that has been accumulating about the automatic processes, which shape many of our cognitive operations in a fast and implicit manner with the discoveries about slower and more deliberated controlled cognitive processes. Convergently, James K. A. Smith gives a Christian philosophical and theological account of this precognitive aspect to worldviews, arguing that our knowledge of God and our capacity to see God and think in Christian categories is related to our desires. That is, to be human is to be a "desiring animal" who is formed by the habits we commit ourselves to. We are "embodied, material, fundamentally desiring animals who are . . . everyday being formed by the material liturgies of other pedagogies" (Smith, 2009, p. 33). In Kahneman's terms, our fast processes can shape our worldview associations and related cognitions just as our slower deliberative ones can.

If our worldview thinking is to be fully and consistently aligned with a faithfully Christian perspective, we need to align both our intentional, deliberative beliefs and our automatic, habitual, implicit "precognitive" associations. The first sort of alignment process has been the predominant focus of the worldview integration project in Christian thought. The second is more likely to be a process of habit formation that shapes our deep passions. *Deep worldview integration will require integration of our precognitive, implicit associations as well as our explicit thinking.* We suggest, then, that personal integration is perhaps as vital to robust worldview integration as the sort of conceptual analysis exemplified in this chapter. We will focus on this personal domain of integration in chapter seven.

Summary

Worldview integration represents an attempt to reposition psychology within a cognitive frame that is coherently embedded in Christian thought and premised on Christian assumptions. This approach makes use of the modern idea of a worldview. A focus on worldview integration has been present for some integrationists since the start of the integration project. This chapter focuses on worldview analysis rather than worldview apologetics. Worldview apologetics is focused on offering a case for a particular worldview and demonstrating the inadequacies of alternatives. Worldview analysis attempts to identify the common features of a worldview family and to offer comparison/contrasts with other worldview families.

Worldviews play a foundational role in shaping disciplines, delimiting their potential theoretical perspectives, and directing their research programs toward or away from certain topics. If adherents of worldviews are not self-aware of the worldview they hold, then such worldviews function as systematic biases. Despite the wide range of perspectives and theories in academia, there has been growing criticism of a lack of viewpoint diversity of certain types in secular academic disciplines. Although one time serving as a hegemonic faith perspective at most of the first universities, Christian higher education now can and often does represent an addition to academic diversity in the contemporary situation.

Two major worldview families prevalent in contemporary psychology include *naturalism*, in both its classic *materialistic* and *secular humanistic* forms, and perspectives that assert something like *pantheistic monism*, such as if often reflected in *transpersonal psychologies. Christian theism* offers an alternative worldview that has both points of convergence and divergence with naturalistic and pantheistic views. We claim that Christian theism provides a robust basis to understand persons that fits with widespread folk and scientific intuitions about persons.

References

American Psychological Association. (2016). *The Standards of Accreditation*. Author.

Blackwell, B. C., & Hatchett, R. L. (2019). *Engaging theology: A biblical, historical, and practical introduction*. Zondervan.

Brown v. Board of Education of Topeka, 347 U.S. 483 (1954).

Brown, W. S., Murphy, N., & Malony, H. N. (Eds.). (1998). *Whatever happened to the soul? Scientific and theological portraits of human nature*. Fortress.

Bufford, R. K. (1981). *The human reflex: Behavioral psychology in biblical perspective*. Harper and Row.

Collins, G. R. (1977). *The rebuilding of psychology: An integration of psychology and Christianity*. Tyndale House.

Cosgrove, M. P. (2006). *Foundations of Christian thought: Faith, learning, and the Christian worldview*. Kregel Books.

Dewey, J. (1991). *A Common faith*. Yale University. (Original work published 1934)

Ellis, A. (1992). Secular humanism and rational-emotive therapy. *The Humanistic Psychologist, 20*(2-3), 349-58.

Entwistle, D. (2015). *Integrative approaches to psychology and Christianity: An introduction to worldview issues, philosophical foundations, and models of integration* (3rd ed.). Cascade Books.

Erdvig, R. C. S. (2020). *Beyond biblical integration: Immersing you and your students in a biblical worldview.* Summit Ministries.

Evans, C. S. (1977). *Preserving the person: A look at the human sciences.* InterVarsity.

Evans, C. S. (1993). Human persons as substantial achievers. *Philosophia Reformata, 58,* 100-112.

Farah, M. J., & Heberlein, A. S. (2007). Personhood and neuroscience: Naturalizing or nihilating? *American Journal of Biothetics, 7*(1), 37-48.

Farberman, R. K. (1997). Terminal illness and hastened death requests: The important role of the mental health professional. *Professional Psychology: Research and Practice, 28*(6), 544–47.

Farberman, R. K., & Martin, S. (2001). APA's Council of Representatives passes resolution on assisted suicide. *The Monitor, 32*(4), 10.

Friedman, R. L. (2011). Medieval Trinitarian Theology from the late Thirteenth to the Fifteenth Centuries. In G. Emery & M. Levering (Eds.), *The Oxford handbook on the Trinity* (197-209). Oxford University.

Glanzer, P. L., Alleman, N. F., & Ream, T. C. (2017). *Restoring the soul of the university.* InterVarsity Press.

Gray, J. (2018). *Seven types of atheism.* Farrar, Strous, & Giroux.

Harris, R. A. (2004). *The Integration of faith and learning: A worldview approach.* Cascade Books.

Hastings, A. (1999). Transpersonal psychology: The fourth force. In D. Moss (Ed.), *Humanistic and transpersonal psychology: A historical and biographical sourcebook* (pp. 192-208).

Heterodox Academy. (2020). *The problem.* https://heterodoxacademy.org/the-problem/

Kahneman, D. (2013). *Thinking fast and slow.* Farrar, Straus, & Giroux.

Kant, I. (1987). *Critique of judgment* (W. S. Pluhar, Trans.). Hackett. (Original work published 1790)

Kilner, J. F. (2015). *Dignity and destiny: Humanity in the image of God.* Eerdmans.

Koch, C. (2012). *Consciousness: Confessions of a romantic reductionist.* MIT Press.

Legaspi, M., & Glahn, S. (2017). *Evangelical America: An encyclopedia of contemporary American religious culture: In encyclopedia of contemporary American religious culture.* ABC-CLIO.

Loftin, R. K., & Farris, J. R. (Eds.). (2018). *Christian physicalism: Philosophical theological criticisms.* Lexington Books.

MacKay, D. M. (1981). *Human science and human dignity.* InterVarsity.

Marshall, B. (2011). The deep things of God: Trinitarian pneumatology. In G. Emery & M. Levering (Eds.), *The Oxford Handbook on the Trinity* (pp. 400-413). Oxford University.

Maslow, A. H. (1968). *Towards a psychology of being.* D. Van Nostrand.

Matzat, D. (Ed.). (2020, May 26). Meet Dr. Bill Coulson: Thoughts from the man who, together with Carl Rogers, pioneered the practice of "encounter groups." www.issuesetcarchive.org/articles/aissar74.htm

Mill, J. S. (1859). *On Liberty*. J. W. Parker.

Myers, D. G. (2010). A levels-of-explanation view. In E. L. Johnson (Ed.), *Psychology & Christianity: Five views* (49-78). InterVarsity.

Naugle, D. K. (2002). *Worldview: History of the concept*. Eerdmans.

Nielsen, L. O. (2011). Trinitarian theology: From Alcuin to Anselm. In G. Emery & M. Levering (Eds.), *The Oxford Handbook on the Trinity* (pp. 155-67). Oxford University.

Orr, J. (1908). *The Christian view of God and the World as centering in the Incarnation* (9th ed.). Charles Scribner's Sons. (Original work published 1883)

Pieper, J. (1998). *Leisure: The basis of culture*. St. Augustine's Press. (Original work published 1952).

Polanyi, M. (2015). *Personal knowledge: Towards a post-critical philosophy*. University of Chicago. (Original work published 1958)

Poplin, M. (2014). *Is reality secular? Testing the assumptions of four global worldviews*. InterVarsity Press.

Ramm, B. (1985). *Offense to reason: A theology of sin*. Harper & Row.

Rogers, C. R. (1957). The necessary and sufficient conditions therapeutic personality change. *Journal of Consulting Psychology, 22*(2), 95-103.

Ryan, M. B. (2008). The transpersonal William James. *Journal of Transpersonal Psychology, 40*(1), 20-40.

Schlieter, J. (2017). Buddhist insight meditation (*Vipassanā*) and Jon Kabat-Zinn's "Mindfulness-based Stress Reduction": An example of dedifferentiation of religion and medicine? *Journal of Contemporary Religion, 32*(3), 447-63.

Schmalhausen, S. D. (1928). *Why we misbehave*. Macaulay.

Sire, J. (2020). *The Universe next door* (6th ed.). InterVarsity Press. (Original work published 1976)

Skinner, B. F. (1971). *Beyond freedom and dignity*. Hackett.

Smith, J. K. A. (2009). *Desiring the kingdom: Worship, worldview, and cultural formation*. Baker Academic.

Sperry, R.W. (1966). Mind, brain, and humanistic values. *Bulletin of the Atomic Scientists, 22*(7), 2-6.

Steibel, W. (Director). (1971). The case against freedom. [Television series episode]. In *Firing Line*.

Watson, T., Jones, S. L., & Butman, R. E. (2011). Person-centered therapy. In S. L. Jones & R. E. Butman (Eds.,) *Modern psychotherapies*. InterVarsity Press.

Werth, J. L. (2017). *A summary of APA's efforts in the end-of-life arena*. www.apa.org/pi/aging/programs/history.pdf

Williams, T. D., & Bengtsson, J. O. (2020). Personalism. In E. N. Zalta (Ed.), *The Stanford Encyclopedia of Philosophy* (Spring 2020 Edition). https://plato.stanford.edu/archives/spr2020/entries/personalism/

Van Leeuwen, M. S. (1985). *The Person in psychology: A Contemporary Christian appraisal*. Wm. B. Eerdmans.

Vitz, P. (1977). *Psychology as religion: The cult of self-worship*. Wm. B. Eerdmans.

THEORETICAL INTEGRATION

WE NOW TURN OUR ATTENTION to a second integration domain, that of *theoretical integration*. This domain logically follows from our consideration of worldview integration. As we noted in the preceding chapter, human worldviews create the mental frame used to perceive and make sense of the world. Theories can be thought of as what one sees when looking out from one's view of the world at specific aspects of that world. The *Oxford English Dictionary* defines a theory as "the conceptual basis of a subject or area of study." The term derives from the Greek word *theoria*, which means a beholding or a scene that is present to one's perception. Theories are explicit formulations of what one believes to be the case about some aspect of an area of study given the vantage point from one's conceptual frame or worldview. In science, theories constitute the conceptual frame within which a scientist understands, explains, and makes predictions about a topic (Leuridan, 2014). The integration project has been frequently described as the integration of some set of theoretical understandings or knowledge claims from a discipline and *Christian thought*. We define *theoretical integration* as the attempt to construct, synthesize, or correlate Christian thought with psychological theory.

Over the span of Christian history, a vast body of theoretical proposals about the human condition and how to intervene in it have been formulated (Johnson, 2017). The psychology-related fields have developed many theories about human and animal functioning as well. Thus, any effort to integrate these fields and Christianity would naturally bring with it an attempt to integrate the relevant theories from each area.

A key focus of the "model building" era of the integration project in the 1970s and 1980s was on the attempt to describe how Christians could integrate psychological theories. This effort may have been motivated in part by the central place coursework in personality theories played both in undergraduate psychology programs and in the training of clinicians and counselors during that period. For undergraduate psychology majors, required courses in personality theory were commonplace. Students in graduate programs also frequently had courses that offered extensive coverage of theories at a more advanced level. Even for those training for clinical careers, therapy coursework often started with a survey of theories of counseling. Raymond Corsini's (1973) *Current Psychotherapies* became a nearly standard text in practice-oriented graduate psychology programs over the last quarter of the twentieth century, offering its chapter-length treatment of a range of the most influential therapeutic orientations and emphasizing each orientation's key theoretical concepts. Psychological theories have also been influential in the nonclinical areas of the behavioral sciences as they were in many other scientific and applied fields in those years.

A variety of factors have somewhat weakened this emphasis on overarching theories. A contemporary discomfort over metanarratives and a resulting de-emphasis on the importance of grand theories at the same time has opened the door to a plurality of less ambitious theories focused on a more limited range of phenomena they were attempting to explain. This has been particularly evident in the field of motivation psychology. Reeve (2018) points out that contemporary psychology has moved through three grand theories of motivation, first inheriting the idea of motivation as a function of *volition or human will* from the older philosophical and theological accounts of human nature. As psychology became a distinct discipline aspiring to be a science in the latter half of the nineteenth century, it moved away from explanatory models relying on the concept of will, as the concept of will seemed to invoke nonnatural mysterious forces.

In place of the older, will-based accounts of motivation, psychology turned to the concept of *instinct* inspired by a combination of Darwin's theory and the older faculty psychology, which had already proposed the idea of the mind as a composite of modules each tailored to a different mental task or operation. For the Christians who had propounded faculty psychology, this tailoring was an artifact of providence. Psychology kept a similar understanding of modularity but utilized Darwin's theory to account for development of the mental faculties in naturalistic terms. However, this seemed to be a strategy with little explanatory power. The instinct theories simply labeled the various motives they saw in humans and animals and acted as though this naming was some sort of explanation. For instance, eating behavior was attributed to an *eating instinct* as though this mere act of attribution explained the behavior. But as critics noted, naming is not explaining.

Instinct theory was succeeded by the last grand theory of motivation: *drive reduction theory*. This notion appeared more explanatory, arguing that organisms strive to maintain balanced biological states of various types (e.g., homeostasis) and when this balance is disrupted, a felt urge or "drive" is experienced that pushes the organism to restore balance. Based on this drive reduction view, psychology students in the mid-twentieth century learned to keep their rats hungry prior to various experiments so they would be strongly motivated to learn. Yet this drive reduction view was also seen to be incomplete. There seemed to be nonhomeostatic motivational processes such as attractive environmental incentives that were difficult to account for in the drive reduction view. Studies also showed animals could be motivated by nonnutritive substitutes for food that did not alter the underlying physiological imbalance, such as saccharine. There was also a growing appreciation for the role of social and cognitive factors in motivation in at least some cases.

What followed in the 1960s and after was what Reeve refers to as the era of "mini-theories." There were now many different theories proposed not of motivation as one universal thing but of what could be expected to lead to particular patterns of behavior in very limited contexts. "Mini-motivation" theories like self-efficacy theory, achievement motivation theory, goal theory, stress and coping paradigms, and many other such ideas were proposed.

In its early decades, the Christian psychological integration movement often took the form of various proposals for how theological perspectives could be integrated with grand psychological theories. Thus, the influential integration introduction from this period by Carter and Narramore (1979) was titled *The Integration of Psychology & Theology* connoting the notion of a cognitive engagement. Various models were proposed of how to interface these two conceptual frames. As was common in psychological education, theories were often engaged one at a time. The integration task was often presented as one of figuring out how to have a Christian approach to this or that theory. We will first review some of the models of theoretical integration advanced to facilitate that task. We will then consider two disciplinary developments that herald a needed shift in the theoretical integration project: the psychotherapy integration movement and the impact of postmodernism.

Early Integrative Models for Christian Theoretical Integration

The classic goal of Christian theoretical integration is captured in this quote from Brian Eck (1996): " . . . to come to a greater, more holistic and unified understanding of human persons and their social/ecosystemic worlds than is possible through any unitary disciplinary window alone" (p. 102). Much of the early psychology integration models were influenced by longstanding and even ancient Christian discussions of how to relate faith and learning or faith and reason. The early evangelical efforts at integration often consisted of typologies of *theoretical* integration approaches.

Larry Crabb's (1977) influential *Effective Biblical Counseling* text outlined four approaches to integration: "Nothing Buttery," "Separate but Equal," "Tossed Salad," and "Spoiling the Egyptians." It should be noted that while biblical counseling is now often contrasted with integrative approaches to Christian counseling, Crabb's model was integrative, valuing contributions from secular psychology and counseling. He proposed a model delineating four approaches to how "truths" from both psychology and Christian counseling might be interrelated:

- *Nothing Buttery*: Rejection of anything "but" the Christian approach (or alternately anything but the secular approach).

- *Separate but Equal*: Proponents of this model view both secular psychology and biblical truth as legitimate, but they argue that they should not be mixed. They represent distinct domains that are each valid in their own sphere.

- *Tossed Salad*: This metaphor for this model indicates a mixture of separate elements that retain their distinctiveness. In terms of integration, the "tossed salad" proponents might use both spiritual and secular psychological approaches to help a client but argue that the approaches need to retain their separate characteristics and not inform each other.

- *Spoiling the Egyptians*: The collection of bounty from the Egyptians given to the Israelites as they left the land of Egypt is proposed as a metaphor for the legitimacy of mining secular domains of learning for useful truths.

C. Stephen Evans (1977), a prominent Christian philosopher and an interdisciplinary contributor to integration in psychology, offered an influential typology. He identified three broad categories of integration approaches that also appeared to focus on conceptual or theoretical integration:

- *Reinterpreter*: This group accepts either secular psychology or Christian theology and tries to incorporate the other by reinterpreting to fit in with whichever domain is accepted as dominant. This may be done by simply replacing traditional meanings for concepts within one domain with concepts from the other domain (capitulator) or by finding points of agreement. Example: Reinterpreting original sin to mean Freud's primary narcissism.

- *Limiter of Science*: The limiter of science relates psychology to Christianity by viewing each as having its own turf (territorialism) or distinctive point of view (perspectivalism). Because of this, there can be no real conflict between the two domains.

- *Humanizer of Science*: This approach requires a critical synthesis of psychology with Christianity by revamping psychological science to make it compatible with a Christian anthropology. Evans, as a psychologically minded philosopher, has been building on this approach over the years by unpacking Kierkegaard's Christian existentialism for inspiration.

John Carter and Bruce Narramore's (1979) typology was another widely utilized early classification scheme propounded by foundational faculty at Rosemead School of Psychology. These categories drew inspiration from Christian ethicist H. Richard Niebuhr's (1951) models of the different ways Christians have attempted to relate to culture (viz., see chapter six on *role integration* for more details). While not limited to the theoretical, Carter and Narramore's model also appears to focus on integration of theoretical perspectives or truth claims from both fields (i.e., psychology and theology). Each of the Carter and Narramore categorical types for relating psychology and theology are presented as having both a *sacred* and a *secular* version. The first three are all nonintegrative.

- *Against*: One perspective is adopted to be the final and only arbiter of what is to be included in our understanding of and approach to persons.

- *Secular Against*: Adoption of a rationalist or empiricist epistemology that excludes truth claims based on revealed truth. A belief that religion has a negative relationship with mental health. Only naturalistic explanations or solutions for psychological disturbance are acceptable. Carter and

Narramore cite Albert Ellis, at least in the earlier stages of his career, as a representative of this approach.

- *Sacred Against*: The Bible is the only proper source for our counseling models and approaches; secular psychology has little or no contribution to make in this area. Helping approaches drawn from psychology are dangerous or negative, resulting in adverse effects such as removing valid felt convictions of guilt. Human problems are the result of sin, and the solution is not psychotherapy but biblically faithful spiritual intervention. Jay Adam's views are presented as an exemplar of this approach.

- *Of*: The *of* approach attempts to study Christian topics or concerns using psychological theory and methods. A certain style of psychology of religion exemplifies this according to the authors.

- *Secular Of*: Representatives of this approach find value in religion if understood as a source of metaphors or insights that are broadly true about human experience while rejecting any supernaturalism inherent in religion. Examples of this approach include O. Herbert Mower or Erich Fromm.

- *Sacred Of*: A similar approach is reflected among those who start from a theological perspective, albeit usually a liberal one. They also tend to reject supernaturalism but see religious themes and patterns in psychology. Examples offered of this view include Episcopalian John Sanford's approach to Jung, or Seward Hiltner's psychological reinterpretations of theological concepts like sin.

- *Parallels*: The *parallels* model argues that Christianity and psychology are both legitimate but should not be mixed. They are appropriate in their own independent spheres.

- *Secular Parallels*: Proponents of this version of the model argue that psychology and religion both have value and application but each in their own distinct ways that do not impact the other. The two areas are viewed as in some way isolated from each other or at best in correlation, but neither can be thought to alter or challenge the other. Frederick Thorne is presented as an example of the isolation strategy, while Gordon Allport is viewed as a correlationist by Carter and Narramore. For Allport, the goal is to properly *translate* insights from each area but not to *integrate* them.

- *Sacred Parallels*: The *sacred* version of the parallels' model is often practiced and espoused by persons who hold orthodox, biblical personal beliefs, but who agree with the idea that psychology and theology are distinct and parallel views of the world. Carter and Narramore cite Paul Clement's view as an example. Clement draws here from the statistical concept of orthogonal factors to illustrate variables that are statistically independent of one another (i.e., one cannot predict values of one factor from values of the other). Psychology and theology are orthogonal disciplines operating at different logical levels and so they cannot really conflict. At a more practical level, some Christian psychologists did attempt to find *correlation* but not in this statistical sense. Rather they tried to show how concepts from psychology or theology may be different views of a common phenomenon.

- *Integrates*: This model argues that psychology and Christianity should be united into a unified, integrated Christian psychology that captures what is true in both domains.

- *Secular Integrates*: Carter and Narramore suggest that no secular approach can be truly integrative, but that some secular psychologists have attempted to emphasize a productive view of religion to an extent that seems to go beyond a mere coexistence posture often seen in the parallels strategy.

- *Sacred Integrates*: True integration, Carter and Narramore suggest, requires deep conceptual engagement between theology and psychology to work out a unified account that is richly and fully informed by both. At the time of writing their text, they saw just a few authors who were seriously undertaking this effort, such as William Hulme. Other examples include Larry Crabb or Paul Tournier. Regardless of the proponent, scholars reflecting an integrated-approach derive their view of personhood from the notion that we: are made in the image of God; see all psychopathology as ultimately deriving from effects of the fall (although not to individual willful acts of sin in each case); hold to a balanced view of Scripture that does not neglect its emphasis on God's supernatural operation in redemption or his immanent presence in normal psychological processes through providence; hold a respect for the integrity and relative boundaries of each discipline; maintain a belief that biblical religion is mentally healthy; and have an openness to varied counseling approaches but with an emphasis on biblical themes such as sin or responsibility.

Kirk Farnsworth's (1981, 1985) typology from the 1980s built on concepts from the early typology models and argued for strategies of integration that were critical and transformative. Farnsworth (1985) describes integration as " . . . the process whereby both disciplines retain their own identity while benefiting from each other's perspective and communicating the same truth" (p. 11). He calls for an *embodied* integration that connects to personal integration and disciplinary practices rather than just theoretical integration. Nonetheless, his classification scheme focuses on different ways of relating psychological *findings* or *theories* with scriptural teachings or Christian perspectives and thus remains largely a theoretical integration typology. Farnsworth distinguished five distinct processes for such integration efforts:

- *Credibility*: Psychological findings are accepted only if they are consistent with what is taught from Scripture.

- *Convertibility*: Theological concepts can be accepted but only when "converted" or reconceptualized on purely psychological terms.

- *Conformability*: Psychological findings or theories are *transformed* or reworked in light of Christian perspectives. This approach is broader than credibility because the standard is not merely whether the psychological concept is in accord with a biblical teaching but whether it can conform to Christian concepts drawn from the broader domain of Christian theology.

- *Compatibility*: The compatibility model attempts to identify and relate findings from each discipline that are convergent to provide an enriched understanding of a common area of interest.

- *Complementarity*: This model assumes each field is *separate but equal* in validity. While attempts to correlate findings on similar topics may be present, there is no expectation that theological and psychological claims will always be about the same things or even focus on similar aspects of the same topics they may both embrace. Thus, no unified single account may result but rather a complex account with simultaneously valid psychological and theological perspectives.

A review article in *Journal of Psychology and Theology* by Foster, Horn, and Watson (1988) had judges examine 177 integration articles in the journal's five-year history from 1980 to 1985. They concluded that the "conformability" approach was the most common integrative style. The "compatibility" approach was the next most common integrative approach, and it involves an identification of notions shared in both psychology and Christianity.

Brian Eck (1996) attempted the ambitious task of generating a meta-classification scheme for the several integration models that had arisen. He distinguished between three paradigms: *nonintegrative, nonmanipulative integrative,* and *manipulative integrative*. The nonintegrative paradigm rejects either psychology or theology and so leaves nothing left to integrate. The two integrative paradigms attempt to relate psychology and theology. Some use what Eck refers to as a *manipulative* approach attempting to integrate by changing one or both of the domains. Others utilize a *nonmanipulative* approach adopting interface processes that leave the domains unchanged. Eck emphasizes the differing "processes" that drive subtypes across each of these paradigms. For example, Eck asserted that the nonintegrative paradigm uses a rejective process, while the manipulative integration paradigms use either a reconstruction or transformational process. The nonmanipulative integration paradigms use a correlational process or a "unifies" process. For Eck, the unifies process is the desired form of integration.

All of these early models seemed to assume that theoretical integration approaches would be singularly adopted by individuals. Whether one adopted an integrates approach, correlational process, or conformability approach, one would do so in all integration (or nonintegration) efforts. This presentation of the task, to view theoretical integration as a kind of static Christian posture one adopts to a particular psychological theory, may have been in part an artifact of the emphasis on training clinicians and counselors from within particular theoretical orientations. Regardless of the reason, the models may leave the fledgling integrator with the erroneous impression of "one shoe size fits all" theoretical integration tasks. This picture of integration would be ill-suited to deal with the contemporary state of psychological fields wherein theoretical pluralism and eclecticism have become much more common.

Theoretical Integration in the Context of Theory Pluralism

The psychotherapy integration movement (hereafter, PIM) arose as an attempt to find common ground and to promote synthetic advances over the standalone psychotherapy theories that were prevalent (Stricker & Gold, 1996). (To not confuse the reader, the PIM refers to integration of different psychotherapies, not the integration of psychology and Christianity that is the broader focus of our discussion.) The PIM is complex and reflects varied approaches motivated by multiple historical factors including: research on psychotherapy outcomes that showed a generic benefit for treatment with no clear winners based on therapeutic approach; the growing view that operating entirely within one orientation was too limiting to contend with the full range of clinical problems; the detection of common factors that were important for human change across theoretical approaches; and the explosion of new therapies, making the attempt to master more than a small subset impractical for most clinicians and counselors. The *Journal of Psychotherapy Integration* was launched in 1991 to provide a dedicated forum for this movement. In the opening article of the journal, Arkowitz (1991) noted: "In psychotherapy integration, representatives of different therapy approaches have shown a willingness to look beyond the confines of their own orientations to discover what can be learned from other ways of thinking about psychotherapy and change" (p. 1).

Of the various ways this has been approached, Stricker and Gold (1996) observed that theoretical integration is perhaps the most ambitious attempted: "Theoretical integration involves the synthesis of novel models of personality functioning, psychopathology, and psychological change out of the concepts of two or more traditional systems"(p. 50). The attempt to pull this off in many ways parallels the challenges facing the Christian integration project in the theoretical domain. Stricker and Gold (1996) described some of the PIM strategies. One approach attempted integration by ". . . . translation of concepts and methods of one psychotherapeutic system into the language and procedures of another" (p. 47). Paul Watchel's (1977) *Psychoanalysis and Behavior* therapy served as a watershed moment for this effort. Another approach arose from the common factors tradition, which attempted to identify " . . . generic change factors that were common to all therapies" (p. 48). The PIM has continued to evolve in many complex ways such as: systematic eclecticism; formal identification and promulgation of empirically supported treatment strategies; transtheoretical approaches; empirically identifying beneficial aspects of therapeutic relationships; and evidence-based practice models. Much of these developments engage many other aspects of treatment and therapy than just the theoretical, but they have had a dramatic impact on theoretical efforts nonetheless.

Stricker and Gold (1996) described their own PIM approach as assimilative theoretical integration. It is assimilative:

because a single theoretical structure is maintained, but techniques from several other approaches are incorporated within that structure. As new techniques are employed within a conceptual foundation, the meaning, impact, and utility of those techniques are changed in powerful ways. (p. 50)

Such an effort indicates that multitheoretical borrowing and engagement is a well-recognized part of the theoretical landscape even within the psychologically related disciplines.

Thus, as a discipline, psychology has been striving to *integrate* multiple theoretical views in ways that advance the understanding of the phenomena that field engages beyond what Watchel accomplished by any one theory alone. Similar projects have also occurred in some areas of theology. For instance, *kaleidoscope* views of the atonement argue that no one theory of the atonement captures the scriptural reality of the salvation wrought by the work of Jesus through his incarnation, death, burial, and resurrection. Instead, multiple views are thought as offering added illumination on the nature of the atonement in a way that expands, but does not exhaust, what Jesus accomplished.[1]

If efforts at finding a constructive appreciation for theory pluralism are now influential in both of the areas (i.e., psychology and theology) we are attempting to integrate, then we likely need to think in more complex ways about our theoretical integration project than simply focusing on how Christians should think about any particular standalone psychological theory. This appreciation for theory pluralism has been a hallmark of postmodernism that has increasingly been impacted by the psychology-related fields and theology.

The Impact of Postmodernism

Postmodernism is a famously difficult thing to define. It would be far beyond the scope of this text to offer anything like an adequate introduction to this topic. Yet some observations about postmodernism are necessary to understand another substantial set of factors impacting theoretical integration. We are here referring to postmodernism as a period worldview. Period worldviews are themes or

---

[1]See Baker and Green (2011) for an example of a *kaleidoscope* view. As with some synthetic integrative efforts in the PIM in psychology, some Christian scholars have argued there is value in multiple atonement theories (i.e., Christus Victor, Penal Substitution, or even Moral Example views) but still assert that one framework should be given greater emphasis than the rest. Burnhope (2012) attempts to spell out what a synthesis might look like that would draw from the insights of the kaleidoscopic view but still retains key features of singular and objective views of the atonement, such as the notion salvation is wrought in the atonement by the work of God alone.

constellations of ideas that characterize a period of time, what the Germans refer to as a *zeitgeist*. Attempts to define postmodernism typically contrast it with modernism. Modernity reflects an unbridled confidence in human progress wrought through scientific advance and rationalist enlightenment. It impacted every area of Western culture and thought. Everything was up for challenge and no tradition was viewed as off-limits to the great leveling resulting from the application of scientific method to all spheres of life. The modern ideal was the discovery and commitment to scientifically discerned objective truth with no sacred cows being exempted from its dissections. On a modern view, theories are attempts to accurately describe the way things *really are* or the way things *appear to be*. Theories can be tested empirically or rationally for their adequacy in capturing reality or *saving the appearances*. Various dates are offered for the modern period. Some connect to the earliest signs of the scientific revolution. Others see modernism has symbolically born with the fall of the Bastille during the French revolution in 1789 and lasting until the Iron Curtain fell in 1989, signaling the end of the hypermodern Soviet social-political experiment.

Postmodernism represents a loss of confidence in scientific method to achieve objective truth that will yield inevitable progress. Instead, it is asserted that our views of reality are social constructions—word pictures we create together in our increasingly overlapping cultures and subcultures. Since every theoretical perspective is simply a story told—and perhaps believed—by an individual, or more likely some community of persons, the search to vindicate or even determine the truth of a single theory is little more than one person or group trying to assert the supremacy of their fanciful stories about the world over another. Theoretical ascendency is, on such a view, a kind of imposition or oppression. A theory that pretends to be a singularly true account is depicted in postmodernism as a 'metanarrative.' In his landmark text on postmodernism, Lyotard (1979/1984) concisely defines postmodernism as an "incredulity about metanarratives" (p. xxiv).

A common theme in postmodernism is the placing of a greater emphasis on skeptical deconstruction of grand theoretical perspectives and reality claims than on construction of novel big picture theories. In place of overarching grand metanarratives, postmodernists typically aspire to a plurality of more local, midrange narratives that coexist and overlap. Furthermore, it often asserts that even in the postmodern situation people are rarely defined by a singular narrative, local or grand, but typically represent an intersectionality of multiple story lines. The contemporary condition is suggested to be one in which people exist as *saturated selves* (Gergin, 1991) with *multiphrenic* identities pieced together from an explosion of possible selves that flood our perceptual world and interpersonal situations.

Evangelical Christians reacted to this postmodern turn in varied ways. Some engaged in polemics against it, seeing it as deeply contrary to a biblical worldview and erosive of truth (Groothuis, 2000). Others were more open, seeing it as an opportunity to usurp modernism's hegemony in cultural thought and potentially reopening the door for the importance of tradition that had been muted by modernism (Grentz, 1996; Smith, 2006). Often the discussions over postmodernism proceed as if postmodernism has somehow won the day. But to deconstruct that metanarrative a bit, there is no postmodern consensus that has been uniformly or even pervasively embraced in culture. While postmodernism gives all a seat at the conversation table in theory, it does so at the cost of allowing anyone to say anything *real*. Furthermore, it is not even clear that postmodernism does welcome all comers to a seat at the table. Although it has no ideologically coherent basis for doing so, it tends to be welcoming selectively to those who espouse a particular range of perspectives and rejecting of those outside of its preferences (see our earlier discussion in chapter one about viewpoint diversity).

Still we appreciate postmodernism's dethronement of scientific naturalism with that latter's antipathy toward religious or other truth claims. We also appreciate the emphasis on nuanced aspects of human experience that were likely too hastily glossed over in the past in search of grand theories. While we retain the idea that an objectively true theoretical perspective exists, namely the view of reality in the mind of God, we recognize that we as humans never are able to obtain with limitless clarity that view of the world. Even in the "new creation," when the corrupting influences of sin are removed from our knowing faculties, we will have true understandings of the world but never ones that match the understanding in the mind of God. We suspect there will always be a multiperspicuity to human theoretical constructions differentially informed by our different life situations.

Thus, we appreciate Neff and McMinn's (2020) call for an integrative vision that is conversational and more attuned to varied contextual features of people's lived experiences than the abstracted universals that have often been the focus of the grand theories. A key draw to postmodernism in the psychological-related fields, and among some integrationists, is its openness to divergent, marginalized perspectives. Consequently, postmodern methods, frameworks, and perspectives have been increasingly connected to concerns about promoting equity, diversity, and inclusion (hereafter EDI) in contrast to older modern sensibilities that often excluded not only these perspectives but the representatives of communities that commonly held them. We appreciate this concern and will return to it in our chapter on personal integration.

Still, we would not surrender to postmodern sensibility the notion that the unity of truth is a real thing. All human efforts at understanding, for those who profess to be disciples of the One who is truth, must aim to be faithful to the divine *theoria* in the mind of God. We recognize this to be a regulative ideal and not an expected outcome for any human academic endeavor in this present age. Still, this does not mean there are no anchor points. Some core Christian ideas are more rooted and firmly settled (Wolterstorff, 1988). It would be an act of hubris for a postmodern to dismiss those lightly in favor of idiosyncratic life experience or fad cultural narratives.[2]

The Hermeneutical-Process Approach to Integration

Both of us have appreciated the scholarly trends that have given rise to discontent with modernism and its enlightenment affection for a secularized metaphysical naturalism. We believe the emphasis on interpretation prevalent in postmodernism provides productive resources for reframing of the theoretical integration project. Yet, we also think this can be done in a way that preserves a commitment to *objective truth* as a regulative ideal for that project.

Hathaway (2002) has offered a hermeneutical-process account of integration that attempted to extend the early work on Christian theoretical integration while navigating the complex landscape more recently impacting theory building. A key starting point for this proposal was the observation that early evangelical theoretical typologies all assumed that integrators could be categorized into relatively discrete and fixed integrative types. Also, Eck's helpful emphasis on integrative processes raises the possibility that multiple processes of integration might

---

[2]The reader may detect from our summary that we do not reject postmodernism in toto as a group of varied perspectives with no contribution to offer to the construction of authentic and biblically faithful worldviews. On the other hand, we remain concerned about the relativistic leanings common in postmodernism. We do reject postmodern proposals that reduce to what Plantinga (1994) has called *creative antirealism*: the idea that reality is merely a human construction. Plantinga sees this perspective as naturally resulting in relativism and *anticommitment* to beliefs. He sees perspectives in the creative antirealism camp as the predominant other contemporary error for Christian scholars besides the naturalism so characteristic of modernism that we discussed in our worldview chapter. As Plantinga puts it: "Perennial naturalism and creative anti-realism are related in an interesting manner: the first vastly underestimates the place of human beings in the universe, and the second vastly overestimates it."

be deployed rather than exclusive reliance on one type. What if we reframe the proposed types in the models as *postures* adopted for particular integrative situations at a specific moment? Any given Christian psychologist may adopt multiple integrative postures at the same moment with regard to different theoretical integration tasks.

Hermeneutics is the study of interpretative understanding and the process of interpretation. Since the nineteenth century, hermeneutics has been thought of as the study of all understanding, since it is widely asserted that all understanding is a process of interpretation. Since theoretical integration is about interpretative understanding, it can be properly thought of as a hermeneutical endeavor.

There are resources in contemporary hermeneutics (the field that studies interpretative understanding) that can help us flesh out this proposal.[3] One of the first lessons biblical literature students learn about interpreting Scripture is that the Bible is composed of multiple types of literature called genres. Each genre has interpretative praxes appropriate to it; therefore, one needs to read the text in accord with its genre. For instance, the book of Proverbs contains a collection of aphoristic statements that have long been read differently than historical narratives, such as the book of Joshua, by biblical sages of both Jewish and Christian faiths.

Similarly, we assert that different types of psychological theorizing may pose different theoretical integration challenges for psychology. These different domains are not different genres in the literal sense but do represent different ways of understanding and explaining that have something analogous to their own interpretative rules and discourses (Gerkin, 1984; Ricoeur, 1981). Based on the theoretical area, there may be close enough overlap between psychological and theological understandings to motivate attempts to translate concepts from one domain to another. For instance, efforts to understand the nature of sin and pathology has led both Christian thinkers and secular mental health professions to attempt a translation of these categories in terms that fit the preferred perspective or some integrated view (Menninger, 1973; McMinn, 2008; Ramm, 1985; Stanford, 2010). Similar work has been done on concepts like forgiveness

---

[3]The field of philosophical hermeneutics now is frequently presented as a nonrealist enterprise that eschews any possibility of progress in human understanding of an objective reality. However, hermeneutical realism is a view that argues that hermeneutical understanding in science and other forms of inquiry can be conceptualized as a form of knowing the real world while simultaneously appreciating the interpretative context of all such understanding (Heelan, 1982; Wachterhauser, 1994). Hathaway's model aligns with this hermeneutical realist school.

(Worthington & Wade, 2020) and gratitude (Emmons & McCullough, 2004). On other occasions, the work done in theology and psychology on seemingly related theoretical areas may be too dissimilar in conception to attempt any such translation. However, if the ideas from both seem relevant and not in conflict, then the theoretical perspectives may simply add in the concepts from the other perspective without altering the key features of one's theory. For instance, a Christian dealing with psychobiological features of functioning may be much more likely to simply talk like a secular neuropsychologist when making sense of this sort of natural scientific data. Navigating theoretical perspectives from Christian thought and psychology-related fields that appear to offer divergent or competing theoretical understandings of a closely related subject involves a more challenging process (viz., Yarhouse, 2015, 2019). Thus, in a truly relevant sense then, Christian theoretical integration in the psychology-related fields is much like attempting to make sense of multiple texts representing diverse genres.

The seminal hermeneutical philosopher, Hans George Gadamer, described interpretation as a *fusion of horizons*. A *horizon of understanding* is everything we can see from a particular vantage point. It is like a worldview but includes every aspect of our understanding and experience, not just the foundational assumptions. A reader approaches the text from a particular horizon. But the text also represents its own horizon—that of the author or the original audiences. For Gadamer, interpretation requires the horizon of the reader to become *fused* with the horizon of the thing being interpreted. For instance, the reader cannot step outside of themselves to understand a biblical passage. The person reads the passage with their contemporary eyes. Yet if the readers do not get at least some glimpse of what the text meant in its original horizon (i.e., for its first readers or its author), then they have not interpreted it. They have only imposed their meanings on the text. Interpretation has occurred when the original understandings expressed in the text are faithfully present in the revised contemporary perspective that the reader develops when reading it. When this happens, a fusion of the horizons has occurred.[4] There is an expansion of understanding that is greater than the sum of the two independent horizons.

---

[4]Imagine that you, as a reader, with all of your knowledge and experience were to enter a time machine and return to the first century to visit the apostle Paul just after he wrote 1 Corinthians. Suppose you could have a conversation with him about what the text meant. As he explained it to you, you would no doubt have a much deeper understanding than we do now. Yet as the apostle got to know you and heard about the history of Christianity after his era, applications, implications, and novel ways of understanding what he had written would likely occur even to him. For instance, imagine how he

Paul Ricoeur is another prominent thinker who has helped us understand hermeneutics and whose insights inform Hathaway's model. A few key concepts from Ricoeur include attendance to distance and alien meanings and the production of new understanding:

- *Attending to distance*: One thing that is important in good interpretation is for the reader to pay attention to "distance" between their horizon and the horizon of the text. For instance, when we assume we know what the author means by their use of terms, it is possible that we would read back into the text contemporary meanings that are not correct.

- *Alien meanings and the production of new understanding*: One of the ways we learn from the text, according to Ricoeur, is to give special attention to things that do not fit our easy understanding. When we read a Bible passage and come upon something unclear, we often are tempted to skip over and move on to things that make more sense. But it is precisely these things that "don't fit" that are most able to challenge our preconceptions and grow our understanding. In order to do this, we have to dwell with the tension and not try to assimilate alien meanings too quickly. The tension serves a productive purpose of forcing us to grow in our understanding to faithfully capture the meaning of the text.

Hathaway (2002) sees in hermeneutical theory a resource for an account of theoretical integration that synthesizes the earlier theoretical integration models. This account is depicted in figure 4. On this metamodel, there are three broad stages in understanding in the integrative process. Rather than viewing each of these as competing or alternative models of integration, it is better to see them as different aspects of interpretative understanding. They may each be perfectly valid or invalid depending on the nature of the interpretative task facing the person.

---

would understand the "love chapter" (1 Cor 13) or the "gifts of the Spirit discussion" (1 Cor 12 & 14) differently if he heard about Pentecostalism. Of course, God inspired the Bible and God was aware of our contemporary horizons even when the Bible was being written. But this does not mean that the Apostle was personally mindful of every future application of the message he was given by the Spirit. So, a valid contemporary reading of Scripture requires faithfulness to the message of the text but may result in novel insights that did not necessarily occur to the original first-century audience.

| ASSIMILATION | POTENTIALLY PRODUCTIVE TENSION | | EXPANDED HORIZON |
	Compartmentalization	Complementarity	
Carter & Narramore (1979) Against Carter & Narramore (1979) Of Crabb (1977) Nothing buttery Eck (1996) Rejects Farnsworth (1985) Credibility, convertibility	Carter & Narramore (1979) Parallels Crabb (1977) Separate but equal Evans (1977) Territorialism Farnsworth (1985) Compatibility	Crabb (1977) Tossed salad Eck (1996) Reconstructs, transforms, & correlates processes Evans (1977) Perspectivalism Farnsworth (1985) Complementarity	Carter & Narramore (1979) Integrates Crabb (1977) Spoiling the Egyptians Eck (1996) Unifies Evans (1977) Humanizer of science Farnsworth (1985) Conformability?

RANGE OF UNDERSTANDING   **RANGE OF UNDERSTANDING**

Fusion of Horizons

|---- range ----| |--------- range ---------| |-------- range --------|

Figure 4. Integration typologies as moments along an interpretive continuum

The three postures are *assimilation, productive tension*, and *expanded horizon*. *Assimilation* occurs when one horizon understands another by assimilating perspectives, observation reports, concepts, or other products of the other horizon completely within existing schemes and worldviews. No transformed understanding results from this mere assimilation process. It is appropriate when no schema altering knowledge is offered by the other horizon.

Productive tension occurs when there seems to be something valid in a new horizon that does not fit well within one's existing schema. If the person moves too quickly to assimilate in such cases, then they may get the perspective of the other wrong and fail to learn some new understanding of the world. On the other hand, if they quickly abandon their prior understanding in favor of the new (accommodation), they merely replace one perspective with another, and no growth has occurred for either perspective. But when we dwell in the tension and do not foreclose, we increase the chances that some transformative insight may result in the truth from both perspectives being integrated into an expanded understanding. If we do not know how to faithfully embrace the truth in either our preunderstanding or the new perspective we are trying to understand, it is most respectful of truth to not jump to conclusions. Holding such a state of tension can prompt new insight and produce expanded understanding. But it is only potentially productive. Some ways of living in tension may not be as likely to result in growth. An overly comfortable compartmentalization, such as may be implicit in the notion of territorialism or parallel integration, may not prompt the sort of comprehension effort required to be productive of new understanding. We would speculate that a robust complementarianism may be more productive than a parallelist approach because it would presumably keep both the Christian theological and psychological perspectives in mind as it engages the same phenomenon.

Finally, the *expanded horizon* is the ideal telos (goal) of integrative understanding.[5] We reach this point when novel insights are produced that faithfully receive the truth in the perspective of the other in the context of everything true about our prior understanding of the world. This is a regulative ideal that is approximated to varying degrees by faithful integrative efforts.

One objection that is sometimes offered by those with a high view of the authority of the text is that Gadamerian-inspired models of interpretation seem to relativize all horizons of understanding without any overriding authority. But that is a misreading of the situation when a person views one of the horizons as the Word of God. It is quite understandable when we reject any given person's arrogant assertion of superior judgment, all things being equal. But for someone who holds to a high view of the authority of Scripture, that particular horizon can never be faithfully viewed as on a level playing field with other human horizons, including our own prior ones. It is not merely our own religious insights versus those of Paul or Solomon. It is our own insights versus those of a revelation inspired and providentially mediated through a human writer by the all-knowing, perfect Creator and sustainer of the universe.

If any two people disagree about a topic, they may see the disagreement as arising from potential errors on either of their parts and be humbly open to correction. But in attempting to fuse our psychological horizon with that of Scripture, the intertextuality cannot be viewed as on equal footing by anyone who authentically believes Scripture is the divinely revealed word. Many people who do not believe the Bible to be the infallible revealed Word of God will reject such a way

---

[5]We make repeated use of the notion of a telos. *Telos* literally means an "end" or destination. For Aristotle, the telos referred to the purpose for which something exists. We embrace that Aristotelian idea to a degree but also use the term less precisely to refer to merely the proper end toward which a process is aimed. In this passage, by telos we mean that, when properly functioning, human epistemic (i.e., knowledge providing) faculties produce a truth approximating understanding of the world. Because the only exhaustively true understanding of reality is that contained in the mind of God, all human knowledge acquisition will only approximate that objective and exhaustive understanding.

of viewing the horizon of Scripture. But if exegetes are correct who assert the text of the Bible itself assumes it to be such revelation, then such revelation skeptics will not be pursuing a fusion of horizons with the Scriptures. Instead, they will be seeking to assimilate into their preexisting schema. Of course, even if two interpreters agree that the Bible is the authoritative Word of God, this does not mean they will automatically accept each other's understanding of the text.[6]

It should also be noted that, on this hermeneutical metamodel, it can be legitimate, indeed virtuous, to use different postures with different issues. In contrast to the earlier models of integration, one is not necessarily a certain type (e.g., a perspectivalist or an integrator). A Christian psychologist may naturally assimilate some aspects of psychology without altering their preexisting understandings. When it comes to identifying the lobes of the brain or describing what is known about the neurochemistry of behavior, we would quite naturally adopt a largely assimilationist strategy. Other things may require growth and expansion in both their theological and psychological understandings. For instance, issues such as a Christian integrative view of self-regulation theory or gender identity require a more prolonged and sustained interpretative process to be faithful to the full range of truth.

Based on the insights of hermeneutics literature, this model of integration as interpretative understanding guided by a Christian worldview results in some practical strategies for integration. We will discuss a wider range of spiritual disciplines and related practices and habits for the students in chapter seven (personal integration), but practical strategies include the following:

- Pray for guidance and listen to the Spirit.
- Become a responsive truth seeker: commit but put your beliefs at "risk."
- Immerse yourself in subject matters to be integrated.
- Be patient with tension, avoid premature closure on views.
- Develop a tolerance for ambiguity.
- Track the integrative efforts of other Christian psychologists.
- Test ideas against a community of Christian professionals.

---

[6]Arthos (2009) unpacks the implications of a key part of Gadamer's interpretative model that draws on the concept of the *inner word* illuminated by the Christian doctrine of the incarnation and the Trinity. While Gadamer was not formally affirming the Christian doctrines, he found in them a clue about how language can externally convey an aspect of the world with diminishing it, despite elements of language being distinct from the experience to which they refer.

Does Faithful Integration Mean Monolithic "Unity"?

Returning to our integrative assumptions, it is reasonable to ask whether faithful integration means monolithic "unity." In other words, does our work in integration assume we will have as Christians one voice, one answer in the field of psychology? We do not expect theoretical unity to be achieved by human scholars anytime soon, although some convergence and progress would not be surprising. Rather, our work in integration aims more realistically at finding harmonic convergence from a plurality of situated takes on the human condition. Why?

We should keep in mind that the *unity of truth* notion assumes the appropriate standard for Christian knowledge is the mind of God. But even if this is a correct definition of truth, it does not mean we expect it can be currently achieved in our psychology theory building. First, classic Christian theology holds that we can never fully comprehend God. Even in our eternal state, we will not have omniscience but some form of creaturely knowledge. Differing perspectives (a plurality of voices) can be thought of as an indicator of imperfection. But it is also possible that noncontradictory and complementary pluralism provides a way for a community of finite knowers to have a greater appreciation of truth.

On this view, human understanding and apprehension of divine truth, even in perfection, would be a process collectively distributed across individuals. If this later account is true, then it would also make it very understandable why God would make us as communal creatures. This alternative view does not deny the *unity* of *truth* or that humans can know what God allows them to know truly. Rather, it denies that God designed humans so that they can, in their own human understanding, have an omniperspectival, uniform, and exhaustive apprehension of truth.

The following quote from Calvin University philosopher James K. A. Smith illustrates this alternative vision of a pluralistic but truth complementary regulative ideal for integration:

> Creational-pneumatic hermeneutic is a hermeneutic that celebrates humanity, but it is one that also mourns it rupture and roots its lament precisely in its belief in a good creation. The heart of a creational-pneumatic hermeneutic is space, a field of multiplicitous meeting in the wild spaces of love . . . where there is room for a plurality of God's creatures to speak, sing and dance in a multivalent chorus of tongues. (Smith, 2000, p. 184)

We would expect theoretical integration done well to faithfully resonate the concordant revelation of God in the two books of revelation through a multiphonal chorus. In this picture, we welcome some key aspects of postmodernism and theoretical pluralism implicated by our account of the theory integration project. Yet against postmodernists who embrace epistemological anarchy, we would add that such a multiphonal chorus, if led by the one Spirit and tracking the unity of truth detectable through the many vantage points that are present in the body of Christ, will not result in a cacophony.

Examples of Local Theoretical Integration

We will draw this chapter to a close by briefly mentioning some examples of the more local theoretical projects we believe may more fruitfully characterize this domain moving forward. Theoretical or scientific efforts have been described as *local* when aimed at explaining this more restricted and limited range of phenomena than at explaining functioning at a more universal level (Hathaway, 2004). Some years ago, Bill worked with his postdoctoral mentor, Russell Barkley, to develop a theory of how Attention-Deficit/Hyperactivity Disorder (ADHD) might relate to spiritual development. Barkley's (2003) influential theory of ADHD as a self-regulation disorder was fused with common Christian understandings of spiritual formation to develop this local theory in an early contribution in the mental health fields to what some have called the *theology of disability* (Grcevich, 2018).

Mark has for many years worked to formulate a theoretical understanding of gender and sexual minorities that is faithful to Scripture and empirically accurate. His sexual identity framework represents the fruits of that effort (Yarhouse, 2019). In 2008, we were both asked to review the draft document of the APA's (2009) report on *Appropriate Therapeutic Responses to Sexual Orientation*. We provided feedback that was included in that final adopted document that is now APA policy. We noted that even if a religious community fully accepts the psychological data and conclusions that sexual orientation change efforts are unlikely to be successful and may be harmful in some cases, this does not mean that adherents would authentically or autonomously choose to identify with their bottom-up organismic sexual motivations rather than their religious values or ideals. Maddi (1996) defined organismic valuation as a "biological pressure to fulfill the genetic blueprint" (p. 106). Drawing on this Rogerian-inspired note, one can define *organismic incongruence* as a "discord between phenomenal self and self-concept."

In contrast, we suggested *telic incongruence* is a discord "between experience and 'ultimate goals'" (Hathaway, 2009). We offered this distinction that was incorporated into the policy report to capture this difference in a way that fit with the empirical data. The report cited our theoretical distinction stating "the conflict between psychology and traditional faiths may have its roots in different philosophical viewpoints. Some religions give priority to telic congruence (i.e., living consistently within one's valuative goals)" (American Psychological Association Task Force, 2009, p. 18). Of course, this contribution was not an effort at constructing an entire Christian personality theory but rather a theoretical integration of a much more delimited type.

Numerous other examples can be cited as well of more delimited or *local* theory integration projects. Coe and Hall (2010) and Hall and Hall (2021) have been working out a model of *transformational psychology* that is deeply informed by relational neuroscience, spiritual formation theology, attachment theory, relevant emotion-focused clinical paradigms, and other areas of psychology. Their work offers something like a sophisticated current effort toward the construction of a Christian integrative personality theory. In the field of personality psychology, Emmons (1999) has drawn on goal theory and theologically informed understandings of spirituality to flesh out a measurable theory of human strivings. Psychological scientists, such as Barrett (2012), have research-fertile cognitive science of religion theories that have been highly influential in that field developed in dialogue with Christian and other theological understandings. The substantial work done on religious coping, while not explicitly understood as a part of the Christian integration project, is still relevant here. This work was most seminally conducted by the Jewish psychologist Ken Pargament and many of his students, including a number who were Christian. It produced theoretical elements that are far more open to an explicitly theistic worldview than is often the case in contemporary psychology. For instance, Pargament (1997) and his colleagues found that people often engage in religious coping not to just resolve their problem situation or improve their mental health but rather for specifically spiritual reasons like learning what God wants to teach them or feeling closer to God.

Summary

Theoretical integration is the attempt to construct, synthesize, or correlate Christian thought with psychological theory. If worldview integration is about construction of a faithfully Christian view of the world, theoretical integration reflects the conceptual snapshots of our world that emerge from such a view. The theoretical tradition in the psychology-related fields has a long lineage. During the early decades of the integration project, integration was frequently conceptualized as a project of integrating various psychological theories and Christian thought. Most often the theories being integrated were personality theories (e.g., psychodynamic, humanistic, or cognitive theoretical orientations) or major paradigms of psychological science, such as behaviorism. This early integrative project often was pursued by creating typologies reflecting different ways one might interrelate Christian thought and psychological theories.

However, these integrative models typically focused on integration of stand-alone psychological theories and Christian thought. In recent decades, there has been a shift in psychological fields away from an emphasis on grand theoretical orientations. The movement has been toward a theory of pluralism where ideas from many perspectives are drawn on to attempt to understand more delimited and local—as opposed to universal—aspects of psychological functioning. The psychotherapy integration movement and the impact of postmodernism have been important influential accelerants for this trend.

Hathaway's hermeneutical-process model of integration offers a framework that may subsume insights offered by earlier theoretical integration models. It also depicts when and how different integrative postures may be appropriate. The model distinguishes different integrative postures including those efforts that merely assimilate, hold the theological and psychological in productive tension, and that fuse both in an expanded understanding. All of these integrative *postures* may be appropriate for some specific theoretical integration task but not for others at the same time. Thus, a hermeneutical-process model provides an appreciative framework for theoretical pluralism and a humble caution about our ability to achieve full theoretical integration while retaining a belief in the pursuit of objective truth and theoretical progress as a goal.

References

American Psychological Association Task Force. (2009). *American Psychological Association Task Force Report: Appropriate therapeutic responses to sexual orientation.* American Psychological Association. www.apa.org/pi/lgbt/resources/therapeutic-response.pdf

Arkowitz, H. (1991). Introductory statement: Psychotherapy integration comes of age. *Journal of Psychotherapy Integration, 1*(1), 1-3. doi.org/10.1037/h0101205

Arthos, J. (2009). *The inner word in Gadamer's hermeneutics.* University of Notre Dame Press.

Baker, M. D., & Green, J. B. (2011). Recovering the scandal of the cross: Atonement in New Testament and contemporary contexts (2nd ed.). InterVarsity Press.

Barkley, R. A. (2003). *ADHD and the nature of self-control*. Guilford.

Barrett, J. L. (2012). *Born believers: The science of children's religious beliefs*. Atria.

Bufford, R. K. (1981). *The reflex arc: Behavioral psychology in biblical perspective*. Harper & Row.

Burnhope, S. J. (2012). Beyond the kaleidoscope: Towards a synthesis of views on the atonement. *Evangelical Quarterly, 84*(4), 345-68.

Carter, J., & Narramore, B. (1979). *The integration of psychology & theology: An introduction*. Zondervan.

Coe, J. H., & Hall, T. W. (2010). *Psychology in the Spirit: Contours of a transformational psychology*. InterVarsity Press.

Corsini, R. (1973). *Current psychotherapies*. F. E. Peacock Publishers.

Crabb, L. (1977). *Effective biblical counseling: A model for helping caring Christians become capable counselors*. Zondervan.

Eck, B. E. (1996). Integrating the integrators: An organizing framework for a multifaceted process of integration. *Journal of Psychology and Christianity, 15,* 101-15.

Emmons, R. A. (1999). *The psychology of ultimate concerns: Motivation and spirituality in personality*. Guilford Press.

Emmons, R. A., & McCullough, M. E. (Eds.). (2004). *The psychology of gratitude*. Guilford Press.

Erdvig, R. C. S. (2020). A model for biblical worldview development in evangelical Christian emerging adults. *Journal of Research on Christian Education*, doi:10.1080/10656219.2020 .1816517

Evans, C. S. (1977). *Preserving the person: A look at the human sciences*. Baker Books.

Farnsworth, K. E. (1981). *Integrating psychology and theology: Elbows together but hearts apart*. University Press of America.

Farnsworth, K. E. (1985). *Whole-hearted integration: Harmonizing psychology and Christianity through word and deed*. Baker Books.

Foster, J. D., Horn, D. A., & Watson, S. (1988). The popularity of integration models: 1980-1985. *Journal of Psychology and Theology, 16,* 3-14.

Gadamer, H. G. (1984). *Truth and Method*. Crossroad.

Gergin, K. (1991). *The saturated self: Dilemmas of identity in contemporary life*. Basic Books.

Gerken, C. V. (1984). *The living human document: Re-visioning pastoral counseling in a hermeneutical mode*. Abingdon.

Grcevich, S. (2018). *Mental health and the Church: A ministry handbook for including children and adults with ADHD, anxiety, mood disorders, and other common mental health conditions*. Zondervan.

Grentz, S. J. (1996). *A primer on postmodernism*. Wm. B. Eerdmans.

Groothuis, D. (2000). *Truth decay: Defending Christianity against the challenges of postmodernism*. InterVarsity Press.

Hathaway, W. L. (2002). Integration as interpretation: A hermeneutical realist view. *Journal of Psychology & Christianity, 21*(3), 205-18.

Hathaway, W. L. (2004). Two paradigms of clinical science. *Journal of Mind & Behavior, 25,* 167-86.

Hathaway, W. L. (2009, August 7). *The Clinical Psychology of Religion and Spirituality.* Division 36 presidential address. The American Psychological Association Annual Convention, Toronto, Ontario.

Hathaway, W. L., & Barkley, R. A. (2003). Self-regulation, ADHD, & child religiousness. *Journal of Psychology & Christianity, 22*(2), 104-11.

Hall, T. W., & Hall, M. E. (2021). *Relational spirituality: A psychological-theological paradigm for transformation.* InterVarsity Press.

Heelan, P. A. (1982). Hermeneutical realism and scientific observation. *Philosophy of Science, 1982*(1), 77-87.

Johnson, E. L. (2017). *God and soul care: The therapeutic resources of the Christian faith.* InterVarsity Press.

Leuridan, B. (2014). The structure of scientific theories, explanation, and unification. A causal–structural account. *British Journal for the Philosophy of Science, 65,* 717-71.

Lyotard, J. F. (1984). *The postmodern condition: A report on knowledge,* G. Bennington & B. Massumi (Trans.), University of Minnesota Press. (Original work published 1979)

Maddi, S. R. (1996). *Personality theories: A comparative analysis* (6th ed.). Waveland Press.

McMinn, M. R. (2008). *Sin and grace in Christian counseling: An integrative paradigm.* InterVarsity Press.

Menninger, K. (1973). *Whatever became of sin?* Hawthorn Books.

Neff, M. A., & McMinn, M. R. (2020). *Embodying integration: A fresh look at Christianity in the therapy room.* InterVarsity Press.

Neihbur, H. R. (1951). *Christ & Culture.* Harper & Row.

Pargament, K. I. (1997). *The psychology of religious coping: The theory, research, and practice.* Guilford Press.

Plantinga, A. (1994). On Christian scholarship. In T. Hesburgh (Ed.), *The Challenge and Promise of a Catholic University.* University of Notre Dame Press (pp. 267-95). University of Notre Dame Press.

Ramm, B. (1985). *Offense to reason: A theology of sin.* Harper & Row.

Reeve, J. M. (2018). *Understanding motivation and emotion* (7th ed.). John Wiley.

Ricoeur, P. (1981). *Hermeneutics and the human sciences.* (J. B. Thomson, Ed. & Trans.), Cambridge University.

Slife, B. D. (2000). Theoretical psychology. *Encyclopedia of Psychology.* Oxford University Press.

Smith, J. K. A. (2000). *The fall of interpretation: Philosophical foundations for a creational hermeneutic.* InterVarsity Press.

Smith, J. K. A. (2006). *Who's afraid of postmodernism? Taking Derrida, Lyotard, and Foucault to church* (The Church and Postmodern Culture). Baker Books.

Stanford, M. S. (2010). *The biology of sin.* InterVarsity Press.

Stricker, G., & Gold, J. R. (1996). Psychotherapy integration: An assimilative, psychodynamic approach. *Clinical Psychology: Science and Practice, 3,* 47-58.

Wachterhauser, B. (Ed.). (1994). *Hermeneutics and truth.* Northwestern University.

Watchel, P. L. (1977). *Psychoanalysis and behavior therapy: Toward an integration.* Basic Books.

Wolterstorff, N. (1988). *Reason with the bounds of religion.* Eerdmans.

Worthington, E. L., Jr., & Wade, N. G. (Eds.). (2020). *Handbook of forgiveness* (2nd ed.). Routledge.

Yarhouse, M. A. (2015). *Understanding gender dysphoria: Navigating transgender issues in a changing culture.* IVP Academic.

Yarhouse, M. A. (2019). *Sexual identity and faith: Helping clients achieve congruence.* The Templeton Foundation.

5

APPLIED
INTEGRATION

LET US BRIEFLY RECAP. We see integration as bringing psychology-related fields and the Christian faith into a meaningful dialogue and interchange. We recognize that the contemporary psychological disciplines and Christianity are two distinct approaches to the human experience, despite their historical interconnections and areas of overlap. These distinct approaches bring with them their own epistemic assumptions and methodologies, but they also share more in common than is commonly understood, a point we have alluded to in our earlier chapters. We have examined how worldviews fuel and give context to the theoretical conjectures that psychologists and others formulate in an attempt to understand, explain, and predict psychological functioning. In this chapter we focus on the domain of application of the psychological disciplines to address practical tasks such as treating mental illness or providing data-based change consultation to individuals, groups, or societies. As with the worldview and theory domains, there are relevant developments in the Christian integration project we will review specific to *applied integration*.

We earlier defined applied integration as *the attempt to either culturally adapt or accommodate secular interventions or helping approaches for use with a Christian population or to develop explicitly Christian interventions and helping approaches derived from Christian thought and practice*. Such applied integration engages the practical and functional dimensions of both the Christian faith and the psychology-related fields in an intentional and coordinated way. Although the possible areas of application are many, they have most often taken the form of clinical integration to date.

Having a chapter on an applied activity immediately following a discussion of a theoretical one is in keeping with a traditional view of scientific disciplines that distinguishes between basic and applied science. On this view, basic science is thought of as *pure* or theoretical science that strives to acquire new knowledge with no particular practical aim in mind. It is the pursuit of knowledge for knowledge's sake. In contrast, applied science strives to acquire new knowledge but for the purpose of a practical aim adopted from the outset. Roll-Hansen (2017) notes that often this distinction has included a corollary *linear model* of knowledge in which knowledge flows unidirectionally from basic science to be used later by those applying it. However, it is now common for scholars to deny that science ever followed the linear model. The critics of the basic-applied dichotomy point to historical counterexamples of applied science being intermixed with discovery or to case studies that show how practical social concerns impact even "ivory tower" science, rendering it anything but *pure* (Roll-Hansen, 2017).

By including a distinct theoretical and applied integration domain, we do not intend to convey that we are accepting or promulgating a traditional linear model or even a neat distinction between basic and applied science. The term *applied psychology* arose early in contemporary psychology. While this term reflected the traditional basic versus applied science distinction, psychology itself had early voices that presented a different understanding of applied science. For instance, Witmer (1907) coined the phrase *clinical psychology* drawing on the clinical method from medicine. He protested any model of psychological practice that would derive its principles from philosophical ideas or its practices by directly applying results from laboratory experiments. Instead, he conceptualized clinical psychology as a field of science that should operate by accumulating knowledge through careful experimental work in real-world settings with real service recipients. Substantial developments have occurred in clinical research in the psychology-related fields since that time (Wright & Hallquist, 2020). While the foundational science areas of the psychological sciences (e.g., cognitive psychology, social psychology, developmental psychology, etc.) still inform applied work, sophisticated research paradigms now exist to sort out what enhances treatment effectiveness in a way that generalizes to the real world. Clinical models also are developed explicitly from research in the clinical context. Psychology, counseling, social work, and similar fields have been increasingly embracing the notion that their applied work should be *evidence based*, defined in a manner that draws from both research and clinical expertise (viz., APA Presidential Task

Force on Evidence Based Practice, 2005). A growing emphasis on practice-based research has been emerging, which stresses the importance of the context of real-world practice for discovery in clinical science just as Witmer (1907) suggested over a century ago (Codd, 2018).

Although much of what we will cover in applied integration is clinical in application, we use this label in the older sense that predated clinical psychology as any psychological intervention in a natural setting aimed at meeting a practical need. While this includes all clinical or counseling applications, it also spans beyond clinical application to other applied areas, such as community psychology and industrial-organizational psychology.

Applied Integration: Implicit, Explicit, and Intentional

Many Christians who consider applied integration today make a distinction between *implicit* and *explicit* applied integration (Tan, 1996). *Implicit integration* is present when a clinician chooses between a range of clinical decisions and techniques that are recognizable facts of standard secular practice, because one set of options is more consistent with a Christian worldview or Christian values. An implicit approach would be a "more covert approach that does not initiate the discussion of religious or spiritual issues and does not openly, directly or systematically use spiritual resources" (Tan, 1996, p. 368). For example, a Christian sex therapist who elects not to utilize homework assignments based on viewing erotica as a treatment technique but rather pursues the use of other established secular approaches that are less value-discordant. This might be viewed as a negative example, by which we mean it reflects what a Christian might *not* do if his or her practice were compared to secular peers.

A positive example of what a Christian might *add* to what is done in secular practice is the Christian clinician who recognizes religion as a significant domain of adaptive functioning and so assesses whether existing mental health concerns affect functioning in this area (Hathaway, 1999). The rationale for doing so is that religion is a significant area of functioning for many people, and just as clinicians assess occupational and social functioning, they can also assess religious functioning. Extending the language of the American Psychiatric Association's (1994) *DSM-IV*, Hathaway (2003) suggests that when mental illness adversely impacts religious/spiritual functioning to a sufficient extent, a *clinically significant religious impairment* could be present. He argues that, based on decades of data about the connections between religiousness and psychological outcomes, clinicians should be as concerned about impairments in the religious or spiritual domain as they would be about impairment in social or occupational functioning.

Explicit integration is present when some aspect of Christianity or the Christian faith is formally and openly included in clinical practice. Tan (1996, p. 368) puts it this way:

> Explicit integration . . . refers to a more overt approach that directly and systematically deals with spiritual or religious issues in therapy, and uses spiritual resources like prayer, Scripture, or sacred texts, referrals to church or other religious groups or lay counselors, and other religious practices.

There are many examples of explicit integration, some of which we will highlight below. In their review of the literature on religious techniques in psychotherapy, Worthington et al. (1996) discussed in detail the use of (a) prayer (including studies on the effect of prayer on global functioning, purpose in life, length of sobriety, and so on); (b) forgiveness (including studies on the benefit of forgiveness as related to improved interpersonal relationships and positive mental health); (c) meditation (including studies on its effectiveness as compared to progressive relaxation); and (d) Black religious approaches that differ from those of a Eurocentric background (e.g., the use of "spiritual mourning" among members of the Black Baptist church in the West Indies) (cited in Yarhouse & VanOrman, 1999).

An additional concept that is related to both explicit and implicit integration is what Tan (2001) refers to as *intentional* integration, which he describes as

> prayerfully depending on the Holy Spirit to lead and guide the therapeutic session, using implicit or explicit integration or both in a professionally competent, ethically responsible and clinically sensitive way for the benefit and growth of the client. This is done with clear informed consent from the client, and hence without forcing the therapist's beliefs or spiritual practices on the client. (Tan, 2001, pp. 22-23)

Intentional integration is almost akin to a professional mindfulness exercise in which the Christian clinician deliberately expends energy to seek assistance in their therapeutic work by direct appeal to the Holy Spirit for their clinical practice. What is interesting is that a clinician might be led to more explicit integration in some cases and to more implicit integration in other cases. Another clinician may feel led to switch between explicit and implicit integration with the same client over time. Indeed, the key is an openness to discerning God's direction for care through special, ongoing dialogue with the Holy Spirit about what is in the best interest of the client at a specific time.

Some Forms of Implicit Clinical Integration

We will first examine some forms of implicit clinical integration. We see this in the development of religiously sensitive clinical practice, as when a clinician is trained to think of religion and spirituality as potentially important domains of identity and diversity. We see this, too, in specific protocols that serve as alternatives to existing models of care that may be value incongruent for the client or the practitioner.

Religiously sensitive clinical practice. The past several years have witnessed increased awareness of and sensitivity to religious and spiritual considerations in clinical practice, even by mainstream mental health organizations. For example, in 2007, the American Psychological Association's Council of Representatives voted to approve the *Resolution on Religious, Religion-Related, and/or Religion-Derived Prejudice* (APA, 2007). This document addressed a considerable range of topics and included in it an awareness that psychology as a scientific discipline cannot adjudicate religious issues and theological matters.

Perhaps further awareness of religion in clinical practice is seen in the publication by the American Psychological Association of a number of applied resources that specifically address religion and spirituality, including *Spiritual & Religious Competencies in Clinical Practice* by Cassandra Vieten and Shelley Scammell; *Spiritually Integrated Psychotherapy* by Kenneth Pargament; *A Spiritual Strategy for Counseling and Psychotherapy* by P. Scott Richards and Allen Bergin; and *Religion and the Clinical Practice of Psychology* edited by Edward Shafranske.

In these resources and elsewhere (e.g., Yarhouse & VanOrman, 1999), we see several practical suggestions for adapting clinical services to the preferences of religious clients. Although not limited to a discussion of religious clients, Tjeltveit (1999) discusses how psychotherapists and their clients benefit from a discussion of values in psychotherapy. He would like to see clinicians work with clients in ways that help clients understand why they believe as they do. He sees psychotherapists as *ethicists*, which is someone "who reflects on, has convictions about, and/or attempts to influence others about ethical questions and issues" (p. 35). For Tjeltveit, ethicists themselves think well about meaning, values, and ethical issues. They may teach others about ethics, but they often consult and coach people in thinking through the ethical contours of difficult decisions.

Along these lines, simply initiating a discussion about the values clients hold—and which may be founded upon religious or spiritual beliefs and values—is one way to be respectful of religion. This has been discussed by Doherty (1999) as one way to address values in psychotherapy. Indeed, Doherty distinguishes between the clinical world, moral world, and spiritual world, and the language and meaning associated with each domain as well as potential overlap. For example, clinical language includes words like "dysfunction," "communication," and "self-esteem," while spiritual language includes "God's will," "calling," and "grace." Moral language includes "right and wrong," "obligation," and "fairness." Of course, these domains often overlap, as when clinical and spiritual considerations are discussed. The language used there includes "wholeness," "hope," and "trust," while the language associated with the clinical and moral domains include "commitment," "responsibility," and "honesty" (see Doherty, 1999, p. 185, fig. 10.1). For Doherty, these domains or words do overlap considerably, and when clinicians rely only upon clinical language, they do a disservice to the many dimensions of persons and what it means to be truly human.

In any case, Doherty (1999) suggests that these various domains ought to be in the clinician's mind when providing services, particularly when clinicians work in secular settings. They can be mindful of the language used by the client and can match the language by domain as appropriate. Further, clinicians can use some of the language associated with the overlap between domains when they are unfamiliar with the faith tradition and religious beliefs of their clients. For example, a clinician could discuss "hope" in marriage (an overlap between clinical and spiritual domains), and this may provide a bridge to constructive discussions and a more holistic view of the persons seeking services.

Doherty (1999) summarizes the role of language:

> An appreciation of the language differences and points of connection among the clinical, moral, and spiritual domains can serve as a guide for therapists through these waters. Since therapy is basically a form of conversation, the appropriate role of spirituality in therapy will have to be played out in terms of the language we learn to use with our clients and the language they use with us. (p. 188)

Doherty (1999) also offers ways to address spirituality by degrees of intensity in clinical consultations:

- Acknowledge the client's spontaneous statements of spiritual beliefs.
- Inquire about the client's spiritual beliefs and practices.

- Inquire about how the client connects the spiritual, clinical, and moral dimensions of his or her life or problems.

- Express agreement with the client's spiritual beliefs or sensibilities when such self-disclosure could be therapeutic.

- Articulate the client's dilemma without giving your own position.

- Point out the contradictions between the client's spiritual beliefs, or between spiritual beliefs and clinical realities or moral issues.

- Challenge the client's way of handling spiritual beliefs on the basis of your own spiritual beliefs, your moral beliefs, or your clinical beliefs. (pp. 189-90)

In the end, Doherty's belief is that spiritual, moral, and clinical considerations are all important aspects of the clinical work. From this perspective, "Therapy that neglects any of these threads truncates the human personality" (p. 191).

Another consideration is to routinely engage in spiritual assessment in client intakes. In an implicit context, this will often take the form of a probe question such as, "Is religion or spirituality important to you?" or "Are you religious?" It has been common practice to recommend further exploration of client religious or spiritual functioning only if a client answers in the affirmative to such a probe question. However, a study conducted by Rosmarin, Forester et al. (2015) at Harvard's McLean Hospital noted a substantial portion of clients who indicated in that secular setting that they were not religious still expressed a desire to address spiritual issues in treatment. As we noted above, Hathaway's (2003) clinically significant religious impairment construct also calls for all clinicians to conceptualize religious functioning as a typical adaptive domain of functioning, such as occupational or social functioning. While not everyone has an occupation, clinicians routinely assess whether a client's difficulties impact the occupation for clients that work, even if the client does not spontaneously report such concerns. In the same report, should clinicians not probe for a potential adverse impact on client religious or spiritual functioning if clients report symptoms of a psychological disorder?

Religious sensitivity can also be demonstrated by offering interventions that have been adapted to the language and experience of religious clients (Yarhouse & VanOrman, 1999). This might include recognizing and addressing categories of thinking and behaving that are related in meaningful ways to a particular religious tradition (e.g., forgiveness and repentance in Christianity).

In addition to religiously sensitive clinical practice, we also see implicit integration in efforts to foster collaboration between psychologists and clergy.

Psychologist-clergy collaboration. Collaboration between psychologists and clergy has been another expression of implicit integration. The history of the relationship between psychology and religion has been one of some tension (Bland, 2003), and psychologists interested in cultivating collaborative partnerships often have to take care in how they proceed. Recommendations have included establishing working relationships that are mutually beneficial and characterized by respect and clear and consistent communication, identifying shared values/goals, and recognizing and respecting complementary expertise (McMinn & Dominguez, 2005).

The rationale for collaboration is often framed as one that reflects a convergence of needs for a specific population (e.g., Bland, 2003). Collaboration can take many forms, including assessment of courses in a church community (e.g., Howell, 2005) and broader assessment of churches with respect to their resources and ministry experiences (Dominguez & McMinn, 2003), collaborative research (e.g., Flannelly et al., 2003), and clinical or applied collaboration (e.g., Budd & Newton, 2003).

Additional innovative models that have been discussed include when psychologists are also trained as clergy and vice versa (depending upon primary identity within a community) (Serrano, 2003; Tan, 2005). The perspectives offered here vary considerably, but some psychologists-pastors have discussed how their training has uniquely equipped them to be sensitive to the needs of their faith community while improving the overall quality of services being provided (e.g., Serrano, 2003).

In addition to increased sensitivity to how religion and spirituality may be of importance to clients and the potential benefits to psychology/clergy collaboration, we also see implicit integration in protocols that are alternatives to mainstream models of care that may be value incongruent for clients or for practitioners.

Implicitly integrative protocols.

Sexual Identity Therapy. Sexual Identity Therapy (SIT) is a client-centered, identity-focused model of care to help clients who experience a conflict between their sexual identity and their religious identity (Yarhouse, 2019). SIT is implicitly integrative because it was developed in response to the needs of clients for whom mainstream gay affirmative therapy as offered by some practitioners was not engaging conventional religiosity in a constructive manner. The only alternative to gay affirmative therapy had been sexual orientation change efforts (SOCE), which were increasingly viewed with suspicion and concern (APA, 2009). Indeed, the 2009 APA task force on appropriate therapeutic approaches to sexual orientation recognized that some clients who identify as conventionally religious may be in need of approaches that are sensitive to their religious and spiritual beliefs and values and provide a therapeutic space for sorting out conflicts they may report between their religious beliefs and values and their same-sex sexuality. SIT incorporates elements of a narrative approach to identify problem stories from both a client's religious community (that same-sex sexuality is an abomination, for example) and from the mainstream gay community (that same-sex sexuality and behavior are to be celebrated, for example), so that a person can begin to develop a counternarrative in identity and behavior that aligns with their beliefs and values, which is referred to as congruence (Yarhouse, 2005; 2019; Throck-morton & Yarhouse, 2006).

Supervision. Supervision is an extension of the clinical integration efforts that is often overlooked in discussions of applied integration. Research has shown that most secular mental health training programs provide no systematic training in doing clinical work with religious or spiritual issues (Schafer et al., 2011). Yet when such training is reported, it is typically in the context of supervision. Some recent Christian integrative scholarship in the area of supervision has explored the integration touchpoints for Christians interested in how their faith may intersect with the supervision process.

Supervision can be an integration endeavor in explicit ways, as when supervisors facilitate discussion and reflection on Christian considerations throughout the discussion of theories and in the selection of protocols (Watson, 2018). Indeed, integrative supervision can also explicitly facilitate character formation and promote specific virtues with respect to a proper view of ourselves and others. Watson describes character formation in supervision as the fusing of Christian virtues in the supervisee. She discusses this along the lines of classic Christian virtues, such as faith, hope, and love (theological virtues), as well as wisdom, justice, temperance, and courage (moral virtues). Additional supervision resources can include the use of spiritual formation practices so that there is a more holistic perspective on both professional and personal/spiritual growth.

Supervision can also be implicitly integrative in shaping discussions toward responsible clinical care and faith-congruent considerations but without having the services provided or supervision provided that would reflect explicit Christian constructs. Ethical principles, such as demonstrating respect for the dignity and rights of others can be modeled and taught without an explicit tie-in to love/charity or justice. Likewise, practicing beneficence and nonmaleficence can shape the contours of good supervision without directly connecting these concepts to hope and temperance (see Watson, 2018, pp. 31-32, table 3). Implicit integration can also mean identifying assessment strategies that take religion and spirituality seriously as demographic considerations and domains of functioning. It can also entail identifying intervention strategies and protocols that are more value congruent with that of the client, the clinician, or the supervisor.

Some Types of Explicit Clinical Integration

We turn our attention now to primarily explicitly integrative approaches in the clinical setting. We do not presume that there is but one form of applied integration even in a particular context, like clinical mental health practice. Possible forms of clinical integration include (1) mining Christianity for protocols and therapist interventions (e.g., hope-focused couples approach), (2) mining Christianity for adjunctive interventions, and (3) co-opting spiritual formation strategies for clinical purposes.

Mining Christianity for protocols and therapist interventions. One form of applied integration is to look to the Christian faith for therapist intervention, whether these are incorporated into an overall treatment plan or whether these comprise full-blown protocols.

Forgiveness. One example of a therapist intervention is the use of forgiveness. Forgiveness refers to the act of giving a person a pardon for a wrong that they do not deserve. From a Christian perspective, the act of forgiveness traces to the pardon of sins the Christian experiences in relation to God by virtue of having faith in Jesus Christ. The forgiveness one benefits from is then a model of what can be offered to others in interpersonal relationships. In therapy, this often means some psychoeducation on the concept of forgiveness—what it is and what it is not—while also working through a process of forgiveness of persons who have hurt or done wrong to the client.

We have seen several Christian and non-Christian researchers study forgiveness (e.g., Armour et al., 2008; DiBlasio & Benda, 2008; Enright, 2001; Worthington et al., 2007) and provide useful protocols on implementing forgiveness interventions in clinical practice.

One of the most widely used models to promote forgiveness is the REACH model (Worthington, 2003). It is a five-step process of emotional forgiveness developed by Everett Worthington and his colleagues (Worthington, 2003). The five steps are R (recall the hurt); E (empathize with the transgressor); A (altruistic gift of forgiveness); C (commit to forgive); and H (hold onto forgiveness).

The REACH model is based upon the view that forgiveness is both a decision process and an emotional process. The decisional aspect reflects a changed intention about how one will act toward an offender. It is an intention, not a behavior. (For instance, one could decide to forgive one's deceased father.) The emotional process occurs as people neutralize negative, resentful, unforgiving emotions with positive other-oriented emotions like love, empathy, or compassion for an offender. During emotional forgiveness, people experience lessening of unforgiving emotions. They may cease to try to forgive emotionally after eliminating all negative emotions (such as with a stranger who has harmed one) or may continue to build positive emotions (such as with a spouse or loved family member). Experiences of decisional and emotional forgiveness occur within a person's skin and should not be confused with behaviors like saying one forgives (one may be lying). Several more expanded protocols have been published in recent years that are derived from Christian constructs and integrated with other findings from the fields of psychology and counseling. These include the hope-focused couples approach (HFCA) to working with couples (Ripley & Worthington, 2014), the grace-based marital restoration model (Sells & Yarhouse, 2011), and Christian cognitive-behavioral therapy (CCBT) (Pearce, 2016) (see Worthington, Johnson, Hook & Aten, 2013).

Hope-Focused Couples Approach (HFCA). The HFCA is a strategic couples therapy approach that focuses on identifying and targeting "key behaviors, beliefs, or dynamics that maintain relationship dysfunction" (Ripley et al., 2013, p. 194). HFCA incorporates attachment theory and elements of positive psychology by anchoring its approach in the concept of hope, which emphasizes both agency ("cognitive motivation for a goal with a sense of efficacy for that change") and pathways ("means by which goals [are] achieved") (p. 195). The explicitly Christian foundation is described as faith, work, and love, and the pursuit of virtues in relationships, as well as sanctification (Ripley & Worthington, 2014).

Grace-Based Marital Restoration Model. The grace-based marital restoration model draws on Christian concepts and related virtues such as grace, compassion, faith, forgiveness, and justice. These concepts are integrated with elements of emotion-focused couples therapy and contextual family therapy as couples are aided in identifying their goals, identifying their sense of "us" or cohesion as a couple, identifying pain/hurt/vulnerability, recognizing how each partner manages pain, giving voice to the pain cycle, learning about and extending grace to one another, recognizing the concomitant need for justice, expression of empathy, facilitating forgiveness, and forming trust in a couple dyad (Sells & Yarhouse, 2011).

Christian Cognitive-Behavioral Therapy (CCBT). Cognitive-behavioral therapy has long been used to treat common concerns, such as depression, and it has for many years been modified to incorporate religious content.[1] Pearce (2016) provides a more recent, extensive adaptation of cognitive-behavioral therapy for Christians with depression. This explicitly Christian protocol provides guidance for assessment of religiosity, as well as how to discuss a Christian adaptation with the client, and the specific tools that can be used throughout the middle stages of treatment, such as identifying unhelpful thoughts and replacing them with more helpful, adaptive thoughts, increasing social support, providing forgiveness, incorporating gratitude into one's life, and serving others (see also, Jennings et al., 2013).

These are just three of many different, more expanded, and explicitly Christian treatment protocols that have emerged in recent years. Worthington et al. (2013) offer a good introduction to evidence-based approaches, including more extensive Christian-integrative protocols and Christian accommodative trauma-focused cognitive-behavioral therapy for children and adolescents (Walker et al., 2013), Christian accommodative group forgiveness interventions (Kidwell & Wade, 2013). Additional, more comprehensive models that are also explicitly Christian include transformational psychology (Coe & Hall, 2010) and integrative psychotherapy (McMinn & Campbell, 2007).

Aspects of Christian faith as interventions. In addition to what we might view as comprehensive protocols or adaptations of comprehensive treatment approaches, we also see examples in the applied literature of aspects of Christian

---

[1]For example, Propst (1996) reviews the research she has done in this area. In an earlier study (Propst, 1980), she reported that for religious clients, both a cognitive-behavioral therapy-related religious imagery treatment and a religious placebo (group discussion of religious issues) showed a more positive effect than did a cognitive-behavioral related nonreligious imagery treatment. Similar results were found in a later study comparing a variety of religious and nonreligious interventions with religious clients (Propst et al., 1992). Those who received either religious cognitive-behavioral treatment or pastoral counseling reported significantly lower scores on measures of depression and higher scores on measures of adjustment than did those who took part in either the nonreligious cognitive-behavioral treatment or were in the control group (although these differences disappeared at three-month and two-year follow-up).

faith functioning as interventions in the course of therapy. These include interventions having to do with prayer, the incorporation of Scripture, fellowship, and the use of forgiveness.

Prayer. Christian integrationists often incorporate prayer as a therapy intervention. In terms of direct intervention, some Christian psychologists pray aloud with their clients, while others intercede through prayer silently for their clients during session or ask for divine guidance for the work they are doing (McMinn, 1996). Still others intercede on behalf of their clients outside of session. Contemplative prayer by clients outside of session has also been considered helpful to some clients (Finney & Malony, 1985).

More recent work on prayer has focused on Christian devotional meditation (sometimes referred to as contemplative prayer) for concerns like anxiety (Garzon, 2013). Such an approach

> may be defined as a variety of strategies designed to enhance focused attention on God, Scripture or oneself with the intent of deepening one's relationship with the Lord, cultivating emotional healing, and/or growing in love toward one's neighbor and oneself. (p. 60)

Garzon (2013) discusses three Christian devotional meditation strategies: (1) Scriptural truth meditation (meditating on the character of God or on specific biblical passages that are sources of truth and encouragement and comfort); (2) Scriptural drama meditation (utilizing one's imagination to enter into specific biblical moments so that Scripture becomes more of a "multisensory experience" (p. 64); and (3) Christ-centered present moment awareness or essentially the use of mindfulness principles and strategies while incorporating increased awareness of God's presence in the here-and-now (Garzon, 2013).

Reading of Scripture. Scripture reading is another common spiritual practice for Christians that has been used in contemporary psychotherapy. This has parallels with the familiar strategy of *bibliotherapy* that has long been used by some in the mental health fields as part of the treatment.[2] In therapy, the use of Scripture

---

[2]We recognize there are important differences between the therapeutic use of a sacred text and standard forms of bibliotherapy. Bibliotherapy tends to function as either a kind of psychoeducation, providing readers with well-vetted information about a psychological topic, or as an evocative stimulus the therapist believes may trigger a therapeutically relevant reaction or insight in a client. The Bible is not a textbook on a particular disorder, and it can be misread by the reader. Thus, therapeutic uses of Scripture, at least from a professional mental health perspective, would likely need to be guided or structured in intentional ways by the professional. Of course, the Holy Spirit may use Scripture as a healing force in a person's life in surprising ways. So, we would not want to foreclose

has been to relate stories with themes relevant to the issues being discussed in treatment, as well as to dispute thoughts that have been identified as irrational or dysfunctional (Richards & Bergin, 1997). Still other uses of Scripture are to have clients memorize key verses or read Scripture outside of session to augment the work that is occurring in session. Still others incorporate Scripture into devotional meditation or contemplative prayer practices, as we noted above, either through meditation on biblical passages or through the use of biblically based meditation on key moments in Scripture that may be of relevance (Garzon, 2013).

Promoting trust in God/Reducing distrust in God. A paper published in 2011 by Jewish psychologist David Rosmarin and his colleagues highlighted the potential value of using faith narratives to promote a sense of trust in God and to reduce mistrust in God among theists. The clinicians explained that:

> Trust in God has its origins in traditional Jewish thought (Ibn Pakuda, 1996) but is nevertheless applicable to all monotheistic traditions. Principally, trust in God involves the notion that God, or a Higher Power, is taking care of one's best interests. In particular, it involves the beliefs that the Divine (a) has regard for all worldly affairs (omniscience), (b) is greater than other powers/forces (omnipotence), and (c) is merciful and generous (omnibenevolence). (p. 629)

In a randomized clinical trial described in the paper, the authors found that promoting faith in God through a spiritually integrated treatment using religious stories, teachings, and other interventions resulting in reduced mistrust of God also resulted in lower levels of worry in a Jewish sample.[3]

Mining Christianity for adjunctive interventions. Although much attention has been paid to direct interventions, there has also been interest expressed in adjunctive interventions. This involves looking to Christianity and to the Christian community for care or services that function as adjuncts to the primary clinical services being provided. Adjunctive services include appropriate referrals to church, parachurch, or other religious organizations (Tan, 1996).

Self-help and peer-support groups. Probably one of the most frequently tapped adjunctive resource involves work with clients struggling with substance use

---

on a client reading Scripture for their own devotional practices. We would just note a mental health professional would likely utilize Scripture in treatment in a more circumscribed way.

[3]Rosmarin's work offers an outstanding example of the inclusion of explicitly spiritual interventions and other treatment elements into standard well-supported treatment protocols in an evidence-based way. His work has been researched with clients from a variety of faith traditions. While not specifically Christian, we would suggest it has clear relevance for the Christian clinical integration project. See Rosmarin (2018) for a book-length treatment of his approach.

disorders. It is quite common for clinicians working with a client struggling with a substance use disorder to identify local twelve-step groups that might provide adjunctive support. Such groups are typically religiously congruent, having foundations in Christianity and being quite supportive of religion and spirituality as resources in recovery (see Richards & Bergin, 1997; Yarhouse & VanOrman, 1999).

Specialized religiously affiliated ministries. There are also specialized ministries in areas that are less frequently being addressed in professional psychology or counseling. For example, when clients report conflicts with a child who has come out as gay or transgender, some psychologists and counselors have referred clients to religiously affiliated ministries (e.g., *Embracing the Journey* (McDonald & McDonald, 2020); *Guiding Families of LGBTQ+ Loved Ones* (Henson & Baatz, 2018)), or they might make such a referral while providing supportive professional services. These ministries often provide more than peer-support groups, although they often also provide this level of support. They also often provide reading resources for parents, spouses, and other family members and supportive friends.

Spiritual directors. Spiritual directors are also a resource from Christianity that can be a useful adjunctive to professional clinical services. Spiritual directors provide spiritual guidance and an opportunity for self-examination. Such a practice is often modeled after Paul's relationship with young converts to Christianity and his relationship with Timothy (see 1 Cor 4:15; Rice, 1991). As Rice indicates, the practice is less common among Protestants as it has been among Roman Catholics.

Lay counselors or helpers. It may also be helpful to consider the role of lay counselors or lay helpers in providing a supportive presence. Mental health professionals are simply not available in all settings, nor are they always affordable depending upon a number of factors. Lay counselors or lay helpers can either provide an additional presence or be the primary support person in the life of some people who would benefit from a supportive presence.

Tan (2013) reviewed the considerable empirical support for lay counseling or paraprofessional help. While professional therapists tend to do better at reducing client recidivism and in the use of manualized treatments with more difficult presenting concerns, lay counselors are generally considered as effective as therapists for some of the most common concerns people seek help for. Lay counseling has evolved into different forms and can include more active-listening approaches, cognitive and solution-focused approaches, inner healing approaches, and mixed approaches that draw on more than one of the preceding approaches (Tan, 2013, pp. 44-47).

Fellowship. Fellowship refers to being together in relationship with other Christians. This seems to us to be related to social support, which is a common consideration in clinical practice, but it is not identical to social support. Richards and Bergin (1997) discuss "use religious community" as a religious intervention; this refers to "using the client's religious community as an extra-therapy resource" (p. 234). According to the authors, this might mean a referral to the pastor to address spiritual concerns or consulting with a Christian attorney. But what we mean by fellowship is more of regular time of friendship and camaraderie with others who share similar beliefs and values. This might include relationships with church leadership, involvement in small groups, and being active in youth groups, which we will discuss below.

Church leadership. Clinicians working with Christian clients can discuss with them the role of the local church in their lives. It is not uncommon to then sign releases to discuss a person's care with their pastor, minister, or other religious leader.

Cell groups or small groups. In addition to the local church, there is increased interest in the support and fellowship found in what are referred to as cell groups or small groups. These are groups of adults who meet regularly (e.g., weekly, biweekly) for prayer, fellowship, and often the study of Scripture). As valuable as corporate worship can be in the context of a larger church setting, cell groups often provide opportunity for greater intimacy and personal support, which is especially valuable when people attend larger churches in which they might be more likely to "fall through the cracks."

Youth groups. A clinician working with a Christian adolescent might discuss the role of the youth group in the life of the teen. Sometimes teens will visit youth groups in other churches that they do not attend regularly, but they find value in the kind of activities and other programs that are offered in a particular church setting. Such youth activities (e.g., regular weekly meetings, youth retreats, summer camp) provide adolescents a sense of shared identity and fellowship with peers who share their fundamental worldview and faith commitments. While not a Christian treatment, Scott Henggeler's highly effective multisystemic therapy for antisocial youth frequently utilized religious youth groups to offer a prosocial alternative to the destructive peer influences common in the lives of such youth (Henggeler et al., 2009).

As we bring this section to a close, we note that fellowship, broadly defined, may refer to being a part of a corporate faith community, and it may be expressed in a multitude of ways, including active engagement with church leadership, participation in a small group, or involvement in youth group, just to provide a few examples. In any of these kinds of meetings, we are talking about how people in a common faith tradition meet to apply insights from Scripture or sermons or other resources to the daily life of members. These groups are also often characterized by a deepening friendship and activities that cultivate intimacy.

Co-opting spiritual formation strategies for clinical purposes. Christian clinicians also often co-opt spiritual formation strategies for clinical purposes. This occurs when psychologists use various spiritual disciplines in their clinical work.

Meditation. Similar to *holy name repetition* is the broader category of meditation. It is another spiritual formation practice many Christians have historically used and which some contemporary psychologists find useful in the clinical setting. It has been often used in conjunction with relaxation exercises and spiritual imagery exercises to reduce stress and anxiety (Richards & Bergin, 1997). This can occur in session in much the same way relaxation exercises are learned or practiced in session, and meditation can also be part of homework that clients do between sessions.

Holy name repetition is a specific example of meditation that refers to speaking the name of God (Father, Holy Spirit, or Jesus) several times throughout the day. Doug Oman and Joseph Driskill (2003) wrote about the use of "holy name repetition" or "the frequent repetition throughout the day of a holy name" in response to what they have seen as a need for "spiritual sustenance" (p. 5). This can be expanded to other names of spiritual significance, but its ties are to names that reflect the sacred or holy in the life of the person seeking spiritual encouragement and support.

Solitude. Solitude is another historical spiritual formation practice that some therapists co-opt for clinical purposes. This might include encouraging the practice of solitude including taking a personal spiritual retreat or spending time apart from the daily demands associated with work and family. Journaling is often associated with these times of solitude and reflection.

Study. Study is also another common spiritual formation strategy sometimes co-opted for clinical purposes. Study refers most often to the use of the Bible in spiritual formation (Rice, 1991). It might also entail reading other resources that develop biblical themes or apply them more specifically to the presenting concern. Rice describes the role of Scripture in the life of the believer: "When it is used responsibly and carefully, the Bible functions in the life of the church and in the life of the individual believer to nurture, criticize, and reform that life" (p. 96).

Strawn et al. (2018) have referred to clinical integration as the most recent and "fourth wave" of the integration project. Consistent with the emphasis on the unique aspects of the context of application on the field from the context of *pure* science or theory (noted earlier), they state that "clinical integration is not a model or a destination but an emergent phenomenon that is discovered and rediscovered within the intersubjective experience of relating—talking, feeling, thinking, and behaving together" (p. 90). Thus, they emphasize the importance of case study, relationality, and personal development for clinical integration. We will return to those later themes in our final chapter on personal integration.

Nonclinical Applied Integration

The bulk of our discussion this chapter has focused on applied integration in the clinical domain. This is because most work done in this domain has focused on clinical applications. We will look briefly at three nonclinical areas of applied integration before concluding our discussion of this domain: community psychology, Christian integrative social work, and industrial-organizational psychology.

Community psychology. APA's Division 27, now titled *The Society for Community Research and Action,* offers this definition of its applied niche:

> Community psychology goes beyond an individual focus and integrates social, cultural, economic, political, environmental, and international influences to promote positive change, health, and empowerment at individual and systemic levels. (APA Division 27, 2020)[4]

A number of Christian psychologists have been involved in applied integration in community psychology. One of the leading Christian community psychologists is John Fantuzzo at the University of Pennsylvania. He has often spoken of the connections between being a Christian and doing justice in community-based research (Canning, Manz et al., 2007). The Christian faith motivates believers to intervene through community-based research to address the concerns of the underserved. Very much in keeping with biblical themes of justice and peace in the lives of those who are marginalized, Christians in the field of community psychology develop and implement programs to address the social justice issues facing the most vulnerable among us.

---

[4]We present community psychology here as something distinct from clinical psychology. But in reality, it is common for a community psychologists to be licensed and trained in clinical contexts. One of us (Hathaway) was trained in a clinical psychology program that at the time was called a clinical-community psychology program with required community psychology course work and themes incorporated in clinical psychology. In some mental health professions, such as social work, the applied work done by practitioners may parallel those of community psychologists.

These themes have been picked up by other Christians involved in what has been termed "praxis-oriented" integration (Canning, Pozzi et al., 2000). In short, these are community psychologists motivated by their Christian convictions and desire to see justice and peace "embrace" (Wolterstorff, 1983) in social policies and in services to the "least of these." Who are the recipients of such services? Typically, these are people of low socioeconomic status, who, because of their limited resources, are often at greater risk for mental and physical health concerns. They might be in inner-city environments or rural or sparsely populated environments. Among these are children, older adults, ethnic/racial minorities, and people with serious mental illnesses (Canning, Case et al., 2001).

In any case, Christians interested in "faith-praxis" integration (Canning, Pozzi et al., 2000, p. 205) see it as an extension of a Christian kingdom mandate, by which they mean "those endeavors that are biblically directed, teleologically focused, Holy Spirit inspired, and surrendered to the Lordship of Christ" (p. 205). Such language suggests a very explicit integration emphasis; however, the practice of integration in community psychology often occurs implicitly, as it is directed toward the underserved and the marginalized. When it is tied explicitly to the Christian faith, as indicated above, we might see it as an example of explicit integration. However, when it occurs in the context of supporting existing policies and intervention strategies (e.g., Head Start), we would see it as more implicit in its approach to integration (e.g., Fantuzzo et al., 2007).

This distinction between explicit and implicit ties to the Christian faith provides us the opportunity to discuss how implicit integration is often context and role dependent. When we use God's words or develop community interventions that are direct and forthright in religious context, we are engaging in explicit integration. When we draw on broad kingdom values and a Christian motivation to intervene to promote justice and peace—but do so in a broader social context in which our role expands beyond our Christian identity—we are conducting implicit integration.

Christian integrative social work. We would like to mention here the rich legacy of Christians who have aspired to engage in their profession of social work in an integrated manner. For instance, the North American Association of Christians in Social Work (hereafter NACSW), is a professional association for Christian integration in this field. They hold conventions, publish the academic journal *Social Work & Christianity*, and have other features common for such bodies. While social workers have contributed in their integrative efforts to all of the integrative domains we have been reviewing in this text, we call out their contributions for integration under this domain because, as a field, social work has been so heavily focused on applied caregiving.

Social workers often engage in a practice that is clinical (i.e., clinical social work) but also frequently involves a variety of other forms of applied activity. They are trained to engage a range of practice activities outside of the clinical domain and some function in entirely nonclinical roles. In the 2016 edition of the NACSW text on Christian integration in social work, the editors organize the contributions in the text around their relevance to nine social work competencies whose attainment is expected for social workers trained in accredited programs (Scales & Kelley). A number of these overlap with those common for mental health practitioners, but others reflect distinctive emphases for social work such as: "Advance Human Rights and Social, Economic, and Environmental Justice" or "Engage in Policy Practice." While community psychologists often engage in similar forms of practice, these competencies are not profession-wide expectations for most clinicians in other fields.

Perdue et al. (2016) describe a coalition of efforts that arose in Toledo, Ohio to combat human trafficking of minors. They emphasize the Christian influences on the coalition as Christian social workers partnered with others to advocate for comprehensive social ministry aimed at tackling this problem. As they noted, this required social work interventions at both the micro- and macrolevels. For those unfamiliar with this longstanding dual focus of social work, Rothman and Misrahi (2014) explain:

> Historically, the social work profession took root having a twofold micro—macro mission. Pioneer social worker Mary Richmond represented service to individuals and families needing aid to alleviate difficulties in social functioning. Her contemporary counterpart, Jane Addams, represented social reform through environmental change to meet broad human needs. This dual approach to practice has defined the profession since its inception. (p. 91)

Perdue and her colleagues (2016) described how their coalition worked to address Toledo sex trafficking of minors at all levels. Some of what they developed involved clinical work with trafficking victims at the microlevel. But other interventions were focused more on policy and other systemic issues at the macrolevel. This required advocacy and system change skills that are the focus of social work preparation. The authors also emphasized the Christian mission that motivated them in this project: "For helping professionals, social justice advocacy is a form of practicing spirituality. The fulfillment of one's spiritual life must include engagement with others in the remaking of the world, healing, and creating supportive structures and institutions" (p. 358). We will return to this issue of social justice advocacy as a spiritual discipline below in our discussion of personal integration. But for now, we would like to point out that for Christian integrationists in fields such as social work, advocacy is a common part of the landscape in their applied integration work.

Industrial-organizational psychology. When a member of the general public thinks of someone engaging in the *practice of* psychology, they will likely have images of a clinician in the therapy room. Yet there is a longstanding area of applied psychology that has little or nothing to do with clinical practice. In fact, this area has sometimes been simply identified as *applied psychology.* The most common label for this niche has been *industrial-organizational* psychology (or I-O psychology for short). The Society for Industrial and Organizational Psychology (2020) defines its area of psychology as follows:

> I-O psychology is a dynamic and growing field that addresses workplace issues at the individual and organizational level. I-O psychologists apply research that improves the well-being and performance of people and the organizations that employ them. This involves everything from workforce planning, employee selection, and leader development to studying job attitudes and job motivation, implementing work teams, improving diversity and inclusion, and facilitating organizational change.

Psychologists have training of particular relevance to the needs of organizations in business and other contexts. These strengths can be and have been utilized in working with a normal range of interpersonal and emotional issues that have contributed to organizational impasses.[5] Industrial-organizational (i.e., I-O) psychologists are frequently trained in nonclinical programs. They apply data-based change strategies and a knowledge base that has been built up in their specialty to assist with practical concerns in business and other organizational settings. More recently, a growing number of clinically trained professionals have also started to apply their skill sets to organizational and leadership consulting.

Industrial-organizational psychology has a long history tracing back to the early twentieth century but has excelled in exposure and relevance in more recent

---

[5]Applied psychology increasingly divided into clinical and industrial-organizational psychology by the middle of the twentieth century. Each has become its own distinctive career pathway. An increasing number of clinicians are crossing over this divide and engaging in organizational consulting work (Lowman, 2008; Lowman & Cooper, 2017).

years (Aamodt, 2016). According to Aamodt, the industrial side of I-O focuses on job analysis, employment screening and hiring, performance appraisal, and training, while the organizational side of I-O focuses on leadership and team dynamics, employee motivation and satisfaction, and organizational change and processes. Organizational and business consulting (OBC) psychology, a related professional designation, has a number of practice areas that include test development, assessment, and selection; performance appraisal, management, and improvement; training and career development; leadership and executive coaching; organizational development; organizational surveying; military and national security psychology; managerial psychology; and litigation psychology.

In terms of integration discussions, we have seen an increase in I-O and OBC psychology in integrative Christian programs that have been launched at schools such as Seattle Pacific University, California Baptist University, Grand Canyon University, Liberty University, and Regent University. This raises the question of whether it is time for a formal Christian consulting psychology as an integration project that might include work in pastor and missionary screening and selection; pastor burnout prevention; church leadership development; and spiritual gifts screening and assessment (Hathaway & Hoover, 2019).

Some Christian psychologists have made influential contributions in the areas of organizational and leadership consulting and coaching. AACC has had an executive leadership track as part of its world conference. Most of the contributors in this area have been clinically trained such as John Townsend or Henry Cloud.

An obvious area of applied Christian integration would be to help churches and other faith-based organizations. Pargament's Congregation Development Program (CDP) is an early example of a scientifically grounded church-based consultation project representing an integration of community psychology, psychology of religion, industrial-organizational psychology, and clinical psychology. The CDP was developed in the 1980s by an interdisciplinary and interfaith team. Although not explicitly Christian, it was developed to be of practical benefit to a variety of religious communities that happened to be mostly Christian. Contributors from community psychology, psychology of religion and a premiere industrial-organizational psychology program drew from quantitative I-O measurement models (climate, member satisfaction, mission/priorities, role of leader-pastor) and qualitative, emic strategies from the clinical and community psychology fields to create "a data-based program designed to help congregations assess their areas of strength and weakness and plan for their futures. . . ." using "a collaborative process of consultation, with clergy and leaders as consultees, to interpret the data and consider their implications for congregation life" (Pargament et al., 1991, p. 394).

The CDP developed and validated consulting scales for use with religious congregations. The CDP questionnaire (CDP-q) was validated on over fifty religiously and ethnically diverse religious congregations. The consultations utilized the CDP-q, with some wording tailored for each specific congregation, plus a series of structured interviews. An intentional process was set up to systematically sample the congregations and make sense of data using a "resource collaborator" approach (Tyler, Pargament, & Gatz, 1983).

Summary

This chapter provided the reader with an understanding of applied integration. On a traditional understanding, applied science is the application of discoveries first made in basic science to a later real-world practical task or setting. Current thinking tends to reject this linear view. Instead, it is now common to note that knowledge discovery can occur in the context of applied field science and that basic science is often informed by such discoveries. Christian integration in an applied context involves not only accomplishing a Christian integration of the worldview and theories that might be applied but also integration of the distinctive approaches, data collection, and practice habits that emerge specifically in the context of applied work.

We also introduced the reader to the differences between implicit and explicit clinical integration, as well as what it means to be intentional in integration. We then discussed various forms of clinical integration. Most of these have been examined or developed in clinical practice. Examples of implicit clinical integration included *religious-sensitive practice* (e.g., spiritual probes during intakes), *psychology/clergy collaboration*, the use of *implicitly integrative protocols* (e.g., Sexual Identity Therapy), and addressing spirituality in supervision. Examples of explicit clinical integration included *mining Christianity for clinical interventions* (e.g., prayer protocols), *mining Christianity for adjunctive interventions* (e.g., lay counseling), and *co-opting spiritual formation strategies for clinical purposes* (e.g., solitude).

Applied integration outside of clinical areas has been less often a focus in applied integration project with the possible exception of the integrative social work literature. Some work has been done by Christians in community psychology and industrial-organizational psychology but much more needs to be done. We suggest the time is right for emergence of robust Christian consulting psychology that brings the best scientific resources of the I-O tradition to bear on the organization needs of Christian faith communities.

References

Aamodt, M. G. (2016). *Industrial/organizational psychology: An applied approach* (8th ed.). Cengage.

American Psychiatric Association. (1994). *Diagnostic and statistical manual-IV* (4th ed.). Author.

American Psychological Association. (2007). *Resolution on religious, religion-based and/or religion-derived prejudice.* Retrieved from www.apa.org/about/policy/religious -discrimination.pdf" www.apa.org/about/policy/religious-discrimination.pdf.

American Psychological Association. (2009). *Appropriate therapeutic responses to sexual orientation.* Retrieved from "https://www.apa.org/pi/lgbt/resources/therapeutic -response.pdf" www.apa.org/pi/lgbt/resources/therapeutic-response.pdf.

APA Division 27. (2020, October 30). *What is community psychology?* www.scra27.org/what -we-do/what-community-psychology/

APA Presidential Task Force on Evidence-Based Practice. (2005). Evidence-based practice in psychology. *American Psychologist, 61,* 271-85.

Armour, M. P., Windsor, L. C., Aguilar, J., & Taub, C. (2008). A pilot study of a faith-based restorative justice intervention for Christian and non-Christian offenders. *Journal of Psychology and Christianity, 27*(2), 159-67.

Bland, E. D. (2003). Psychology-church collaboration: Finding a new level of mutual participation. *Journal of Psychology and Christianity, 21,* 299-303.

Budd, F., & Newton, M. (2003). Healing the brokenhearted: Cross and couch together. *Journal of Psychology and Christianity, 21,* 319-22.

Canning, S. S. (2003). Psychological resources in faith-based community settings: Applications, adaptations, and innovations. *Journal of Psychology and Christianity, 22*(4), 348-52.

Canning, S. S., Case, P. W., & Kruse, S. L. (2001). Contemporary Christian psychological scholarship and "the least of these": An empirical review. *Journal of Psychology and Christianity, 20*(3), 205-23.

Canning, S. S., Manz, P., McWayne, C., & Fantuzzo, J. W. (March 2007). *Beyond the institutional review board: Doing justice in community-based research.* Symposium presented at the conference "Transformation of the Person in Christ," sponsored by the Christian Association for Psychological Studies, Philadelphia, PA.

Canning, S. S., Pozzi, C. F., McNeil, J. D., & McMinn, M. R. (2000). Integration as service: Implications of faith-praxis integration for training. *Journal of Psychology and Theology, 28*(3), 201-11.

Codd, R.T., III (Ed.). (2018). *Practice based research: A Guide for clinicians.* Routledge.

DiBlasio, F. A., & Benda, B. B. (2008). Forgiveness intervention with married couples: Two empirical analyses. *Journal of Psychology and Christianity, 27*(2), 150–58.

Doherty, W. J. (1999). Morality and spirituality in therapy. In F. Walsh (Ed.), *Spiritual resources in family therapy* New York: The Guilford Press, 179-92.

Dominguez, A. W., & McMinn, M. R. (2003). Collaboration through research: The multimethod church-based assessment process. *Journal of Psychology and Christianity, 21*, 333-7.

Enright, R. D. (2001). *Forgiveness is a choice: A step-by-step process for resolving anger and restoring hope.* American Psychological Association.

Fantuzzo, J., Stevenson, H., Kabir, S. A., & Perry, M. A. (2007). An investigation of a community-based intervention for socially isolated parents with a history of child maltreatment. *Journal of Family Violence, 22*, 81-89.

Finney, J. R., & Malony, H. N. (1985). Contemplative prayer and its use in psychotherapy: A theoretical model. *Journal of Psychology & Theology, 13*(3), 172-81.

Flannelly, K. J., Weaver, A. J., Smith, W. J., & Handzo, G. F. (2003). Psychologists and health care: Chaplains doing research together. *Journal of Psychology and Christianity, 21*, 327-32.

Garzon, F. (2013). Christian devotional meditation for anxiety. In Everett L. Worthington, Jr., Eric L. Johnson, Joshua N. Hook, & Jamie D. Aten (Eds.), *Evidence-based practices for Christian counseling and psychotherapy* (pp. 59-76). IVP Academic.

Hall, T., & Coe, J. (2010). *Psychology in the Spirit: Contours of a transformational psychology.* InterVarsity.

Hathaway, W. L. (2003). Clinically significant religious impairment. *Mental Health, Religion & Culture, 6*(2), 113–29.

Hathaway, W. L., & Hoover, J. (2019). Christian psychologists as organization and leadership consultants. Workshop conducted at the American Association of Christian Counselors World Conference, Nashville, TN.

Henggeler, S. W., Schoenwald, S. K., Borduin, C. M., Rowland, M. D., & Cunningham, P. B. (2009). *Multisystemic therapy for antisocial behavior in children and adolescents* (2nd ed.). Guilford Press.

Henson, B., & Baatz, M. (2018). *Guiding families of LGBTQ+ loved ones* (2nd ed.). Lead Them Home.

Howell, S. H. (2005). Using psychology to facilitate Christian living: Description of a first step in building a program of collaboration. In M. R. McMinn & A. W. Dominguez (Eds.), *Psychology and the church* (pp. 41-47). Nova Science.

Jennings, D. J., Davis, D. E., Hook, J. N., & Worthington, E. L. (2013). Christian-accommodative cognitive therapy for depression. In E. L. Worthington, E. L. Johnson, J. N. Hook, & J. D. Aten (Eds.), *Evidence-based practices for Christian counseling and psychotherapy* (81-100). InterVarsity.

Johnson, W. B., DeVries, R., Ridley, C. R., Pettorini, D., & Peterson, D. (1994). The comparative efficacy of Christian and secular rational-emotive therapy with Christian clients. *Journal of Psychology and Theology, 22*, 130-40.

Kidwell, J. E. M. & Wade, N. (2013). Christian accommodative group interventions to promote forgiveness for transgressions. In E. L. Worthington, E. L. Johnson, J. N. Hook, &

J. N. Aten (Eds.), *Evidence-based practices for Christian counseling and psychotherapy* (255-78). InterVarsity.

Lowman, R. L. (Ed.). (2008). *The California School of Organizational Studies handbook of organizational consulting psychology: A comprehensive guide to theory, skills, and techniques.* Jossey-Bass.

Lowman, R. L., & Cooper, S. E. (2017). *The ethical practice of consulting psychology.* American Psychological Association.

McDonald, G., & McDonald, L. (2020). *Embracing the journey.* Howard Press.

McMinn, M. R. (1996). *Psychology, theology, and spirituality in Christian counseling.* Tyndale House.

McMinn, M. R., & Campbell, C. (2007). *Integrative psychotherapy: Towards a comprehensive Christian approach.* InterVarsity.

McMinn, M. R., & Dominguez, A. W. (Eds.). (2005). *Psychology and the church.* Nova Science.

Nielsen, S. L., Johnson, W. B., & Ellis, A. (2001). *Counseling and psychotherapy with religious persons: A rational emotive behavior therapy approach.* Lawrence Erlbaum.

Oman, D., & Driskill, J. D. (2003). Holy name repetition as a spiritual exercise and therapeutic technique. *Journal of Psychology and Christianity, 22*(1) 5-19.

Pargament, K. I. (2008). *Spiritually integrated psychotherapy: Understanding and addressing the sacred.* The Guilford Press.

Pargament, K. I., Falgout, K., Ensing, D. S., Reilly, B., Silverman, M., Van Haitsma, K., Olsen, H., & Warren, R. (1991). The congregation development program: Data-based consultation with churches and synagogues. *Professional Psychology: Research and Practice, 22*(5), 393-404.

Pearce, M. (2016). *Cognitive behavioral therapy for Christians with depression.* Templeton Press.

Perdue, T., Prior, M., Williamson, C., & Sherman, S. (2016). Social justice and spiritual healing: Using micro and macro social work practice to reduce domestic minor sex trafficking. In T.L. Scales & M.S. (Eds.). (2016). *Christianity and social work readings on the integration of Christian faith and social work practice.* (5th ed., pp. 355-69). NACSW.

Propst, L. R. (1996). *Cognitive-behavioral therapy and the religious person.* In E. P. Shafranske (Ed.), *Religion and the clinical practice of psychology* (391-407). American Psychological Association.

Propst, L. R. (1980). The comparative efficacy of religious and nonreligious imagery for the treatment of mild depression in religious individuals. *Cognitive Therapy and Research, 4,* 167-78.

Propst, L. R. (1988). *Psychotherapy in a religious framework: Spirituality in the emotional healing process.* Human Sciences Press, Inc.

Propst, L. R., Ostrom, R., Watkins, P., Dean, T., & Mashburn, D. (1992). Comparative efficacy of religious and nonreligious cognitive-behavioral therapy for the treatment of clinical depression in religious individuals. *Journal of Consulting and Clinical Psychology, 60,* 94-103.

Rice, H. L. (1991). *Reformed spirituality: An introduction for believers.* Louisville, KY: Westminster John Knox Press.

Richards, P. S., & Bergin, A. E. (2005). *A spiritual strategy for counseling and psychotherapy.* American Psychological Association.

Ripley, J. S., & Worthington, E. L., Jr. (2014). *Couple therapy: A new hope-focused approach.* IVP Academic.

Roll-Hansen, N. (2017). A historical perspective on the distinction between basic and applied science. *Journal for General Philosophy of Science, 48*, 535-51.

Rosmarin, D. H. (2018). *Spirituality, religion, and cognitive-behavioral therapy: A guide for clinicians.* Guilford Press.

Rosmarin, D. H., Forester, B. P., Shassian, D. M., Webb, C. A., & Björgvinsson, T. (2015). Interest in spiritually integrated psychotherapy among acute psychiatric patients. *Journal of Consulting and Clinical Psychology, 83*(6), 1149-53.

Rosmarin, D. H., Pirutinsky, S., Auerbach, R. P., Björgvinsson, T., Bigda, P. J., Andersson, G., Pargament, K. I., & Krumrei, E. J. (2011). Incorporating spiritual beliefs into a cognitive model of worry. *Journal of Clinical Psychology, 67*(7), 691-700.

Rothman, J., & Misrahi, T. (2014). Balancing micro and macro practice: A challenge for social work. *Social Work, 59*(1), 91-93.

Scales, T. L., & Kelly, M. S. (Eds.). (2016). *Christianity and social work readings on the integration of Christian faith and social work practice* (5th ed.). NACSW.

Schafer, R. M., Handal, P. J., Brawer, P. A., & Ubinger, M. (2011). Training and education in religion/spirituality within APA-accredited clinical psychology programs: 8 years later. *Journal of Religion and Health, 50*(2), 232-39.

Sells, J. S., & Yarhouse, M. A. (2011). *Counseling couples in conflict: A relational restoration model.* IVP Academic.

Serrano, N. (2003). A psychologist-pastor: A bridge for churches at a Christian community health center. *Journal of Psychology and Christianity, 21*, 353-56.

Shafranske, E. P. (Ed.). (1996). *Religion and the clinical practice of psychology.* American Psychological Association.

Society for Industrial and Organizational Psychology (2020). *About the Society for Industrial and Organizational Psychology (SIOP).* Retrieved from "http://www.siop.org/" www.siop.org/.

Strawn, B. D., Bland, E. D., & Flores, P. S. (2018). Learning Clinical Integration: A Case Study Approach. *Journal of Psychology & Theology, 46*(2) 85-97.

Tan, S. Y. (1996). Religion in clinical practice: Implicit and explicit integration. In E. P. Shafranske (Ed.), *Religion and the clinical practice of psychology* (pp. 365-87). APA.

Tan, S. Y. (2001). Integration and beyond: Principled, professional, and persona. *Journal of Psychology and Christianity, 20*(1), 18-28.

Tan, S. Y. (2005). Psychology collaborating with the church: A pastor-psychologist's perspective and personal experience. In M. R. McMinn & A. W. Dominguez (Eds.), *Psychology and the church* (pp. 49-55). Nova Science.

Tan, S. Y. (2013). Lay Christian counseling for general psychological problems. In Everett L. Worthington, Jr., Eric L. Johnson, Joshua N. Hook, & Jamie D. Aten (Eds.), *Evidence-based practices for Christian counseling and psychotherapy* (pp. 40-58). IVP Academic.

Throckmorton, W., & Yarhouse, M. A. (2006). The sexual identity therapy framework. sit-framework.com/wp-content/uploads/2009/07/sexualidentitytherapyframeworkfinal.pdf

Tjeltveit, A. (1999). *Ethics and values in psychotherapy*. Routledge.

Tyler, F. B., Pargament, K. I., & Gatz, M. (1983). The resource collaborator role: A model for interactions involving psychologists. American Psychologist, 38(4), 388-98.

Walker, D. F., Quagliana, H. L., Wilkinson, M., & Frederick, D. (2013). Christian accommodative trauma-focused cognitive-behavioral therapy for children and adolescents. In E. L. Worthington, E. L. Johnson, J. N. Hook, & J. N. Aten (Eds.), *Evidence-based practices for Christian counseling and psychotherapy* (101-21). InterVarsity.

Watson, T. S. (2018). *Developing clinicians of character: A Christian integrative approach to clinical supervision*. IVP Academic.

Witmer, L. (1907). Clinical psychology. *The Psychological Clinic, 1,* 1-9.

Worthington, E. L., Jr. (2003). *Forgiving and reconciling: Bridges to wholeness and hope* (rev. ed.). InterVarsity Press.

Worthington, E. L., Jr. (2006). *Forgiveness and reconciliation: Theory and application*. Taylor and Francis.

Worthington, E. L., Johnson, E. L., Hook, J. N., & Aten, J. D. (Eds.). (2013). *Evidence-based practices for Christian counseling and psychotherapy*. InterVarsity.

Worthington, E. L., Kurusu, T. A., McCollough, M. E., & Sandage, S. J. (1996). Empirical research on religion and psychotherapeutic processes and outcomes: A 10-year review and research prospectus. *Psychological bulletin, 119*(3), 448-87.

Worthington, E. L., Witveit, C. V., Pietrini, P., & Miller, A. J. (2007). Forgiveness, health, and well-being: A review of evidence for emotional versus decisional forgiveness, dispositional forgivingness, and reduced unforgiveness. *Journal of Behavioral Medicine* 30(4), 291-302.

Wolterstorff, N. (1983). *Until justice and peace embrace*, Eerdmans.

Wright, A. G. C., & Hallquist, M. N. (Eds.). (2020). *The Cambridge handbook of research methods in clinical psychology*. Cambridge University.

Yarhouse, M. A. (2005). Same-sex attraction, homosexual orientation, and gay identity: A three-tier distinction for counseling and pastoral care. *Journal of Pastoral Care & Counseling, 59*(3), 201-12.

Yarhouse, M. A. (2008). Narrative sexual identity therapy. *American Journal of Family Therapy, 36,* 1-15.

Yarhouse, M. A. (2019). *Sexual identity and faith: Helping clients achieve congruence*. Templeton Press.

Yarhouse, M. A., & VanOrman, B. T. (1999). When psychologists work with religious clients: Applications of the general principles of ethical conduct. *Professional Psychology: Research and Practice, 30*(6), 557-62.

6

ROLE
INTEGRATION

WE NOW TURN TO AN INTEGRATIVE DOMAIN that has been largely un-
named and underaddressed in the Christianity-Psychology Integration project.
Yet we note with some irony that this domain represents an ancient focus on
discussion in Christian thought as we will see by looking at the way it was addressed by Augustine, the influential North African bishop and prolific Christian
scholar from antiquity. We have called this domain *role integration.* In the first
chapter, we defined integration in this domain as the effort *to live out in integrity
role expectations and patterns that arise from a psychological vocation in a particular context in a way that is simultaneously faithful to one's Christian identity.*
In this chapter, we will provide the reader with a definition of some relevant
terms and a brief discussion of pertinent theological issues such as Augustine's
concepts of "two cities" and the Anabaptist response. We will also consider what
role integration may mean in this context of Christ's instruction to "render unto
Caesar."[1] Further, we discuss accountability and integrity as bridge principles for
both Christian discipleship and ethical practice in the psychological professions.
We close the chapter with an extended discussion of the complexities, challenges,
and considerations by use of several case examples.

---

[1]We will describe some details about these influential Christian scholars and traditions in our text.
For the reader who is unfamiliar with Saint Augustine, Saint Boniface, or the later Anabaptist tradition, McGrath's (2012) introductory text on historical theology can provide more context. The "render
unto Caesar" phrase is an allusion to the famous reply of Jesus that is presented in each of the synoptic
Gospels to interlocutors who were attempting to catch him in opposition to a Roman tax thus
engendering a conflict with Roman authorities.

In *Awaiting the King*, James K. A. Smith recalls an exchange of letters between influential early church scholars and leader, Augustine, and Boniface, a general in the Roman army. Boniface had written to Augustine for guidance on his being a follower of Christ and a soldier. Part of Augustine's reply was this: "Do not suppose that no one can please God who as a soldier carries the weapons of war" (Smith, 2017, p. 198). Smith reminds the reader of the biblical precedents for this specific vocation, including David and Cornelius, but there is more to the charge than that. He offers, "Be, therefore, a peacemaker even in war in order that by conquering you might bring to the benefit of peace those whom you fight" (p. 199). After his wife died, Boniface considered leaving his role and entertained the idea of monastic life. Augustine encouraged Boniface to stay true to his calling to public office. As Smith observes, there is no "Holy Roman empire" here; Augustine is able to "relativize" Rome without "demonizing" Rome.

This is an early discussion of what we are referring to as role integration. Whenever we enter into a public life and weigh what it means to be faithful to God, we are in a discussion of role integration. The challenge of professional role integration arises when Christians committed to be faithful disciples of Christ attempt to adopt established roles within a secular profession. These roles often involve serving the public or serving the profession in some capacity.

To get at the question of what it means to be a faithful Christian in established professional roles, it is first helpful to understand role theory in social psychology. The concept of a role is drawn from dramaturgy, a sociological perspective that all of life is a play in which people play out socially defined parts. Role theory "explains roles by presuming that persons are members of *social positions* and hold *expectations* for their own behaviors and those of other persons" (Biddle, 1986, p. 67).[2]

Roles here can refer to behaviors that are characteristic of psychological scientists, or roles and obligations associated with a designated professional role as a psychologist or related regulated mental health profession. To be a psychologist is to hold a designated professional and social position in which there are shared norms for our conduct. When students train in the profession, they are learning to adopt a way of relating and behaving that has specific expectations for conduct and defined ways of relating when in that role.

---

[2]We acknowledge that feminist and sociological criticism of role theory has suggested it insufficiently accounts for other economic, social, and familial complexities that both constrain and facilitate human behavior (Jackson, 1998). For the purposes of introducing role integration, however, a basic understanding of role theory, as incomplete as it may be, will suffice.

The need for professional role integration arises when Christians voluntarily enter a profession that requires fidelity to ethic codes, professional practice standards, relevant legal statutes, or regulation. Many aspects of these professional role requirements naturally converge with a Christian caregiving ethos, but sometimes role tensions or even conflicts may arise between one's Christian callings, values, beliefs, or practices and one's professional standards or norms. In such conflictual moments, there are parallels to the ancient discussion about whether a converted Roman soldier could properly remain a soldier.

What are the professional roles in psychology, counseling, marriage and family therapy, and related professions that need to be considered? Professional roles may involve conduct expectations that can arise in one of two different types of ways: *de jure* and *de facto*. *De jure* standards or role expectations are explicitly delineated and required by some authoritative body. *De facto* standards/role expectations are not explicitly stated but arise from the common conduct patterns that characterize a profession. It may be the case that students most often think of professional ethics codes as the primary thing that explicitly governs their roles in the professions (i.e., as what we are here calling a *de jure* standard). Professional ethical codes are certainly a major source of role requirements and will be discussed more below. However, for most professionals in North America, it is governmental regulations and codes that have greater force in actually giving form and consequence to the roles that must be fulfilled by licensed or registered mental health professionals. Professional ethics codes and other factors are more pivotal for those in the nonlicensed psychological careers, for instance, as a research psychologist in a nonclinical field.

Functioning as a licensed psychologist, professional counselor, marriage and family therapist, or in some other related licensed mental health field is the most common endeavor that creates the need for role integration for those who seek to conduct themselves as Christians in their professional calling. This is not unlike Boniface serving Rome in a public capacity. By entering a government-regulated profession, the Christian is entering into what is sometimes referred to as fiduciary space of public trust. Licensed professional practice of psychology, counseling, or family therapy is a societally granted privilege that creates special obligations and role expectations for the practitioner. To be a licensed mental health professional is to be a trustee of a public trust. One voluntarily accepts the obligations arising from civil, and sometimes criminal, legal codes that apply to those entering these professions. In the United States and Canada, the professions are typically regulated by state or provincial licensing boards that consist of politically appointed peer professionals and other political appointees. The Association of State and Provincial Psychology Licensing Boards (ASPPB) is an organization that includes delegates from these boards. While ASPPB is not itself a regulating body, it provides a common forum for regulatory bodies to share and promulgate common standards and best practices in the psychological profession. The purpose of licensing boards is not to promote the guild interests of a profession such as psychology but to protect the public. As the ASPPB website notes:

> To practice psychology in a state, province, or territory (jurisdiction) of the U.S. or Canada, an individual must be licensed or registered as a psychologist according to the laws and regulations in effect in that particular jurisdiction. The legal basis for licensure lies in the right of a jurisdiction to enact legislation to protect its citizens—in this case to identify qualified psychologists and to discipline or remove from practice incompetent or unethical psychologists. Licensure as a psychologist generally involves meeting requirements in three areas: education, examination(s), and supervised experience. (ASPPB, 2020)

Bill served some terms as a member of the Board of Psychology for the state of Virginia and as a delegate to ASPPB while a member of that board. A formal orientation to this role and its requirements was provided by the state. Board members are given specific instructions about the role they must enact, and they are also informed of how the board's role is to regulate with the force of state law and regulation the conduct of professions consistent with their roles. As with any governmental body, there are detailed procedures in place for promulgating regulations; implementing changes in statutes that impact the profession; conducting disciplinary procedures when concerns arise about psychologists violating practice regulations or statutes; ensuring appropriately qualified individuals enter the profession; overseeing processes to ensure competence is maintained, such as requiring and monitoring ongoing continuing education; and many other aspects of public protection. While the Board routinely receive input from state psychological associations and others, board members are reminded by state officials that their duty is one of public protection and enforcing applicable state law, not representing a profession's interests.

Let us return to the issue of professional ethics codes. Most contemporary professions have ethics codes that stipulate how the members of their professions are, or are *not*, to conduct themselves. Yet given how common such codes are, it may surprise some readers to hear that the professional codes are relatively recent parts of the professional landscape. Baker (1999) provides an informative discussion of the history of professional codes. While some ethical principles were included in the oaths one took to enter particular professions, such as the Hippocratic Oath, these oaths were "honorific." They had no force of regulation and were often tied to principles such as *doing no harm* rather than focusing on specific behavioral expectations. This changed in 1794, when Thomas Percival wrote *A Code of Conduct for Physicians and Surgeons.*

Percival was put in charge of a committee at Manchester Infirmary after infighting between apothecaries, physicians, and surgeons resulted in a dramatic interruption of services to the public during an influenza outbreak. Each group felt the other group was deficient in practicing proper medicine. A volley of insulting essays were distributed through pamphlets followed by, in some cases, duels. Percival, a physician who was also trained in philosophy and who possessed Anglican/Unitarian sensibilities, felt such conduct had to be prevented among professionals who aspired to medical roles. His code was quite different from the honorific oaths and other aspirational notions in medicine that were the main guidance up to his time. In his code, he laid out clear expectations for how health care providers were to conduct themselves, such as the obligation to do rounds at the infirmary "early and often," and to ensure patients were not abandoned. His code was expanded a few years later (1803) and included the first use of phrases such as "professional ethics" and "medical ethics." It introduced the concept of a *health care system* and the specific behavioral expectations for those who are part of it. The overarching moral principle was that care for the sick was a binding duty not only on physicians and other providers, but also the lay trustees of the hospitals and anyone else influencing the provision of care.

Percival's code had an enormous impact on contemporary professions starting with medicine but then going far beyond it. In 1808, the Boston Medical Society formulated an ethics code modeled after Percival's. Then, when the first national medical association was formed in the United States in 1847, the American Medical Association adopted a Percivalian code of ethics, the first ever adopted by any professional society. Within a century of that development, having a professional code of ethics to which members were expected to conform became the defining feature of the professions. As Baker (1999) put it:

> From accountants to zookeepers, professionals of all sorts seem to have a code of ethics these days. It was not always so. Until about 1800, ethics, especially professional ethics, was about character, honor and dishonor, virtue and vice. Ethics had

nothing to do with formal codes of conduct. A true professional, being a gentleman, needed no written instruction in how to behave . . . (n.p.)

Religion was not a central focus of most of Percival's code. While Percival moved away from orthodox trinitarian belief in his adult life, theistic faith remained a vital framework that supported and gave motivation to the moral imperatives in his code (Gregory, 2001). Anyone familiar with contemporary codes of ethics in the health care–related fields will find much that is familiar in Percival's code. Yet unlike the purely secular emphasis in the current codes, Percival indicated that the spiritual development of the medical student was an ethical issue. He noted in the 1803 edition of his code that medical students who came to study in the urban teaching centers, by virtue of being away from home and being exposed as young people to the harsh realities of the sick and dying, sometimes became calloused and uncaring. Percival believed "non-attendance of public worship will lead to coldness of heart and moral insensibility" (Gregory, 2001, p. 40). To guard against this, his code stipulated they should not neglect active participation in "public worship." It will likely come as no surprise to readers living in our secular age that this emphasis of professionals maintaining active religious observance was not retained in the widespread professional codes that Percival's code inspired.

In the wake of this ethics sea change wrought by Percivalian codes, people who enter contemporary professions now are bound by an agreement to follow specific ethical standards articulated by their professions. Since the early 1950s, the American Psychological Association has had an ethics code that governs all of its members, both clinicians and nonclinicians. Many state regulations and/or statutes have modeled their psychologist practice standards on the APA Code, and some even explicitly enforce the code as a requirement for all license holders in their jurisdiction. Similar codes exist in other mental health professions including counseling and social work. There is much in these codes that conform with standard Christian morality and virtues. That is no accident. Biomedical ethics have evolved in an ethical space impacted for millennia by Christian deliberation on ethics. APA's ethics code includes both aspirational principles and enforceable conduct standards that are thought to embody the ethical principles in concrete ways. What many psychologists quite familiar with the code may not realize is how aligned the APA ethical principles had been to the biomedical ethical philosophy of two of the leading contemporary Catholic Bioethicists, Beauchamp and Childress (2019; Lozano, 2004; Knapp & Vandecreek, 2004). They have defended an approach to biomedical ethics committed to four principles: autonomy, nonmaleficence, beneficence, and justice. APA's (2016) general principles are beneficence and nonmaleficence (benefiting and doing no harm), fidelity and responsibility, integrity, justice, and respect for people's rights and dignity.[3]

We are not suggesting here that the contemporary professional ethics codes are Christian moral systems, but rather that there is convergence on some key principles perhaps in part because of the historical residue of Christian thought in Western culture (Fitzgerald, 2019). In many cases, it is quite natural to echo the ethical expectations in the professional codes from a Christian moral perspective. What Christian would object to being expected to do no harm, obtain informed consent for treatment, refrain from sexual behavior with our clients, or limit our practice to interventions within our competence, for instance? Yet in other cases, the way the ethics principles are applied in practice does sometimes create tension for Christians in the mental health and health care professions as we will discuss below.

In addition to roles arising from the *de jure* standards for conduct that apply to our professions, we can also have patterns of expected behavior arise from the social and institutional professional cultures in which we function. The public frequently understands the role of the psychologist to be something like a counselor in a therapy setting. But there are also many other venues with quite different roles that psychologists may inhabit. Examples include functioning as parts of professional societies, associations, colleges, scholarly venues, and other formal parts of the profession. Mental health professionals and psychological scientists are sometimes elected to governance in the American Psychological Association (APA), the American Counseling Association (ACA), the American Association for Marriage and Family Therapy (AAMFT), state professional associations, or many other membership bodies. They also might be appointed to professional service and policymaking roles on working groups or task forces. They might serve their profession by becoming an ad hoc reviewer of a scientific journal or even serving as an editorial board member, so that they are functioning as a gatekeeper on behalf of the professional for what is published and what is representative of the profession in areas of scientific publication.

---

[3]At the time of writing this text, APA is in the process of a major revision of its code. A review of the draft of the principles for the new version out for public comment appears to reflect less alignment with Beauchamp and Childress. Still, some of the core principles from this tradition appear to be present and the Percivalian emphasis on concrete ethical standards appears to remain.

In academia and other training settings, professionals teach the next generation of emerging professionals, socializing them into the same or evolving roles in the professions they have already adopted. They could represent their professions to those outside the profession in various consulting roles. In virtually all of these contexts, there are orientation procedures and processes—sometimes formal, other times informal—that acculturate professionals to the expected roles. Some settings have highly specialized role expectations that require special pathways for entrance. For instance, active duty military psychologists must be prepared for this unique area of professional service and become dual qualified as both psychologists and military officers.

Thus, the issue of role integration, even in a single profession like psychology or social work, is a complex matter that could take on substantially different forms across any of the specific roles in the profession. In cases where a specific set of role expectations arise from voluntary entrance into a regulated practice field, such as licensure, a Christian who seeks and obtains licensure has made an explicit commitment to practice consistent with the applicable professional standards. So, a willingness to conform to professional standards becomes, in most instances, a matter of basic integrity. Will the Christian professional keep their word in their professional conduct? If a Christian enters the profession with their fingers crossed, intending to conform to the professional standards only selectively, then how could that reflect the biblical virtues of honesty and truthfulness that disciples of Jesus are expected to evidence? The public trust placed on the licensed mental health professional also creates in us a spiritual obligation (given biblical teaching) that obligates the follower of Christ to civic submission as a rule. As Christians weigh entering into professionally regulated practice, we weigh committing ourselves to obligations defined by custom, policy, code, and law applicable to this fiduciary space. The civic and professional obligations are also Christian obligations in light of biblical teaching. We are to "Give back to Caesar what is Caesar's, and to God what is God's" (Mt 22:21).

In addition to the formal *de jure* aspects to the roles a psychologist may adopt, it is possible that other aspects of roles arise tacitly, from the widely recognizable patterns of behavior we have instilled in us by training or the habits of others. Role theory also suggests there are public expectations for our behavior when we adopt publicly recognized roles in society. What do our clients expect when they come to see a psychologist? In general, professional expectations are shaped by professional ethical standards, as well as profession-wide competencies defined by accrediting bodies for the profession of psychology. These obligations are supported and enforced by licensing boards.

Some obligations are fixed features of the practice context that arise by law or ethical standards. We can think of examples in which what is shared in therapy is confidential, which refers to the idea that private information shared in this professional context will ordinarily remain between the client and the clinician. However, there are exceptions. If a psychologist is informed of child abuse or if a person is in imminent danger to oneself, the psychologist then has special obligations in that practice context.

It may be that other moral obligations arise from the reasonable role expectations our clients have, given public understandings of psychology, the context of our practice, or other situational factors. For example, in a government-regulated practice context, like a Veterans' Affairs (VA) hospital, a client likely has the reasonable expectation that explicit Christian integrative approaches or heavy presence of religious stimuli favoring a particular faith (e.g., crosses, Christian magazines, etc.) will not be the dominant experience for all clients walking in the door.

Even in this practice context, it may be perfectly legitimate to use explicit integrative techniques or protocols when they are consistent with client preferences and values and when such techniques or protocols are clinically indicated. Yet, there are other layers of obligation that have to be considered having to do with whether we have agreed to function within certain constraints as a condition of employment in that practice setting.

Practicing in an explicitly Christian context may create a reasonable expectation of more explicitly integrative activity, but even in these instances, the Christian should not automatically assume this to be the case. A secular client may elect to come into a Christian site but have no idea or any interest in "Christian psychology"; they may not distinguish a Christian site as a specialized practice context but expect standard (i.e., secular) mental health services.

Christ and Culture

As we noted in chapter four (theoretical integration), in H. Richard Niebuhr's influential text *Christ and Culture*, Niebuhr categorized various ways Christians throughout history have responded to the enduring problem of how we are to live in culture. Many interested in the mental health fields will have encountered versions of the famous serenity prayer: "Father, give us courage to change what must be altered, serenity to accept what cannot be helped, and the insight to know the one from the other," authored by Niebuhr's older brother, Reinhold (Shapiro, 2014).

Table 1 presents a brief description of his five types. Niebuhr's typology has been especially useful in prompting Christians to think about how others have attempted to function as Christians in their culture in matters that closely relate to what we are calling Christian role integration. Of course, with any overarching typology attempting to categorize so many forms of Christian life over the millennia into a small set of types, it is not without its critics.

Table 1. Niebuhr's (1951) five *Christ and Culture* types

Type	Characteristics	Examples
Christ against culture	Uncompromising assertion of the sole authority of the Christ against any claims to loyalty by culture. Faithful Christians must adopt the extreme to *reject* or *separate* from culture.	Tertullian, Benedictine monks, Mennonites, Quakers, Leo Tolstoy
Christ of culture	Asserts there is no significant tension present between Christianity and the ideal aspects of culture, which are congruent with Christian callings. Faithful Christians must adopt the extreme to fully *assimilate* or *accommodate* within culture.	Early Gnostics, Peter Abelard, Thomas Jefferson, Albrecht Ritschl
Christ above culture	Modal, centrist Christian posture attempts a synthesis between Christ and culture. Culture is a mixed bag reflecting both holy, God-given elements and sinful, bad elements. Christian rely on grace to faithfully affirm the good but not the bad. Faithful Christians selectively adopt their culture.	Clement of Alexandria, Thomas Aquinas
Christ and culture in paradox	The conflicting realities of the demands of Christ, his gracious provision in the world and yet its pervasive sinfulness, requires Christians to live in tension. Faithful Christians participate in culture in a constant state of tension. They must continually ensure that in their personal passions and the life of the Church, Christ is their sole focus.	Martin Luther, Søren Kierkegaard, Roger Williams
Christ the transformer of culture	Christians can "redeem" or convert culture to make it more faithfully Christian. Human nature and culture is corrupted but not irredeemable. Faithful Christians attempt to transform or convert culture.	Augustine, Calvin, F. D. Maurice

Bargár (2014) argues that Niebuhr's Christology is inadequate, seeing Christ as a countercultural figure and failing to appreciate the way Jesus reflected his own culture. He also suggests that some of the most influential Christian leaders fit more than one category, so some of the types may be dominant, but they are not usually exclusive. Cultures are not monolithic, fixed unitary things with firm boundaries. D. A. Carson (2008) offers an evangelical assessment of Niehbuhr's typology. He argues an approach to Christ and culture centering on the "non-negotiables" of biblical theology but further notes:

> Until the final resolution in the culture of the new heaven and the new earth, challenging and sometimes painful tensions will afflict us in these domains. Christians living under one particular model of how these matters should be worked out may labor under a too-limited vision of what might be, or what should be attempted, of what can be achieved. . . ." (Carson, 2008, p. 209)

The twentieth century witnessed the rise and intensification of what religious studies scholar Hunter (1991) called the "culture wars": ongoing struggles for the dominance of polarized sets of values and approaches to politics and other aspects of culture as cultural divides became increasingly pronounced. In recent years, many evangelical and other Christian thinkers have been reconsidering how Christians can faithfully live out their call to be disciples of Christ in an increasingly post-Christian culture. Hunter (2010) argued against the culture war-posture and in its place calls for Christians to simply demonstrate a faithful presence of the way of Christ in the world. He asserted:

> If there are benevolent consequences of our engagement with the world. . . . it is precisely because it is not rooted in a desire to change the world for the better but rather because it is an expression of a desire to honor the creator of all goodness, beauty, and truth, a manifestation of our loving obedience to God, and a fulfillment of God's command to love our neighbor. (p. 234)

Rod Dreher (2018) has argued for the *Benedict option* in which Christians refocus from changing the culture at a national level and instead cultivate local expressions of Christian community that evidence a vibrant and authentic witness to Christian forms of life.[4]

Calls to learn from "the way of the exile" are becoming increasingly common in evangelical contexts. This call emerges from those who strove to remain

---

[4]Dreher clarified: "It's a word I use for thinking of ourselves as radically countercultural, and living like monastics in the world . . ." and it is based on the life of Benedict of Nursia. According to Dreher, "St. Benedict of Nursia, . . . left the collapsing Roman Empire, went into a cave, sought the Lord's will, and emerged to start a monastic community. He wrote a famous Rule of monastic life. When he died in the year 547, he had planted twelve monasteries in the vicinity of Rome. From those mustard seeds grew a great monastic movement, one that spread throughout barbarian-ruled Europe, and tended the light of faith through a very dark time." www.theamericanconservative.com/dreher /meaning-of-the-benedict-option.

faithful to the kingdom of God while taken into exile by Babylon after Judah fell to that nation in the sixth century BC. The prophet Jeremiah predicted the captivity. Recall that ancient Israel was divided into northern and southern kingdoms. Unlike the Jewish tribes of the northern kingdom that were previously disbursed and assimilated by their Assyrian conquerors, the Babylonian captives from Judah were taken into exile as a group. This made it possible for them to band together and, for those who had not lost faith in God, to continue to remain faithful to Him in exile. But how were they to do that? Jeremiah enjoined them to " . . . seek the peace and prosperity of the city to which I have carried you into exile. Pray to the LORD for it, because if it prospers, you too will prosper" (Jer 29:7). Here we have a recommendation to remain faithful but to live in a way that promotes the prospering of the secular culture in which the Jewish captives were taken.[5]

Two biblical exemplars, Daniel and Esther, lived out this prophetic instruction. Daniel reflects the dramatic story of a bright young Jewish captive who serves Babylon with the talents and spiritual gifts given to him by God. It is a story of respectful and loyal service for the welfare of the foreign ruler and the people in whose land he found himself. Yet it is also a story of steadfast and uncompromising faithfulness to God that created moments of dramatic conflict resolved by the power of God and with the vindication of Daniel as a faithful civil servant. On matters that did not require a violation of a core of his faith, Daniel served and adapted to the Babylonian culture.

Esther was a Jewish woman during the Persian period who became a princess to the Persian ruler. By this point, the Persian empire had conquered the Babylonians and were now the captors of the Jewish exiles. The biblical depiction of Esther did not present her as having religious clashes in her exilic culture until a plot to attack the Jews emerged. She was then in a unique position to approach the king unsolicited and speak on behalf of her people. The book of Esther is one of the two biblical books that does not mention a name for God. It is clear that this winsome woman was providentially situated to serve the divine plan at an opportune moment "for such a time as this" (Esther 4:14). She had credibility and standing not through overt miracles and demonstrations of divine power but through the way she had lived her life in the Persian court.

---

[5]The phrase "the way of the exile" has been used to demarcate a distinctive posture that Christians might take in a post-Christian cultural context in a variety of sources. See the Bible Project's (2020) video with the title, *For the Life of the World: Letters to Exiles* video series. Griffith (2015) described it *in Christianity* Today as the best video ever made on Christ and culture, or the text by Clark (2019) on doing evangelism as an exile for examples.

Christians in the mental health fields may at times experience being conflicted as disciples of Christ in a post-Christian context. Like Daniel and Esther, if they seek to serve well in their roles, they seek the welfare of both their clients and the profession. Given the enormously influential roles the secular mental health fields now have in many societies, if Christians avoid them because of the periodic conflict and tensions that may arise, then who will be in a position to exert a Christian influence on them? Admittedly, tensions do arise in these fields as with any secular profession. Let us talk now more about the role conflicts.

Role Conflict and Related Terms

Role conflict, according to role theory, refers to "the appearance of two or more incompatible expectations for the behavior of a person" (Biddle, 1986, p. 82). What role conflict seems to reflect are problems in what Biddle refers to as "structural conditions" (p. 83) that can be related to other role-related concepts, including role overload, role malintegration, and role discontinuity (Biddle, 1986). Role overload refers to "when the person is faced with too many expectations" (p. 83). Perhaps more in keeping with our present concerns, role malintegration refers to those experiences "when roles do not fit well together" (p. 83), which role discontinuity refers to "when the person must perform a sequence of malintegrated roles" (p. 83).

Some Christians entering into specific psychology-related fields may experience either role malintegration (i.e., the experience of roles not fitting well), or they may experience role discontinuity (i.e., the normative expectation that they perform a series of malintegrated roles). In such circumstances, we sometimes heard Christians who early in their career professions wonder about the roles they have undertaken.

To make this more concrete, let us consider the case of Sandra Bruff. Bruff, a licensed professional counselor with an Employment Assistance Program, asked her employer to accommodate her religious beliefs about not counseling a lesbian client on her same-sex relationship. After attempts to reconcile her complaint, Bruff was ultimately dismissed of her counseling duties and placed on leave (Hermann & Herlihy, 2006). Bruff filed a lawsuit against North Mississippi Health Service, claiming that according to Title VII of the Civil Rights Act of 1964 (as amended in 1972), the company had violated federal law by not accommodating her religious beliefs (Hermann & Herlihy, 2006). The jury initially awarded Bruff over two million dollars in damages; however, the ruling was reversed on appeal because the judge believed it would have been an undue hardship to accommodate Bruff's religious beliefs (Hermann & Herlihy, 2006). Yet it should be noted that the court's decision actually indicated the employer *did* have a duty to accommodate Bruff's religion-based request if it could be done without exceeding a small burden (literally less than a *de minimis* cost) (Hathaway & Ripley, 2009).[6] It is because Bruff voluntarily agreed to a job where a small number of therapists were responsible to provide counseling to all eligible beneficiaries that the appellate court determined the burden was too great to obligate the employer to grant her the requested accommodation. This case raises the potential issue of role malintegration that can occur when a person may wish to place value-based limitations on their practice and elect to serve in specific roles that are at odds with those limitations.

It is noteworthy that some of the discussion that followed the Sandra Bruff case included the suggestion that Christians perhaps should work only in private practice settings that are explicitly Christian rather than in EAP settings in which it would be an "undue hardship" for the EAP to accommodate religious beliefs. Of course, Christian psychologists could choose to work in only *explicitly* Christian practice contexts, with clients who desire *explicitly integrative* techniques to pursue therapy goals that *comfortably conform to Christian values*. However, such qualifiers, in our experience, would be difficult to pull off even in an explicitly Christian practice context. While explicit integration and explicitly Christian practice contexts have a legitimate place in psychology, it is implausible to think that all Christian practitioners can or may even feel called to restrict their practice entirely to such domains.

Perhaps more importantly, some Christians may think integrative practice will allow them to isolate themselves from the world, but we have to ask at what cost and whether such a posture really reflects broader Christian values having to do with engaging the culture. In other words, even if they could, it may not be appropriate for other reasons. Incarnational discipleship calls us out of our insular sacred refuges and into the world. Explicit integrative activity and practice

---

[6]The *de minimis* phrase was used in the court decision. Gregory (2011) discusses how this standard has been used to indicate when employers may face an undue burden if an employee's religious practices were to be accommodated. The *de minimis* standard is a relatively low bar. If the accommodation is more than just a small or trifling difference, then an employer may not be obligated to accommodate under federal civil rights law. After commenting on the Bruff case, Gregory explains, "In determining whether a cost is more than *de minimis*, EEOC guidelines provide that the cost of the accommodation should be considered in relation to the size of the employer, its operating costs, and the number of employees who will need such an accommodation (p. 201).

contexts are appropriate only when they serve the function of enhancing service provision. Any motivation to withdraw into a Christian practice bubble that keeps us separate from the world puts us at odds with the incarnational mandate.

There are additional concepts in role theory that may aid our thinking about role integration. For example, *role ambiguity* refers to "a condition in which expectations are incomplete or insufficient to guide behavior" (Biddle, 1986, p. 83). This is probably the more common point of tension for Christians. For example, A few years ago, Mark was asked to serve as a subject-matter expert to the National Institute of Corrections (NIC). Staff from the NIC were asking for help because Mark's specialty is in working with people of faith who are navigating sexual or gender identity concerns. What they were wanting was some insight into training corrections staff to work with LGBTQ+ inmates despite coming from more conventionally religious backgrounds. What they were finding was that religious staff members were not being abusive to LGBTQ+ inmates; rather, they tended to turn a "blind eye" when abuses to LGBTQ+ inmates did occur. The out-briefs tended to reveal attitudes of, "Well, you are getting what you deserve," or, "Well, you are gay, so you like that kind of behavior." Mark agreed to participate in the development of a training for staff on LGBTQ+ persons in corrections.

One of the most interesting experiences was the focus on wanting to change the theology of staff who viewed same-sex sexual behavior as morally impermissible. Not only did Mark think that a three-hour training would be unable to change the doctrinal positions of conservative Christians, but he felt it was beyond the competencies of those conducting the training to adjudicate complex and controversial theological and ethical positions in which a range of views exist in a diverse and pluralistic society. However, what was the purpose of the training? To increase safety and security for all inmates, including those who identify as part of the LGBTQ+ community. Rather than focus on altering a religious doctrinal view of what is or is not morally permissible behavior, Mark suggested appealing to conventionally religious persons' work ethic and desire to serve God in meaningful ways. That is, to pitch the training around the idea that when a guard puts on their uniform, they are serving the interests of the NIC and their particular correction facility, which has as one of its charges to protect the welfare of its inmates. *This is their charge.* Guards and other staff can say to themselves, "No one is going to be harmed on my watch. Not on my shift." Christians work as *unto the Lord*, and appealing to their work ethic is a better angle of entry into a discussion than chastising them for their doctrinal views, which would only serve to make those in attendance more defensive. This training, then, would be able to stay within the competencies of the NIC staff and not extend beyond those competencies into areas of theological and ethical discourse.

Before they were able to make this the focus of a part of the training, Mark felt deep ambivalence about developing the training. He was the only evangelical Christian in the consultation group, and the overall training was to be quite affirmative in ways he was unsure he could support. There was a kind of role ambiguity Biddle refers to. This is one example of what we mean more broadly by role integration or role-related integration. In this case, Mark was invited to serve people beyond the church, beyond those who agreed with him. Indeed, he was to work with others who largely disagreed with him on important topics to serve superordinate goals that included the safety and welfare of LGBTQ+ inmates. These role-related tensions exist for all Christians who serve the public good in some way.

We turn now to specific professional role recommendations for the Christian in psychology and allied mental health fields.

Professional Role Integration Recommendations

As we have both had considerable experience in professional role integration, both as licensed clinical psychologists and in service to various profession-related leadership and service roles, we would like to offer a few recommendations for Christians who are thinking through role integration, perhaps for the first time.

Faithfulness. Christians should be faithful in the roles they accept without deception or evasion. This first principle goes back to the spiritual obligations of the Christian who elects to serve the public or the profession. We honor God by how we function in our professional capacity.

Example: Consider a Christian psychologist who does deliverance prayer ministry with clients he believes are facing spiritual attack from demonic forces. The psychologist charges an insurance company for this activity and presents it as standard psychotherapy. Would this be a faithful enactment of one's professional role?

Being careful. Since some role obligations are elective, be careful to agree to only those roles you can fulfill in good conscience.

Example: Consider a pro-life Christian who takes a job at a Planned Parenthood clinic and is required to help women resolve guilt over choices to have abortions. Why would this Christian accept such a position?

Being aware. Advocacy and professional leadership around issues of Christian concern.

Example: Consider that Christian psychologists quietly practice without being active in regional, state, or national psychology organizations. Professional policies get passed that require all psychologists to do gay affirmative therapy. Although Christian voices may have been able to temper this policy when it was being formulated, they were not present. The policy gets written in such a way that anyone operating with respect for a traditional Christian sexual ethic will either have to compromise their Christian values or risk violating professional standards. Would this not be, at least partially, a self-inflicted role conflict?

Each of the examples we have chosen illustrates conflicts that may arise between professional roles and one's Christian faith. The suggestions are intended to help navigate the twin demands of faithful Christian discipleship and professional integrity. Two of the examples reflect hot-button issues from a conservative evangelical perspective. They are not meant to imply that Christians will always be pro-life but to indicate the challenges that might arise when Christian values conflict with professional psychological mores.

It has also been helpful to both of us to remember that roles are not static, eternal forms. They are created and maintained through role formation processes. Christians in a profession can help to create roles, not just passively respond to the roles they are given. Christians can also play a role in producing incremental changes in existing roles to make those roles more harmonious with Christian ideals. Professions are made up of the professionals that constitute them. When Christians are in the professions, does it not make sense to proactively seek to be salt and light in those professions, helping to shape them in ways that will allow Christians to serve the profession for the common good with integrity?

We turn now to specific recommendations for producing roles and incremental changes in existing professional roles.

Recommendations for Producing and Shaping Roles

In light of our experience in professional role integration, we wanted to offer a few recommendations for Christians who wish to produce or shape roles so that those roles are more congruous with Christian ideals.

Prayerfully respond to role-related invitations. Sometimes professional roles are not sought so much as we receive invitations that we may want to prayerfully consider. These are often doors through which we enter into some of the most challenging role-related integration moments, so we take invitations seriously, recognizing that not every door is one we have the time or capacity to walk through.

Prayerfully consider role-related strategic initiatives. While we may be invited to serve in some professional roles, we may also seek to be elected to some roles or otherwise put ourselves in position to serve for strategic reasons. The difference between this recommendation and the first one is that this recommendation is about identifying important, strategic positions. For example, Bill has been able to serve on APA task forces that crafted APA policies on anti-Semitism and on both religion-derived and antireligious prejudice. He also participated in APA Board of Educational Affairs working groups that created guidance documents for how psychology educators can constructively navigate potential trainee value conflicts with particular clinical situations.

Outward- Versus Inward-Facing Role-Related Integration

We have been discussing role-related integration with respect to the challenges a Christian may face when they enter into a profession in which there are profession-wide characteristics of mental health professionals or roles and obligations associated with a designated professional role as a psychologist, counselor, or family therapist. This is a kind of *outward-facing* role-related integration that has to do with functioning in professional roles as a Christian. Returning to the notion of the way of the exile, when we are in such outward-facing roles, it is important that we not function merely as advocates for Christian interests. We should not compromise our Christian integrity in our positions or actions in such roles. Yet we are unlikely to be effective if we are perceived as only self-interested antagonists who care little for the welfare of those with whom we may differ.

There are also role-related considerations that are *inward-facing*. What we mean by this is that there are role integration challenges associated with Christians serving the church when we are also a licensed mental health professional. Put differently, we want to recognize the challenges faced by Christians in the mental health fields when they are asked to serve in more explicit ministry capacity in which designated clerical or otherwise ministry role considerations may pose additional challenges.

Returning to role theory: we recognize there are expectations from Christian faith communities for the role of the elder, deacon, Sunday school teacher, or small group leader, and that there are corresponding congregational expectations for one's behavior. What do people within our faith communities expect when they see us in ministry settings?

Both of us have served as elders in our local churches, for example. Serving as an elder is a ministry role that may vary to some extent from faith community to faith community but carries with it a localized set of assumptions and role-related behavioral expectations. This may entail role-related expectations surrounding teaching, shepherding, pastoral counseling, administration of sacraments such as the Lord's Supper, baptism, church discipline, and so on. Other ministry roles, such as being a deacon, small group or life group leader, Christian educator, or Sunday school teacher, serving on the worship team, and so on, also carry with them various role-related behavioral assumptions and expectations for ministry.

With inward-facing role-related integration, the questions that arise have to do with boundaries between functioning in a ministry capacity in which there are established roles and expectations, and functioning as a licensed mental health professional. There are many possible ministry roles, and when any of us enters into that ministry role, we bring with us advanced knowledge in our field that may enhance our ministry, but our ministry is distinct from and separate from our professional role as a mental health professional.

One important consideration on the front end of inward-facing integration is the extent to which you as a mental health professional will serve in specific ministry roles and what contact you will have with clients or former clients in that capacity, as well as whether you will see people from your church for professional services. These are important questions we all wrestle with, and there are no easy answers, as some of the answers depend on the size of the church, the nature of your professional practice (e.g., short-term versus long-term therapy, therapy versus testing, and so on), and the nature of your ministry role and associated role-related obligations (e.g., worship team, small group leader, elder).

Ministry Role Recommendations

As we have both had considerable experience in ministry role integration, both as elders and small group leaders, but also work as psychologists in a professional role, we would like to offer a few recommendations for Christians who are thinking through inward-facing role-related integration.

Set boundaries. Christians should set clear boundaries around their ministry roles. This first principle goes back to the professional responsibilities of any mental health provider who serves the body of Christ in a ministry capacity. We honor both our professional roles and God by establishing clear boundaries around our ministry roles.

Example: Consider a Christian mental health professional who serves as a deacon and is asked by a member of the church (who was seen by this professional for a comprehensive psychological assessment three years ago) to visit and pray with their eighty-four-year-old mother who is sick in the hospital.

Anticipate conflict. Christians should anticipate ministry role-related conflicts and plan accordingly. The second principle points to the professional and ethical responsibilities mental health professionals have to anticipate multiple roles and potential role-related conflicts and to take steps to mitigate those conflicts.

Example: Consider a Christian who serves as an elder and has knowledge—obtained through professional services—of a church member who is now receiving church discipline. These are moments when the elder may need to recuse him- or herself from any role of church discipline with a professional client.

Inward-facing integration considerations come to the fore when we think about role-related expectations for ministry roles when we are also licensed mental health professionals. As in most other ethical and professional practice tensions, much of what can be done is to anticipate and think through in advance the challenges that could arise depending on role expectations, while remaining open to how God might direct you to use your gifts in various ministry capacities.

Proselytization: A Role Integration Test Case

Should Christian mental health professionals proselytize their clients? Since Jesus is the only path to salvation and to realization of our ultimate purpose and potential, should we not share the gospel with our clients and set the salvation of their souls as a professional goal? Many Christians, particularly those of conservative leanings, may expect such a proselytizing posture would or should be a natural part of the helping roles of Christian mental health professionals. It may surprise some to learn that many in the secular world who are most distrusting and hostile to Christianity also believe that Christian mental health professionals set a priority on converting their non-Christian clients. While some Christians may think proselytization in the professional context would be a good thing, the latter group expresses deep concern over it.[7]

---

[7]The *Secular Therapy Project*, for instance, warns against the promulgation of religious therapists who bring religious elements into treatment. They express particular concern about graduates of

Contrary to the perception or expectation of both groups, our experience is that Christian mental health communities widely hold that proselytization of clients is unethical and improper. We suspect this is a product of role integration. The ethical codes of the mental health professionals all enjoin a professional obligation to respect the beliefs of our clients and in some fashion or another prohibit imposition of personal therapist values. Additional guidance, such as from practice guidelines or other resources, reinforce this expectation. For instance, the American Psychiatric Association (2006) generated a resource document directing psychiatrists to refrain from imposing their own religious views on clients. To engage in such proselytization would be to break faith with the professional role, standards, state regulations, and legal codes, by which one has agreed to abide upon becoming licensed. Consequently, such a practice would likely reflect a lack of integrity and honesty that we believe would be counter to biblical moral standards.

We are not assuming the therapy room can be a value-neutral context. But implicit influence of one's values and an explicit, intentional attempt to convert someone to a professional's religion are two quite different things. While we do not have survey data to support it, we suspect the proselytization of clients would be almost universally viewed as ethical misconduct by mental health professionals. Multiple factors contribute to why this norm is so generally embraced both by secular therapists and professionals who are people of faith. First, given the way the mental health professions have developed, clients expect these professionals to pursue psychological goals through treatment, not other types of goals. Thus, when a counselor exploits a client sexually or engages in another kind of boundary expectation such as entering a business arrangement with the client beyond the therapy contract, it is experienced as a role violation and deep betrayal. The same principle applies to pursuing nontreatment related spiritual goals in treatment.

Second, clients who seek therapy for mental health issues are often vulnerable to exploitation. Roger Williams (1644/2005), the founder of Rhode Island and key contributor to the American religious liberty tradition, argued forcefully that

faith-based programs. They have set up a referral network to help connect secular or nonreligious clients to secular providers. We are not aware of any empirical data that would support this body's contention that there is a systematic problem with religious co-option of treatment among licensed mental health professionals. We are also aware of isolated cases where nonreligious values were imposed in destructive ways on therapy by counselors. So, the problem is not whether religious or secular elements are present in treatment. We would suggest it is rather whether one is doing clinically appropriate practice within one's professional role, consistent with relevant standards and evidence.

coercive means of promoting *religious uniformity* (i.e., that all agree with the dominant party's faith perspective) is counter to the Bible and the purpose of evangelism. He pointed out that such efforts may result in insincere, outward conformity rather than true conversion. They also can harden people to the message of Jesus due to their aversive techniques. If a professional used the client's mental illness as a justification to attempt to convert them, the risk for coercive manipulation would be high.

Now to be clear about what we are saying here: we are both Christians. We believe eternal life comes only through salvation from Jesus. Yet the contemporary role of a mental health professional is one that focuses on psychological outcomes in this life using helping practices that can be justified to a diverse community of regulators and peer professionals to whom they are accountable. If Christians were to refuse to enter the mental health fields, that would relegate the highly influential set of professions entirely to adherents of non-Christian worldviews. While neither of us have engaged in proselytization in our mental health work, we both have viewed our practice as a form of ministry to those in need. We helped bind the brokenhearted, families avoid divorce, widows bear up under grief, drug addicts achieve and maintain sobriety, clients move away from suicide, soldiers recover from the trauma of war, and we have provided assistance to many others facing the range of psychological difficulties that plague the human condition. While we desire all to come to know Jesus as their savior and Lord, we are convinced the assistance we provide in our professional roles, even though not directed toward proselytization as a goal or activity, is still a work of mercy and of love that honors God.

Might there be a time when it would be ethically appropriate for a mental health professional to share their faith with a client? Given the nature of the contemporary professional role in the mental health fields, this would depend on several factors, such as obtaining informed consent, practicing within one's range of competence, and ensuring that self-disclosure is done for a clinical purpose and in a manner that could be justified to a professional peer community and relevant regulators who may not share the therapist's personal faith. In an early integrative article on this topic, Nelson and Wilson (1984) concluded that:

> Christian therapists who do know the reality of God may work within a patient's belief system and utilize the power available to them to affect the healing of those patient problems which have a spiritual origin. Such intervention is permissible if

it is consonant with the patient's ethical belief system and has been carefully defined within the treatment contract. (p. 21)

But note that Nelson and Wilson's model presupposes a shared Christian belief system prior to the sharing, so this remains quite distinct from proselytization.

Mental health professionals are not pastors or evangelists. The religio-legal role of the pastor, that may be guided ultimately by doctrinal or scriptural authority alone, is not a part of the mental health professional role. But we would offer one closing thought on this discussion. There is a kind of preparatory role possible for the mental health professional in evangelism highlighted by the parable of the sower (Mt 13). Jesus indicated that when the gospel is received, it sometimes bears fruit and other times does not. Some who hear the gospel have the message choked out because of the "worries of the world." Effective mental health care may remove or minimize such obstacles to hearing the gospel and help it to take root and produce fruit.

This role integration test case has focused on whether proselytization is proper for the mental health professions. In many nonclinical roles, the opportunity to engage in lifestyle evangelism or to share the gospel, may be quite appropriate just as it can be in any vocation (Alderich, 2006; Gibbs, 2005). We have both made no secret of our Christian faith in our profession and have both had opportunities arise in which we were invited by our non-Christian colleagues to tell them about our faith or some aspect of it. As relationships have been fostered, we also did what it is natural in evangelism to do (Coleman, 2019); we have invited colleagues to home Bible studies or other Christian forums where explicit engagement with the gospel has been quite appropriate. On a broader scale, we engaged explicitly Christian topics in our scholarship and practice in ways that are appropriate for our disciplines. We have found it vital that this be done in a way that is biblically faithful and yet without any violation of our professional integrity if the audience is to give us a continued hearing (Kersting, 2003).

Summary

Role integration is defined as the effort *to live out in integrity role expectations and patterns that arise from a psychological vocation in a particular context in a way that is simultaneously faithful to one's Christian identity.* We explored a variety of role integration issues and considerations for Christians who enter the psychology-related professions. Functioning as a licensed psychologist, counselor, or marriage and family therapist is an activity that raises role integration issues not unlike those faced by Boniface serving Rome in a public capacity. By entering into a regulated profession, the Christian is entering into what is sometimes referred to as fiduciary space of public trust. Licensed professional practice of psychology, counseling, or family therapy is a societally granted privilege that creates special obligations and role expectations for the practitioner. This is what we referred to as outward-facing role integration. This can be thought of in juxtaposition to inward-facing role integration, as when tensions arise when a licensed mental health professional serves the body of Christ in a designated ministry role. Both outward-facing and inward-facing role-related integration reflect endeavors often neglected in the training of students who are entering into the mental health professions.

Good mentoring around ways in which Christians have served the public, the profession, and the church is a necessary next step in guiding students through the challenges they are likely to face. Various proposals for functioning in these roles in relationship to a post-Christian culture were explored. Niebuhr's influential typology of how Christians have related to culture was mentioned and briefly assessed. Models, such as considering the Benedict option or the way of the exile, were explored.

The chapter concluded our discussion by looking at the role integration test case of proselytization. Contrary to what some Christians may advocate and what some others may fear, Christians in the mental health professions have widely embraced the professional norm against explicit value imposition that renders proselytization of clients by their mental health provider as a breach of professional integrity. Yet there are circumstances in which explicit religious disclosures in treatment may be appropriate and clinically indicated. Performing the role of a mental health professional is an opportunity to demonstrate the love of Christ to people at deep moments of pain, even if the explicit gospel message is not shared as with many other secular vocations. Finally, outside of clinical roles there are various ways an evangelistic purpose can be adopted with professional integrity.

References

Alderich, J. (2006). *Lifestyle evangelism: Learning to open your life to those around you.* Multnomah Press.

American Psychiatric Association. (2006). *Resource document: Religious/spiritual commitments and psychiatric practice.* Author.

Association of State and Provincial Psychology Boards. (2020, May 31). *Requirements to Practice*. www.asppb.net/page/ReqPsych

Baker, R. (1999). Codes of ethics: Some history. *Perspectives on the Professions, 19*(1). Online Periodical of the Center for the Study of Ethics in the Professions, Illinois Institute of Technology. http://ethics.iit.edu/perspective/v19n1%20perspective.pdf

Bargár, P. (2014). Niebuhr's typology reconsidered: Reading Christ and culture through the lens of the praxis matrix. *Communio viatorum, 56*(3), 294-316.

Beauchamp, T. L., & Childress, J. F. (2019). *Principles of biomedical ethics* (8th ed.). Oxford University Press.

Bible Project. (2020, October 31). *The way of exile*. https://bibleproject.com/videos/the-way-of-the-exile/

Biddle, B. J. (1986). Recent developments in role theory. *American Review of Sociology, 12*, 67-92.

Carson, D. A. (2008). *Christ and culture revisited*. Wm. B. Eerdmans.

Clark, E. (2019). *Evangelism as exiles: Life on mission as strangers in our own land*. Gospel Coalition.

Coleman, R. E. (2019). *The Master plan of evangelism*. Martino Fine Books.

Dreher, R. (2018). *The Benedict option*. Sentinel Books.

Fitzgerald, J. J. (2019). A considerably common morality: Catholic ethics and secular principlism in dialogue. *Christian bioethics: Non-Ecumenical Studies in Medical Morality, 25*(1), 86-127.

Gibbs, D. (2005). *The legal implications of witnessing at work*. www1.cbn.com/legal-implications-witnessing-work-1

Gregory, R. F. (2011). *Encountering religion in the workplace: The legal rights and responsibilities of workers and employers*. ILR Press.

Gregory, S. R. (2001). *A Place for piety: The role of religion in early Anglo-American texts on medical ethics*. Unpublished thesis for the University of Texas Medical Branch at Galveston.

Griffith, J. (Director). (2015). *For the Life of the world: Letters to exiles*. Acton Institute.

Hathaway, W. L., & Ripley, J. S. (2009). *Ethical concerns around spirituality and religion in clinical practice*. In J. D. Aten & M. M. Leach (Eds.), *Spirituality and the therapeutic process: A comprehensive resource from intake to termination* (25-52). American Psychological Association.

Henggeler, S. W., Schoenwald, S. K., Borduin, C. M., Rowland, M. D., & Cunningham, P. B. (2009). *Multisystemic therapy for antisocial behavior in children and adolescents*. Guilford Press.

Hermann, M. A., & Herlihy, B. R. (2006). Legal and ethical implications of refusing to counsel homosexual clients. *Journal of Counseling & Development, 84*(4), 414-18.

Hunter, J. D. (1991). *Culture wars: The struggle to define America*. Basic Books.

Hunter, J. D. (2010). *To change the world: The irony, tragedy, and possibility of Christianity in the late modern world*. Oxford University.

Jackson, J. (1998). Contemporary criticisms of role theory. *Journal of Occupational Science, 5*(2), 49-55.

Kersting, K. (2003). Religion and spirituality in the treatment room. *The Monitor, 34*(11), 40.

Knapp, S., & Vandecreek, L. (2004). A Principle-based analysis of the 2002 American Psychological Association Ethics Code. *Psychotherapy: Theory, Research, Practice, Training, 41*(3), 247-54.

Lozano, A. J. (2004). Principles of bioethics for Christian physicians: Autonomy and respect. *The Linacre Quarterly, 71*(2), 104-13.

McGrath, A. E. (2012). *Historical theology: An introduction to the history of Christian thought* (2nd ed.). Wiley-Blackwell.

Nelson, A. A., & Wilson, W. P. (1984). The ethics of sharing religious faith in psychotherapy. *Journal of Psychology & Theology, 12*(1), 15-23.

Niebuhr, R. (1951). *Christ and culture.* Harper & Row.

Percival, T. (1803). *Medical ethics; or, a code of institutes and precepts, adapted to the professional conduct of physicians and surgeons.* S. Russell. (Originally published 1794)

Shapiro, F. R. (2014, May 2). Who Wrote the Serenity Prayer? *Chronicle of Higher Education, 60*(33), B14-B15.

Smith, J. K. A. (2017). *Awaiting the king: Reforming public theology.* Baker Academic.

Williams, R. (2005). *The bloudy tenet of persecution.* Bibliobazaar. (Original work published 1644)

7

PERSONAL
INTEGRATION

I

WE HAVE NOW COME TO THE LAST INTEGRATION DOMAIN we will be considering in our review.[1] Personal integration refers to the *organic ways that people integrate as a function of their personality and other individual characteristics in relationship to the living God*. Personal integration is perhaps the most widely used integration approach but also one that is not consistently addressed in an explicit way in the psychology integration literature. In this chapter, we wish to introduce the reader to the concept of personal integration and what it means for the person who is a professional and a Christian to pursue sanctified and Spirit-led professional development.

Among those who explicitly engage the importance of personal integration, a claim is often made that this area of integration is foundational to the whole integration project. For instance, Tan (2001) has expressed the conviction that

---

[1]We have chosen to focus on five integrative domains we believe are most often engaged in the psychological integration project. We do not mean to imply, however, that there are no other domains that may be fruitfully explored to continue the work of integration. Some of these may be more prominent in different fields. We could imagine a *social* or *relational* integration domain could be a prominent area to be further addressed especially in the mental health counseling fields. The *advocacy or public policy* integrative domain may be helpful for social work or community psychology efforts. In non-practice-oriented areas, such as cognitive science, an *interdisciplinary* integration domain may reflect another possible demarcation that could focus integrative reflection and effort. Perhaps the time is ripe for an explicit engagement of the *multicultural or diversity* integration domain as well. The possibilities are many. We would suggest that explicit identification and exploration of an integrative domain is warranted when a case is made that either sufficient-focused scholarship or reflection already exists to cohesively mark out a previously underidentified area as its own domain, and when such identification serves important heuristic functions in furthering the integration project.

personal or intrapersonal integration, including the spirituality of the integrator, is the most fundamental and foundational category of integration, without which biblical integration of psychology and Christian faith in the principled (conceptual-theoretical and research categories) and professional (clinical or practice category) areas cannot be substantially achieved (p. 22).

In one sense, all professionals engage in *personal integration*. That is, their professional identity and praxis are an outworking of their orientating system and what they hold of highest value. For those who hold something other than God sacred, that alternative may still serve similar psychological functions in their personal formation, challenging them to forge professional identities and paths consistent with what they deem of ultimate concern. Still, from a biblical perspective, anything that stands in the place of God as one's sacred focus of devotion is idolatry.

We have both encountered professionals for whom fields like psychology and social work seemed to be not only a professional identity but something sacred or defining for their whole being. In such cases, the profession becomes a kind of idol. In our experience, when this has been done, a person has tacitly presumed some metaphysical or ethical philosophy as part of their understanding of the profession. For instance, a psychologist may be a hedonistic naturalist. The psychological hedonist may see their role as a mental health professional in a manner analogous to that of a priest. Their job is to discern and foster what makes people align with what is allegedly sacred (i.e., happiness) and to be, therefore, ministers of that sacred outcome. For these secular priests, this ministry is not limited to their work with clients but shapes their approach to other areas of life as well.

But for the Christian, personal integration involves faithful discipleship to Christ in all of life including one's profession. Thus, Christian personal integration places a priority on spiritual formation. Dallas Willard (2021) shared:

> Spiritual formation in the tradition of Jesus Christ is the process of transformation of the inmost dimension of the human being, the heart, which is the same as the spirit or will. It is being formed (really, transformed) in such a way that its natural expression comes to be the deeds of Christ done in the power of Christ. (n.p)

Christian discipleship is never merely a matter of outward conformity. While our conduct should reflect that discipleship, it should also flow from our innermost being even in our professional domain. Having an intentional commitment to pursue the path of a disciple in one's profession will motivate Christians to work out the practical challenges that can sometimes arise in the secular mental health fields for Christians. It can engender Spirit-led creativity and may even result in proactive transformation of our mental health professions when they are in tension with biblical forms of life as we discussed with regard to role integration. This possible outcome highlights the importance of personal integration for Christian mental health professionals and psychological scientists, but we also believe there are good reasons to welcome such integration on secular grounds.

Bill was working on an APA task force that was thinking through how to navigate value conflicts that might arise in training for some students with some client issues (e.g., sexual behavior or abortion) that ran counter to the trainee's moral beliefs. As the working group watched various public testimony given to a state political committee considering conscience clause legislation, some of the working group resonated with the comments by a psychologist who identified herself as a Christian. She said, "I'm a Christian but I learned a long time ago that to be a psychologist I have to check my beliefs at the door." Bill suggested that although this was a common sort of thing said in training, meant to imply something like we should not coercively impose our beliefs on our clients, it was fraught with problems. Do we really want our trainees being taught to be ethical in their professions by disconnecting their professional training and roles from their deepest centers of moral motivation? Would it not be far more likely to protect the public and cultivate an ethical profession to encourage trainees to find ways that were congruent and authentic with their deepest moral motivation to function according to professional standards? Rather than checking our beliefs at the door, the goal for trainees should be to find a way to bring their beliefs through the door with full personal *and* professional integrity.

If a Christian is to accomplish this both/and task in a way that is faithfully biblical, God-honoring, and professional, it will require Christians to undergo careful and intentional development at its achievement. As with our discussion in role integration, it is possible that situations could arise where a choice must be made between one's faith and commitment to a profession. Jesus tells us we cannot serve two masters. What we would aspire to is a personal integration path fully congruent with the best standards of one's profession *because of* one's submission to the ultimate lordship of Christ in that career path. Some believe that attempting this in the context of the contemporary mental health professions is too much like trying to sail between Scylla and Charybdis to justify even starting on the journey. We do not believe that to be the case for at least many of the career paths a Christian could pursue in the psychology-related fields.

Exemplarist Personal Integration and Narratives

We also have found that the most common areas of conflict can be effectively navigated with careful wisdom honed out of cognitive complexity and a discerning heart. Aristotle used the term *phronesis* for the kind of skilled ethical know-how that enabled those who possessed it to find creative and effective resolutions for moral dilemmas that may seem insurmountable to others. This idea of phronetic practical wisdom has been commended over the centuries by Christian virtue ethicists (see Zagzebski, 1999, for a recent example). Along these lines, we suggest that faithful personal integration in the psychology-related fields requires a skillful and discerning personal formation project that fosters phronesis in one's professional life. Zagzebski (2017) stresses the importance of learning from *exemplars* for forming such wisdom. She defines exemplars as a " . . . paradigmatically excellent person" whom we are motivated out of admiration to emulate (p. 20). By looking to those who have trod this personal integration path well before us specifically as exemplars of Christian personal integration, we can foster our own practical wisdom at doing so. Such imitation is not mimicry, but rather the grasping of inner logic that allows the exemplar to live wisely. In so doing, we can learn to fruitfully adapt that same wisdom to related situations we face. Such spiritual formation through the imitation of role models or *exemplars* is a longstanding part of Christian spirituality (viz., 1 Cor 11:1, 1 Tim 4:12; 1 Pet 2:21; Heb 13:7; 3 Jn 1:11). We would suggest it is a primary approach in this specialized niche of personal integration in the psychology-related fields as well. Integration in the personal domain will be an integration of the whole individual (i.e., bio-psycho-social-spiritual) with their profession.

The process of professional formation occurs through various formal training settings in a growing number of countries around the world. There are multiple established professional training pathways that aim at socializing students in the professions and abundant exemplars of how to be a wise professional. Yet for the Christian who desires formation in a personally integrative way, it may be more challenging to find appropriate mentors. In North America, there are integrative training programs at the undergraduate and graduate level as we mentioned in our opening chapter. There are also similar programs in several other countries.

For Christians who can enter these programs, they provide a mentoring context for Christian personal integration. In addition, one can find integrative internships, residencies, practicum sites, continuing education offerings, and professional associations that will provide opportunities to connect with those who have gone before us down this integrative road. If no such formal psychology-related integration venue is accessible, then networking informally with Christian professionals in another field may be helpful. Informal networking also takes place at conferences, such as the Christian Association for Psychological Studies (CAPS) national and regional conferences. Readings on the lives and experiences of Christians in psychology may also be a source of encouragement to those just starting out in integration (see Moriarty, 2010). We stress here the importance of not reinventing the wheel. While each professional's personal integration path will have unique challenges and considerations, we can all be guided and benefited from reflecting on the journey of others who have demonstrated wisdom in some area we could emulate.

Psychological formation is another aspect of personal development emphasized to varying degrees in the training pathways for the psychology-related fields (Fowers, 2005). Psychological mindedness, self-awareness, and psychological competence have often been advanced as an important prerequisite for effective functioning in the psychology-related professions (see Knapp et al., 2017, for a review). While mental health professionals are not free of the common psychological frailties that afflict the human condition, it has long been argued that their effectiveness, especially in clinical or counseling roles, depends significantly on their having adequate self-awareness about personal issues that could impact their caregiving. Jung asserted that many therapists enter the field motivated by their own past struggles and thus are "wounded healers." Whether this is the case, psychological health minimally reduces potential sources of adverse impact on our clinical work and can foster more beneficial therapeutic relationships.

Even for those who enter the nonclinical areas of the psychological sciences, psychological formation may play an important role. This case is especially made by those who argue for the importance of cultivating *scientific virtues* such as curiosity, intellectual humility, or generosity in scientists. Such scientific virtue approaches start

> with a philosophy of science but goes on to develop a philosophy of the scientist, looking at what may be thought of as the scientific mindset or as scientific habits of mind. Scientific virtues are those character traits—what we may think of in this

context as practiced dispositions which have a general biological basis, but which are given specific normative content by, and must be learned through, scientific practice—that are necessary for or conducive to achieving the aims of science. (Pennock & O'Rourke, 2017, p. 247)

Let us illustrate this issue of the importance of scientific virtue cultivation by reflecting on the character traits of scholars we have encountered that have impacted their work. We have been privileged to work with researchers who were prolific and highly successful in their research niches. While it is not always the case with well-known researchers, we found their productivity to be fueled in part by their generous collaborations with other researchers. Because they quickly shared ideas and offered help, many talented emerging researchers flocked to them and collaborative projects emerged in turn, further advancing the research of these mentors. In contrast, we have also encountered novice researchers who were possessive and secretive about their research almost to the point of paranoia. That style was deeply alienating and appeared to be a direct cause of their research floundering.

Virtue-based approaches to personal formation provide a natural point of personal integration for Christians. There is a longstanding virtue tradition in Christian spiritual formation. Whether we engage in clinical training that may try to produce wise practitioners or in scientific training aimed to foster *practiced dispositions* that help science to flourish, Christians may find resonance with their own virtue cultivation traditions. Psychology-related fields devote considerable effort to socializing their students into professions (i.e., professional formation) or scientific disciplines. Yet there is rarely a clear emphasis on engaging trainee spirituality in this socialization. Despite this secular socialization pathway for most individuals entering the mental health professions, it remains the case that many trainees and professionals are personally spiritual or religious. Given the relative neglect of the spiritual in professional formation, it is not surprising if the professional landscape is peppered with members who have idiosyncratic and underdeveloped ways of integrating their spiritual lives with their professions.

Neff and McMinn (2020) in their book, *Embodying Integration,* make the case for a conversational approach to integration that is relevant here. As they put it, "conversation is contextual" (p. 9), by which they mean, "Each of us brings a story to the task of integration and those stories influence our ways of understanding God, ourselves, the world around us, and the work we do in counseling and psychotherapy." Their book represents an effort to reflect on integration from a postmodern perspective: one that may resonate well with younger integrationists who are particularly sensitized to how diversity considerations might impact the integration project as it has historically taken place.

The virtue framework we have mentioned here provides a convergent emphasis on the importance of conversational encounter for personal integration. We learn to apply practical wisdom not when we rigidly mimic those who are our examples, but rather when we form relationships of the sort that can foster an intuitive understanding of the virtues that allow the exemplar to flourish in the professional context within which we are trying to function. While this virtue model implies a mentor-mentee pattern to the relationship, at least on what is being emulated, this does not mean the exchange is unidirectional. The exemplar may provide a springboard for personal formation, but our own personal circumstances will often extend the exemplar's wisdom in new ways that may benefit them as well. So, the conversational frame recommended by Neff and McMinn is an apt description of the kind of relationship that may foster personal integration.

Yet we would caution against any approach that makes personal narratives a *metanarrative* for the integration project. The focus in the personal integration domain does indeed connect integration to individual narratives and the enormous diversity that arises from individual and cultural differences. But this does not mean we are prepared to accept *humanity as the measure of all things*, to update Protagoras according to APA style. For instance, we assert that anyone who has authentically experienced the Bible *as the Word of God* cannot elevate any other experience to the same level without a loss of congruence or integrity. One never authentically stands in the presence of God as a presumed equal. Ultimately, as Nietzsche famously proclaimed, the postmodern possibility that truth is our subjective invention is occasioned by an eclipse of authority of God in the psyche. We would assert that the integration project is the antithesis of Nietzsche's eclipse. Christian integration is a matter of walking faithfully within one's profession as a disciple, authentically living out that walk before the face of God (*coram Deo*). Put differently, if God is not dead but experienced as a living God in our phenomenal world, then we could not let anything take priority over what God has said without fracturing our own individual phenomenal fields. When we do give priority to something else, we can only do so by repressing God's voice so to allow an idol to stand in his place.

Still narratives are important. They add perspective that can be lost in larger structures and help us understand the full range of application of divine revelation. Indeed, throughout this book we share our own experiences with various integration endeavors, including below our integration journeys. But we caution the reader to not view narratives in opposition to the integration project but as one aspect of the integration project, so that we include the richness generated from idiosyncratic differences while retaining the capacity to critique and make observations about trends in integration in a postmodern cultural moment.

Personal Integration Must Properly Include the Spiritual

Since personal integration involves integration of the whole person, a Christian must also include spiritual development along with the other aspects of personal development present in training programs in the mental health fields (e.g., the psychological, interpersonal, professional, cultural). While the term spirituality applies to a wide range of forms of life, both Christian and non-Christian, the integration project we have been engaging is specifically delimited to the Christian spirituality and its formation. We agree with Christian approaches to spiritual formation that foster spiritual development of the whole person. For instance, Chandler (2014) explains: "For our purposes, the word spiritual relates to more than simply the nonphysical and mystical components of life lived in God; rather, it is utilized to describe all dimensions of life as influenced by the Spirit" (p. 18). While our personal integration of Christianity and the psychology-related fields may be limited to Christian spiritual formation, this still presents a richly varied set of options (Demarest, 2012). Even within particular Christian traditions, individuals may differ in the spiritual practices and forms they embrace. Simon Chan (1998) noted "different spiritualties may appeal to Christians of different temperaments or even to the same person at different times" (p. 20).

Personal integration will be shaped by the specifics of the Christian spiritual stream(s) in which the integrator swims. Most contributors to the integration project we have been describing in this book have approached it from a broadly evangelical perspective. Tan (2011) has given considerable focus to the Christian spiritual formation in the integration project. Table 2 presents some typologies of Christian spirituality he has drawn from various Christian writers. Tan's approach draws heavily from evangelical and charismatic spiritualities. Spiritual formation approaches could also be distinguished by the Christian traditions within which one exists. Demarest (2012) edited a volume with contributors from four of these (i.e., Orthodoxy, Catholicism, Evangelicalism, and Progressive Protestantism), all discussing how their tradition engages a range of spiritual formation issues. There is overlap among these Christian traditions, but the contributors noted distinctive goals: Orthodox spirituality is aimed at the believer participating in the divine nature (i.e., *theosis*); Roman Catholicism at purgation, illumination, and union with God; Progressive mainline Protestantism with its ecumenical and social justice commitments; and evangelicalism at glorifying God by living in union with God as restored image bearers.[2]

Tan has argued for the importance of spiritual formation and personal integration as foundational to the integration project. But both he and other integrative psychologists, such as Gary Moon, have also contributed heavily to the renewed emphasis on spiritual formation and spiritual direction in the evangelical world. Both their work and this relatively recent renewal has also been influenced by spiritual formation scholars outside of psychology, such as Richard Foster and Dallas Willard, and increasingly by classic Christian sources from a wide range of Christian traditions (Foster, 1978; Moon, 2009; Willard, 1988, 2002).

This is a rich and helpful literature that cannot be covered here more than just in passing. We do wish to note what we perceive to be an overarching theme in this evangelical spiritual formation literature: namely, that regardless of the Christian tradition one engages for Christian formation, such engagement is typically presented as requiring intentional, even disciplined, participation with the aim of spiritual growth.

Christian Psychological Practice as Spiritual Formation?

One question that arises with an emphasis on Christians pursuing sanctified and Spirit-led professional development as key to personal integration is to what extent Christian psychological practice itself should function as spiritual formation. Benner (1988) early on emphasized the connection between depth psychologies and the *spiritual quest*. While this is perhaps most appropriately located as an issue of applied or role integration, we wanted to acknowledge how others in the integration discussion are grappling with it as something that raises the importance of the professional's own spiritual development.

---

[2]The reader unfamiliar with these categories is referred to the Demarest (2012) text for a more extensive discussion. Our purpose in citing them here is only to note the diversity present within Christianity about the goals to which spiritual formation may be directed.

Table 2. Three typologies of Christian spirituality as summarized by Tan (2011)

Six Christian spirituality streams (Foster, 1998)	Twelve facets of spirituality (Boa, 2001)	Nine sacred pathways (Thomas, 2000)
contemplative tradition the prayer-filled life	**paradigm spirituality** focus: cultivating an eternal versus a temporal perspective	**intellectual thought**
holiness tradition the virtuous life	**devotional spirituality** focus: falling in love with God	**vision**
incarnational tradition the sacramental life	**disciplined spirituality** focus: engaging in the historical disciplines	**tradition**
evangelical tradition the Word-centered life	**motivated spirituality** focus: a set of biblical incentives	**service**
social justice tradition the compassionate life		**activism**
charismatic tradition the Spirit-empowered life	**Spirit-filled spirituality** focus: walking in the power of the Spirit	
	nurturing spirituality focus: lifestyle of evangelism and discipleship	**contemplation**
	corporate spirituality focus: encouragement, accountability, and worship	**worship**
	process spirituality focus: process versus product, being versus doing	**nature**
	relational spirituality focus: loving God completely, ourselves correctly, and others compassionately	**relationships**
	holistic spirituality focus: every component of life under the lordship of Christ	
	warfare spirituality focus: overcoming the world, the flesh, and the devil	
	exchanged life spirituality focus: grasping our true identity in Christ	

Tan (2011) has also argued that Christian therapy or counseling should have the spiritual formation of clients as part of its goal. This requires, in his view, that the therapist engage in personal formation:

> In order for the Holy Spirit to do his crucial work in Christian therapy that also focuses on Christian spirituality and the spiritual formation of clients into deeper

Christlikeness (Rom 8:29), Christian therapists must have faith in Christ as Lord of all professional and academic disciplines, including psychology and counseling. . . . As Spirit-filled servants of Jesus Christ, Christian therapists will exercise faith or trust and full confidence in Christ as the most brilliant person in the universe who is also both master and maestro of our field and profession of counseling and psychotherapy . . . (pp. 371-72)

The view that our professional practice as clinicians should have as its goal spiritual transformation is also the thesis of Todd Hall and John Coe's book, *Psychology in the Spirit: Contours of a Transformational Psychology* (Coe & Hall, 2010). They, too, place emphasis on the person providing psychological interventions and stress that they do so within a Christian tradition and anew in the Spirit, an approach that is grounded in distinctively Christian realities. Here is their thesis:

Doing psychology, as one human activity, is a means to the ultimate goal of union with God by which one loves God and neighbor and glorifies God. Thus, we do psychology well to the degree that we are a) more and more transformed by the filling of the Spirit into the image of God, and b) using our abilities in God to observe and reflect upon the reality of the person (the process), c) in order to produce a body of knowledge and wisdom on the person, sin and well-being for the sake of the world and the Church (theoretical product), as well as for the end of the transformation of the psychologist (existential product). (p. 85)

Hall and Coe argue that "the person determines the process." That is, it is the character of the clinician that "grounds, preserves, and guards the process of doing psychology" (p. 86), which they view as underscoring the significance of the spiritual life and vitality of the clinician, as it affects the quality of the process itself as well as the outcome.

Personal Integration, Social Justice, and EDI

The mental health professions are increasingly concerned about issues of social justice. Given this emphasis, let us focus for a moment on social justice pursuit as one of the streams of Christian spirituality noted by Foster (1998). The National Association of Social Workers (2020) has articulated five social justice priorities to which it is committed. APA's strategic plan and ethics code emphasize a concern for human rights and inclusiveness. The American Counseling Association (2020) lists social justice and empowerment as one its core values for its strategic plan.

As Messmore (2010) notes: "Jesuit Luigi Taparelli D'Azeglio first used the phrase social justice in 1840 based on Thomistic thought" (n.p.). The Bible repeatedly emphasizes the vital importance of justice in our social relations and conduct as a key aspect of the divine standard from which we have fallen. For the prophets, exploitation of the poor and other marginalized persons provided clear evidence of the depths of sin and disobedience to which humanity had fallen. Many examples could be given but consider these verses from Amos 2:6-7:

> For three sins of Israel,
>> even for four, I will not relent.
> They sell the innocent for silver,
>> and the needy for a pair of sandals.
> They trample on the heads of the poor
>> as on the dust of the ground
>> and deny justice to the oppressed.
> Father and son use the same girl
>> and so profane my holy name.

Despite these theological and biblical aspects of the Judeo-Christian tradition, a criticism is sometimes raised against forms of Christian spirituality that focus on our eternal state as being "too heavenly minded to be any earthly good." The idea is that when Christians devalue the present age because it is viewed as the smoldering embers of a dying world that will soon be left behind, they have little motivation to be concerned about the current state of our world. This can lead to a weakened environmental ethic; apathy toward unjust social, economic, or political patterns; or even a disregard for one's temporal affairs, so charge the critics. While this may be true about some individuals, we see little evidence that this is an accurate generalization about biblical Christianity or those who embrace it.

What is at issue here, as Francis Schaeffer (1976) often highlighted, is the extent to which Christian spiritual formation should have a practical result in how we live both individually and communally. We share with Schaeffer (1976), Wolterstorff (2010, 2013), Volf (2019), and many other Christians throughout the ages a belief that the biblical message conveys a robust notion of holiness characterized by both vertical and horizontal righteousness—being right in relationship to God and right in relationship to the creation. Wolterstorff's (2013)

Christian account of justice has emphasized this in his unpacking of relevant biblical concepts.

Such discussions go far beyond our disciplinary competence as psychologists or the scope of this book. We allude to them only to note that Christian personal integration will likely require more from those who genuinely want to live out the lordship of Christ than merely finding a congruent form of individual life in the profession. It will lead us to also be concerned broadly about those impacted by our professional life and by our very professions (and those excluded from such impact). A key challenge for Christian integration in the psychology-related professions is the working out of a rigorous biblical understanding of justice. Wolterstorff (2013) offered the following reflection on how a justice ethos has motivated Christians to seek remedy for injustice both through prayer and other actions available to them:

> I submit that Christian hope for the righting of injustice will take the form, among other things, of prayer—prayer and song. It will take the form of petitionary prayer: it will pray in hope for the righting of injustice, not only for the righting of injustice in general but also for the righting of particular injustices. It will have the courage to name injustices, and then to pray for the righting of the injustices named. And if those named injustices are righted, Christian hope will then offer prayers of thanksgiving, not just for the righting of injustice in general, but for the righting of the named injustices. . . . To name the injustices for whose righting one thanks God in Christ is to identify the signs in history of Christ's liberating work.
>
> In addition to taking the form of prayer, Christian hope for the righting of injustice takes the form of struggling for that same righting. *Ora et labora* ("pray and work") has always been the motto of the Christian church. Not just praying and then, in addition, working—praying for one thing and working for another— but working for the very same thing for which one prays. (n.p.)

The integration task on these matters would seem, on the surface, to be a straightforward matter: should not Christians in the psychology and related professions simply be banner carriers for these social justice programs in their respective professions? We would agree enthusiastically that the Bible requires Christians to be champions of justice and champions in particular for those who are marginalized, exploited, or oppressed. Yet it is not clear to all Christians that such full alignment is possible even when one agrees with the priority placed on justice and the concern for the oppressed. Some Christians have taken issue, for instance, with the Neo-Marxist assumptions underlying some of the analyses of the problems and proposed solutions offered in these fields (see the Statement on Social Justice and the Gospel from 2018; Bradley, 2010).

The training focus on social justice in the psychology-related fields has often been embedded in the portions of curriculum related to diversity and multicultural issues. The recent trend has been to move from a primary focus on diversity or multiculturalism to a focus on equity, diversity, and inclusion (i.e., EDI).[3] The EDI framework's growth has been very evident in corporate culture in response to the Civil Rights Act of 1964 and a focus on EDI at the Equal Opportunity Employment Commission (Murphy, 2018). It is now common for larger corporations to have an organizational unit and/or dedicated staff person focused on EDI. The EDI framework has emphasized that a focus on diversity without inclusion risks degenerating to tokenism and a stifling of the contributions and voices of underrepresented members of the workforce or organization. Murphy (2018) notes that effective inclusive practices inculcate a culture that gives voice to those from marginalized and underrepresented groups and thus fosters not token diversity but rather truly diverse corporate cultures. However, effective inclusive practices must take note of those factors that create barriers to inclusion. An emphasis on equity is important to foster a richly inclusive culture according to this understanding. Equity, in this sense, is frequently defined as fairness of opportunity for all.

It is also important to note that diversity is primarily a characteristic of groups. The number of differences on diversity variables represented by a group's membership constitute the groups' level of diversity. Yet the same individual may represent multiple areas of diversity. Thus, two people who share the same ethnic or gender diversity designation may differ from each other on other variables such as religion. This characteristic of a particular individual having a polyform or multifaced diversity identity is referred as *intersectionality*. Intersectionality can produce distinctive identities not only in terms of each diversity category with which that same individual identifies but also because of their particular constellation of those multiple areas of diversity. When each area of identity involves a commonly marginalized group, the intersectionality can have a potentiating effect, multiplying the impact of the marginalization.

---

[3]The still fluid nature of this framework is reflected in part in the differing acronyms used to summarize the designation the three constructs of equity, diversity, and inclusion. Most have moved away from D.I.E., although this acronym may convey the historical sequence in which each construct emerged as a major emphasis in organizational cultures. EDI is now in widespread use, but others have chosen to use DE&I.

When Christian clinicians engage in practice with clients, they do so as an embodiment of all of that they are as a person of faith, to include various individual characteristics of race, culture, ethnicity, sexual orientation, gender, and so on. There is increasing emphasis on understanding how these aspects of identity shape who we are and how we approach our work, our clients, and really all aspects of life. These are broadly understood as a multicultural lens through which we come to locate ourselves and others around us as we grow and develop in psychology. The now relatively longstanding emphasis in training on fostering multicultural competence and awareness for diversity is aimed at fostering a deeper appreciation for such a lens and how it impacts our clinical relationships (McNeil & Pozzi, 2006).

The EDI framework is becoming more explicitly utilized in the psychology-related professions to organize work and training around diversity, multiculturalism, and social justice issues. For instance, an early draft of APA's proposed standards for master's accreditation relabeled the profession-wide competency of *Individual and Cultural Diversity* to an *Equity, Diversity, Inclusion, and Social Justice* competence. Similar engagement with EDI constructs is present in various ways in other mental health fields, although the EDI label may not be used.

We assert that integrative Christian approaches to the psychology-related fields should be affirming of the EDI aspiration. As Hays (2003) concludes from his study of the biblical theology of race: "*the picture of God's people at the climax of history portrays a multi-ethnic congregation from every tribe, language, people, and nation, all gathered together in worship around God's throne*" (p. 205). In EDI terms, the destination of a richly diverse and inclusive community of equally perfected divine image bearers will have been fully achieved in the kingdom of God when the kingdom has fully come. But as so many know from their experiences and history, that full realization of the diverse but unified kingdom is *not yet*. The call for the church now is to increasingly seek to instantiate that kingdom vision through the power of the Holy Spirit (e.g., Mt 6:10)

A Christian integrative approach to this area must develop a faithful Christian worldview, theoretical perspective, practice competencies (i.e., applied integration), and relevant role navigations. We have chosen to locate this discussion under the personal integration domain because of the great deal of personal growth required to foster such a competence at all levels including implicit ones. We do *not* mean to imply that concerns about EDI are purely individual matters, or that no systemic and structural barriers to equity exist.

There is much work to be done to flesh out a faithfully Christian integration on these topics. We would call the Christian community to be champions of justice and of all of humanity's worth and dignity as creatures made in the divine image. We also would call for confession and repentance when individual Christians, communities of Christians, and Christian societies have perpetuated, maintained, or failed to remedy oppression and marginalization of any persons or groups. The increased focus on racial justice in recent years reflects an opportunity for Christians to model a biblically shaped response to the injustices and marginalization that is still too often a part of the world before us. This will require us to be a Holy Spirit–transformed community that proceeds wisely and effectively as we enter the public discourse around such painful, power-invested, and conflict-imbued matters.

As we noted in our discussion of social justice, some Christians have taken issue with some of the proposed analyses and solutions from social justice advocates. Discernment is needed to find a biblically faithful path on these matters as with any movement or school within the psychology-related fields. Some have pursued social justice approaches that attempt to utilize liberation theology concepts, critically engaged from an evangelical perspective, while noting the long-standing evangelical concerns about the Marxist roots of liberation theology (Cannon & Smith, 2019). Others Christian scholars have suggested alternative paradigms for social justice advocacy. For instance, the African American Rutgers legal professor and Dallas Willard–scholar Brandon Paradise (2014) has enjoined returning to a more faith-congruent source and rationale for social justice pursuits than has been offered by the recent trend toward critical theory. The pursuance of racial justice would be better fueled, he argues, by key commitments within the Black church rather than from Marxist ideas at odds with them. He notes that the ". . . civil rights movement was fundamentally a religious movement. Born in the Black church and powered by the Black prophetic tradition" (p. 119). Regardless of where one lands on such matters, we would assert that an integrationist should seek to be biblically faithful. This means echoing the same resounding call for justice evident in the Scriptures *and* conforming our lived-out response to a biblically faithful path in how we pursue justice.[4]

---

[4]We will not suggest the sociopolitical path that such a response must take to be biblically faithful. Christians disagree about such things. We would assert that all Christians should be concerned about EDI and social justice. But what constitutes the barriers to inclusion and the causes of inequity? Should equity be understood as equality of outcome or of opportunity? The dominant perspectives in the psychology-related fields have favored explanations and proposed strategies informed by the

Another caveat to the task for the integration project set out in this section is a candid realization that it is common for members of the psychology-related fields to view the requirement of creedal affinity or conformity to Christian codes of conduct that are present in many Christian colleges and training programs to be in direct conflict with a commitment to inclusivity. Christians will need to be ready to effectively respond to such allegations if they are to avoid problematic repercussions such as challenges to accreditation, ethics complaints, or barriers to inclusion in the profession. We refer the reader back to our earlier discussion of viewpoint diversity and faith-based higher education in chapter three for our thoughts about the form such a response might take.

Integration around issues of EDI and social justice in the psychology-related fields will require a careful but not sluggish engagement with a wide range of issues that impact all of the domains we have engaged in this text. Depending on whether our theologies move us to the left or right of the political spectrum, Christians passionate about an integrated approach to EDI and social justice may find themselves diverging in this domain on the specifics. Yet, as both the biblical record and multicultural counseling literature teach us, we are aware that our thinking on these sorts of evocative topics can be skewed by cultural, systemic, and personal biases of which we may not even be aware. For this reason, we have chosen to raise this integration area and challenge under the personal integration domain.

A recent contribution to the multicultural counseling literature is helpful here. It is the notion of cultural humility. Hook et al. (2013) have it as the "ability to maintain an interpersonal stance that is other-oriented (or open to the other) in relation to aspects of cultural identity" (p. 2). While the work on cultural humility has been done by scholars of varied backgrounds, Christian mental health professionals have been frequent contributors to this domain. Dwiwardani and Waters (2015) discussed the biblical support for valuing cultural humility. They note:

---

sociopolitical left. Yet perspectives more commonly aligned with the sociopolitical right exist among conservative scholars that are also deeply committed to rectifying inequities. They often assert that the leftist approaches perpetuate the inequities that they are attempting to overcome. Because of the relatively greater representation of conservative leaning sociopolitical perspectives among Christians who enter it, particularly in North America, we would not be surprised if the integration community is relatively less aligned with how their professional peers tend to approach social justice issues. We also expect that Christian integrationists who believe that right-leaning responses to EDI/social justice issues are a better path will likely face an uphill climb in developing integrative approaches on these topics that are also professionally viable in the psychology-related fields.

Not only does humility protect against too much of ourselves, it protects against too little. Humility as a character trait includes an accurate assessment of oneself, not a lower view of the self (Tangney, 2000). Instead of being synonymous with self-deprecation, humility has been found to be positively related to self-esteem (Dwiwardani, 2011) and to be predicted by secure attachment (Dwiwardani et al., 2014). Cultural humility, then, does not pretend to know less or demean acquired knowledge. Instead, it holds a respectful stance toward one's own cultural identity while exercising the capacity to genuinely value, engage, and welcome others' cultures. (n.p.).

As Christians who seek to integrate with the psychology-related professions around issues of social justice, the cultivation of cultural humility seems an important personal virtue to cultivate. It appears to be one that, for the Christian, directly implicates spiritual formation into the personal integration project. A key temptation that seems rampant in the cultural wars of the late twentieth century, and perhaps with the more recent increased attention given to social justice advocacy, is the tendency to demonize those who approach heated social issues, such as abortion or the level of systemic racism in law enforcement, with a diverging viewpoint. Likewise, this animus often appears to be reciprocal. We are not here saying all positions are equal morally or that there are no controversies on which one side of the debate is simply correct, but we are objecting to Christians who think it sufficient to speak what they believe to be the truth without a commensurate concern to do so in love. Regardless of how one thinks God would have us seek justice, we believe all Christians should minimally agree that we are to aspire to a God-honoring justice in our personal and professional lives. As Micah reminded us millennia ago:

> He has shown you, O mortal, what is good.
> And what does the LORD require of you?
> To act justly and to love mercy
> and to walk humbly with your God. (Mic 6:8)

Precognitive Considerations for Personal Integration

We now wish to return to the issue of precognitive or implicit cognition that we raised in chapter three. Moon (2009) criticized the hyperintellectualism he believes present in many churches that lead to a Christianity that is intellectual but not lived out. This is an old concern. Seventeenth-century pietists complained that Protestantism had become an overly intellectualized dead orthodoxy.

Whatever the Christian spiritual stream that one partakes to foster personal integration, it will fall short if it does not impact us at both an implicit (i.e., heart) and explicit (i.e., head) level. Not only should our chosen words be faithful to the walk God calls us, but also our knee-jerk heart attitudes should be. The psychological research on implicit bias change shows this to be a complex topic. Some studies find little change is possible for deeply ingrained implicit biases. Others show change can be demonstrated on measures of implicit bias, but this may not be translated into changes in actual behavior. A variety of intervention strategies have been aimed at changing harmful biases, such as those based on race (Mallet & Monteith, 2019).

Removing negative intrapersonal and negative interpersonal or systemic implicit patterns that fail to model the standard to which we are called is important. But personal integration at a heart level is more than just a matter of getting rid of the negative. In Paul's letter to the Ephesians, he calls believers to leave behind patterns of life representing the old self. In their place, we are to adopt patterns representing our new self in Christ. A preacher once humorously summarized Paul's message here. In Ephesians 4:28, thieves are told to stop stealing. But if this is all they did, they would still be thieves: they would just be thieves in between jobs. Paul calls them to be something else. He tells them, "Anyone who has been stealing must steal no longer, but must work, doing something useful with their own hands, that they may have something to share with those in need" (Eph 4:28). In other words, replace thievery with the habit of honest productive work and you are living out your new self in Christ. Providentially, automatic or implicit cognitive processes are not always negative. Such processes can also fuel adaptive functioning that help us navigate the many split-moment behavioral choices we must make throughout the day (Kahneman, 2011).

Far before the age of contemporary psychology, Aristotle emphasized that virtue required the cultivation of moral habits through repeated action. On such an account, a person who is only superficially moral may choose to act correctly under low-pressure circumstances but, caught off guard, their reactions will over time reflect who they really are by nature. Only the habitually moral person can be expected to *react* morally with any consistency on Aristotle's account. Given biblical teaching about the nature of sin, Christians are not surprised that virtue ethics do not typically presuppose we are born virtuous. Virtue has to be cultivated and formed through a developmental process and most do not excel at it. Depending on one's theology of sanctification (i.e., the process of being made holy), one may have different expectations of how likely we are to actually ever change our heart attitudes during our time on earth (White, 2017).

James K. A. Smith, in his book *Desiring the Kingdom*, has developed an interesting and helpful line of scholarship around the idea that human beings feel their way through life; that we do not take so much a cognitive approach to the world around us as we take a noncognitive approach à la Heidegger's concept of attunement. We are "feeling our way around the world" (p. 50). Smith further develops the idea that we actually follow Augustine in terms of our loves. "Our ultimate love is constitutive of our identity," that is, those things we love are those things we worship, the things toward which we are "fundamentally oriented" (p. 51). The habits we form reflect our loves, and our habits are meant to reflect a first and foremost priority of the kingdom of God. We are "fundamentally creatures of desire or love and that our love is always already oriented to an ultimate vision of the good life, a picture of the kingdom that embodies a particular image of human flourishing" (p. 55).

According to Smith, the picture we have of the good life, of the kingdom, is meant to shape the contours of who we are, of our character, and this occurs through our routines. Indeed, the integrative task would be severely truncated if we were to pass over the formation of the psychologist at this deep heart level. Whole person integration then, at both the head and heart level, would have as its goal Christian psychologists who are attuned to a biblical vision,

> To form radical disciples of Jesus and citizens of the baptismal city who, communally, take up the creational task of being God's image bearers, unfolding the cultural possibilities latent in creation—but doing so as empowered by the Spirit, following the example of Jesus's cruciform cultural labor. (Smith, 2009, p. 220)

Recommendations for Fostering Personal Integration

As we bring this section to a close, we want to offer a few recommendations for enhancing personal integration.

Aspire to a life of obedience under the lordship of Christ. The Christian interested in pursuing integration is encouraged to surrender every domain of life to the lordship of Christ. The domain or endeavor approach to integration we have been discussing attempts to highlight how specific aspects of being a psychologist are concretely impacted by the lordship of Christ. We are to surrender to Jesus as Lord in order to faithfully live out our professional and scientific lives under the authority of Jesus.

Cultivate a life of Christian virtues. Christians who wish to faithfully live out professional lives under the authority of Jesus are encouraged to cultivate a life of Christian virtues. We can ask God to expand our capacity for faith, hope, and charity. This means growing in our belief in the right things, as well as trusting that God is providing for us and guiding us, even when that provision or guidance is not readily apparent. We can grow in our capacity to trust that good will prevail, and we can work toward the good of those around us. We can also pray for God to expand our capacity for prudence, justice, temperance, and fortitude. Smith (2009) recommends that individuals conduct a "practice audit" as a helpful step toward targeted virtue formation consonant with a biblical kingdom vision (see table 2).

Embody integration in your own individual characteristics. The integration you live out is a reflection of all of who you are as a Christian, including individual characteristics of your race, culture, ethnicity, socioeconomic status, sexual orientation, gender, and so on. Recognize how individual characteristics interact with your own faith development and how your faith interacts with the field and profession of psychology.

Breakout Box: Consider Conducting a Practices Audit

As suggested by James K. A. Smith in *Desiring the Kingdom*, a practices audit can help us reflect on our habits, time, and rituals. Here are some of the questions he raises for a practices audit:

- What are some of the most significant habits and practices that really shape your actions and attitude—what you think and what you do?

- What does your time look like? What practices are you regularly immersed in each week? How much time is spent doing different sorts of activities?

- What do you think are the most important ritual forces in your life? And if you were honest with yourself, are these positive (forming you into the kind of person who embodies the kingdom of God) or negative (forming you into someone whose values and desires are antithetical to that kingdom, oriented toward another kingdom)?

- What do you think are some of the most potent practices in our culture? Or, if you have kids, what are the cultural forces that you *don't* want your children shaped by? What are the ritual forces that you *do* want to shape their desires? And why on both counts?

- If you step back and look at them, are there some habits and practices that you might have originally thought were neutral or thin, but upon further reflection, you see them as thicker and more significant?

- Is there any way in which you see worship as a thick habit? How so? How not?

- If Christian worship is a thick practice, what do you think are its most significant "competitors"? (Smith, 2009, p. 84)

Endeavor to be guided by the Spirit. Personal integration is enhanced through an intentional posture of seeking guidance by the Spirit. This is more than a superficial process of knowing what is right or wrong, of understanding sin and turning from it; rather, we are discussing fidelity to the divine will that requires nothing less than God's sustaining grace through a moment by moment living in his Spirit. Some have suggested that the Holy Spirit may provide special insights to the Christian caregiver or even miraculously intervene in client outcomes (Decker, 1996, 2002; Tan, 2011). For the Christian who practices in a regulated mental health profession, the counselor must always be prepared to give an account of our clinical practice activities and treatment with our clients to pertinent regulatory bodies. We agree to operate under the authority of these bodies by virtue of voluntarily applying for and practicing under state licensing. Thus, while the Holy Spirit may indeed provide supernatural insight or even miraculous suprapsychotherapeutic change to our clients, the Christian counselor must be prepared to explain in terms cogent to a likely unbelieving regulatory body why we have taken the therapeutic steps we have. In this regard, being competent in the common grace resources available to psychology will be critical. Thus, it is not surprising that even Christian psychologists who are personally charismatic, like Siang-Yang Tan, have often developed extensive secular rationales for their therapeutic approaches. The Holy Spirit is not limited by our practice roles and patterns and can intervene in ways that partner with us and go beyond the most responsible help we can think to offer, given our limited understanding of the human condition. Who better to be a partner in Christian counseling than the Lord and giver of life?

In a sense, all integration is a result of personal integration. Put differently, no domain of integration is likely to be successful without being a byproduct of persons who embody the psychology-related professions and disciplines living out those domains in faithful submission to God.

Making It Personal—Our Integrative Journeys

William L. Hathaway. I (Bill) grew up in a very liberal church that placed no real creedal adherence expectations on its members. I remember being intellectually and socially stimulated in this setting but had no clear sense of God or his designs for my life. Along the way, I kept running into contemporary psychology. The chair of the local state university psychology department was a respectful agnostic who also served briefly as the scoutmaster of my Boy Scout troop at the church. My sister completed degrees in social work, and I remember reading through her psychology textbooks with fascination as a youth. That interest continued as I read books like B. F. Skinner's *Beyond Freedom and Dignity*. In my midteen years, I became friends with some evangelical Christians and was introduced to the biblical Gospel. After about six months of searching, I asked a truly risen Jesus to become a conscious reality in my daily life as my Lord and Savior. It was the mid-'70s—just after the peak of the Jesus Movement—and several spiritual trends were occurring. The Charismatic Renewal was well underway, spanning denominations and introjecting new life into old forms of faith. My spiritual rebirth was followed with an exposure to a smorgasbord of Christian spiritual traditions. I engaged these traditions with the zeal of a new believer.

My interests in psychology were not displaced by my conversion but were deepened and given a new focus: how does one fit these fascinating insights of contemporary psychological science with the eternal truths of Christianity? How did the standard of human functioning set by the life of Jesus relate to the notion of what is normal in contemporary mental health fields? As we discussed Freud, Adler, Skinner, Rogers, and others in my high school psychology class, I wondered how to reconcile these *theories* with the concepts about human nature I was learning from the Bible. About this same time, I attended a viewing of Francis Schaeffer's *How Should We Then Live?* film series at our local state university. It was a wonderful presentation of a wide swath of Western history and culture reinterpreted from Schaeffer's reformed worldview. That experience taught me to be reflective and discerning about the underlying assumptions characterizing the worldviews I was encountering in psychology.

As a relatively new convert, I grew through Bible reading, prayer, Christian study, participating in corporate worship, and learning from others who were further on in their faith journeys with an attentive spirit. During this time, I also met and married my wife. We shared in these approaches to receiving guidance

coping research, I saw an opportunity for a greater emphasis on clinical integration. I was mindful that my studies were continuing on in a secular environment, so my wife and I remained active in a local church, attended retreats, worked as staff at a Christian camp for one summer, maintained our personal devotions and prayer, networked with other Christian graduate students and faculty at the state university, subscribed to Christian periodicals such as *Christianity Today* and *Christian History*, regularly reviewed relevant texts from Christian publishers, and kept up with the few integrative journals in the field such as the *Journal of Psychology and Theology*. Those personal and corporate spiritual disciplines continued to keep me anchored in my Christian formation, both as a believer and an emerging psychologist.

After graduate school, I served as a US Air Force psychologist for seven years and also worked as an adjunct professor in psychology and philosophy. I have never practiced full-time in an explicitly Christian practice setting, but I made no secret of my Christian faith in my secular work settings or of my psychologist identity among the churches I attended in the communities where I was stationed. Consequently, during my years as a full-time military clinician, I was frequently sought out by Christian clients.

Several years into my career, I left full-time practice to assume my current role as a Christian university professor. I have been active in various service roles in psychology helping to write policies and position statements regarding religious issues in psychology. During my professional service roles, I have been able to serve on state licensing boards, in governing roles in the profession, and assisted in federal and professional accreditation rule making. These undertakings have made me keenly aware of the role integration issues I believe are still underdeveloped in the integration literature.

Mark A. Yarhouse. I (Mark) was raised in a Christian home and from an early age was part of the local church community. My mother came from a Baptist background and my father from a Presbyterian background. We attended different churches growing up but were probably more influenced by Reformed theology and an evangelical Christianity that emphasized conviction of sin, personal repentance, and evangelism. I made a personal decision to become a follower of Jesus during high school. This was in the context of my participation in our church youth group and active involvement in our local chapter of Young Life, a parachurch ministry that focuses on introducing teens to the person and work of Jesus Christ.

When I looked into undergraduate degree programs, I was attracted to the idea of studying in a Christian context. I attended Calvin College (now Calvin University) and completed degrees in philosophy and art with a minor in psychology. At that time, I believed I wanted to work as a counselor: I needed to take coursework in psychology, but I also had been active in art and found completing an art degree helped bring that interest into sharper focus. At this time, my sister was completing a degree in English at Duke University, and through her, I was learning the challenges of being a Christian in secular academic contexts. This led me to add a philosophy degree to my education at Calvin, and it was at this time that I first read Nicholas Wolterstorff's book, *Reason within the Bounds of Religion*. This was one of the most influential books for me, as it exposed me to the idea of "control beliefs" and how these assumptions or presuppositions function in our scholarship, as well as recognizing the legitimacy and necessity of Christian control beliefs in distinctively Christian scholarship.

When I left Calvin, I was deciding between two programs—a Christian program and secular graduate training program in clinical psychology. I initially decided to complete my degree at a secular program, but at what was really the last moment, I felt a strong sense of a call to study at a particular Christian graduate school, Wheaton College. I completed my MA and PsyD in Clinical Psychology, as well as an MA in theological studies at Wheaton. One of the first papers I read during the first course I completed in my doctoral studies was perhaps the most influential to my thinking, at least early on. It was "Advice to Christian Philosophers" by Alvin Plantinga, and it was his inaugural address as he was named the John A. O'Brien Professor of Philosophy at the University of Notre Dame. The paper was a call to be the Christian philosophers of the Christian community—to recognize the distinct interests and research agendas among Christians:

> In sum, we who are Christians and propose to be philosophers must not rest content with being philosophers who happen, incidentally, to be Christians; we must strive to be Christian philosophers. We must therefore pursue our projects with integrity, independence, and Christian boldness.

This call to "integrity, independence, and Christian boldness" was applied in my graduate training to the work of the Christian psychologist. Much of my training involved both *worldview* and *theoretical* integration, as we critically engaged and critiqued from a Christian worldview the existing theories of health and abnormality advanced within the field of psychology. During this time, I was most influenced by my work with Dr. Stanton Jones, who at that time was the program director of the doctoral program in clinical psychology. We worked on a project that later would become our first book together entitled, *Homosexuality: The Use of Scientific Research in the Church's Moral Debate*. Stan would later assume the position of provost at Wheaton, and this subsequently meant the many invitations he would receive to write, speak, and consult on homosexuality were offered to me. This shaped my work early on as I launched my own academic career.

My personal spiritual life was influenced by an interest at this time in the liturgical worship I discovered at our local Episcopal church. My upbringing and the emphasis there on personal piety and intellectual assent to orthodoxy left me feeling somewhat disconnected from the experiential component of worship. I found the *Book of Common Prayer* and the structure of the Anglican service a welcome framework for organizing my own spirituality in a church that valued a style of worship that brought together both intellectual integrity and the aesthetics of music and art. Many people I know come out of liturgical traditions and complain of the "spiritual deadness" they witnessed in church. I found just the opposite: the faith I brought into the liturgical structure was given a kind of frame for it to grow and mature. I later would be shaped deeply by my experiences in multiethnic churches: the liturgical structure I found would continue in my private devotional life, while my public and corporate worship experiences would expand in other directions.

In any case, when I left graduate school, I accepted an academic position as a core faculty member at Regent University where I would explore ways to integrate psychology and Christianity in diverse areas of academic interest, including psychopathology, family theory and therapy, professional ethics, and sexual identity. I would later transition to Wheaton College and continue to think about ways to relate psychology and Christianity, particularly in the areas of sexual and gender identity.

In response to what appeared to be gaps in the integration literature at the time, and in collaboration with colleagues, I coauthored integration texts on psychopathology (McRay et al., 2016), family theory and therapy (Yarhouse & Sells, 2017), and sexuality (Yarhouse & Tan, 2014). These resources represent elements of worldview, theoretical, and applied integration, in particular.

My primary integration scholarship, however, is in the complex areas of sexual and gender identity and, in particular, how people navigate these aspects of identity in light of their religious identity (e.g., Yarhouse, 2015, 2019). This has included all of the integration endeavors we discussed throughout the book, but has taken on special significance in the area of role integration, where I have had opportunities to serve in specific roles on behalf of the profession to help various organizations think through the relationship between current trends in lesbian, gay, bisexual, transgender, and queer (LGBTQ+) studies and the beliefs and values of those who identify as conventionally religious.

Summary

Personal integration refers to the organic ways people integrate as a function of their personality and other individual characteristics in relationship to the living God. In this chapter, we have surveyed topics we believe are properly located in this domain. We see the cultivation of Christian virtues through emulation of exemplars as the launching point for much personal integration in the psychology-related fields, both in the mental health practice professions and in the scientific areas. We have emphasized that personal Christian integration requires spiritual formation, and we briefly surveyed some of the varieties of Christian spiritual formation approaches Christians use to pursue such growth. We offered a focused discussion on one spiritual formation tradition that appears to have particular salience for the integration task with psychology-related fields at present: the cultivation of a biblically faithful approach to pursuing equity, diversity, inclusion, and social justice. We examined strategies for formation at an implicit *heart* level and to foster Spirit-filled personal integration. Finally, we told the stories of our own life journeys as we pursued the integration project.

As with many areas of diversity, one of the first steps in acquiring competency is developing self-awareness about one's own relationship to the diversity domain. Psychologists with a reflective and self-aware understanding of their own developed spirituality are more likely to appreciate how spirituality can be a salient feature in the lives of clients or research subjects.

Because of common grace, God can work through any agent, even the nonspiritual secular practitioner. However, Christianity brings rich resources for the psychology-related fields. These include:

- a worldview shaped by the Creator's revelation in Word and world,
- a self-awareness of central dimensions of human existence often neglected by secular psychology,
- a vast and global set of institutions and communities motivated and equipped to be resources for caregiving and world impact,
- a long, multimillennial enterprise of crosscultural reflection on the human condition often guided by these providential resources and many efforts at beneficially intervening in that condition,
- the potential for cultivation of the fruits of the Spirit which, when manifested, facilitate healing relationships, and
- the resources of a supernatural Spirit of God who providentially superintends creation and indwells the body of Christ.

We are aware that our stories, and the story of the integration project itself, are just a small part of a larger story of the kingdom of God and how it has impacted and intersected human lives and cultures. We have been much inspired, instructed, and shaped by the stories of others on the kingdom journey and especially by those for whom this journey overlaps our particular career callings. We look forward to the further unfolding of God's kingdom as it interfaces the psychology-related fields and those who constitute them. We are grateful for the blessings brought to suffering humans through the psychology-related fields and aspire to a sanctifying cultivation of those disciplines as forces for healing and holiness in every domain of the lives they impact. We invite those who similarly feel so called to join us in that mission all for the glory of the One who is the Author and Perfecter of the true integration project.

References

American Counseling Association. (2020). *Our vision and mission: ACA's strategic plan.* www.counseling.org/about-us/about-aca/our-mission

Benner, D. G. (1988). *Psychotherapy and the spiritual quest.* Baker Academic.

Benner, D. G. (2005). Intensive soul care: Integrating psychotherapy and spiritual direction. In L. Sperry & E. P. Shafranske (Eds.), *Spiritually oriented psychotherapy* (pp. 287-306). American Psychological Association.

Boa, K. (2001). *Conformed to His image: Biblical and practical approaches to spiritual formation.* Zondervan.

Cannon, M. E., & Smith, A. (Ed.). (2019). *Evangelical theologies of liberation and justice.* InterVarsity Press.

Chan, S. (1998). *Spiritual theology.* InterVarsity Press.

Chandler, D. J. (2014). *Christian spiritual formation: An integrated approach for personal and relational wholeness.* InterVarsity.

Collins, G. (1997). *The rebuilding of psychology: An integration of psychology and Christianity.* Tyndale House.

Decker, E. E., Jr. (1996). A theology of Holy Spirit empowerment. In J. K. Vining & E. E. Decker, Jr. (Eds.), *Soul care: A Pentecostal-Charismatic perspective* (pp. 59-79). Cummings & Hathaway.

Decker, E. E., Jr. (2002). The Holy Spirit in counseling: A review of Christian counseling journal articles (1985-1999). *Journal of Psychology & Theology, 21*(1), 21-28.

Demarest, B. A. (Ed.). (2012). *Four views on Christian spirituality: Four views.* Zondervan.

Dwiwardani, C., & Waters, A. J. (Spring 2015). Fostering cultural humility in Christian clinical psychology programs. *Society for the Psychology of Religion and Spirituality Newsletter, 39,* 4-8.

Foster, R. J. (1978). *Celebration of discipline: The Path to spiritual growth.* Harper Collins Books.

Foster, R. J. (1998). *Streams of living water: Celebrating the great traditions of Christian faith.* Harper.

Fowers, B. (2005). *Virtue and psychology: Pursuing excellence in ordinary practices.* American Psychological Association.

Hall, T., & Coe, J. (2010). *Psychology in the Spirit: Contours of a transformational psychology.* InterVarsity.

Hays, J. D. (2003). *From every people and nation: A Biblical theology of race.* InterVarsity Press.

Hook, J. N., Davis, D. E., Owen, J., Worthington, E. L., Jr., & Utsey, S. O. (2013). Cultural humility: Measuring openness to culturally diverse clients. *Journal of Counseling Psychology, 60,* 353-66. doi:10.1037/a0032595.

Kahneman, D. (2011). *Thinking fast and slow.* Farrar, Straus, & Giroux.

Knapp, S., Gottlieb, M. C., & Handelsman, M. M. (2017). Self-awareness questions for effective psychotherapists: Helping good psychotherapists become even better. *Practice Innovations, 2*(4), 163-72. doi.org/10.1037/pri0000051

Mallet, R. K., & Monteith, M. J. (Eds.). (2019). *Confronting prejudice and discrimination: The science of changing minds and behaviors.* Academic Press.

McNeil, J. D., & Pozzi, C. (2006). Developing multicultural competency. In Carolyn Porter, Alvaro L. Nieves, and Robert J. Priest (Eds.), *This side of heaven: Race, ethnicity, and the Christian faith* (pp. 81-94). Oxford University Press.

McRay, B., Yarhouse, M. A., & Butman, R. E. (2016). *Modern psychopathologies: A comprehensive Christian appraisal* (2nd ed.). IVP Academic.

Messmore, R. (2010). Real social justice. First Things. Retrieved from "https://www .firstthings.com/web-exclusives/2010/11/real-social-justice" www.firstthings.com /web-exclusives/2010/11/real-social-justice.

Moon, G. (2009). *Apprenticeship with Jesus: Learning to live like the Master*. Baker Books.

Moon, G., & Benner, D. G. (2004). *Spiritual direction and the care of souls: A guide to Christian approaches and practices*. InterVarsity Press.

Moriarty, G. L. (Ed.). (2010). *Integrating faith and psychology: Twelve psychologists tell their stories*. InterVarsity Press.

Murphy, W. (2018). Distinguishing diversity from inclusion in the workplace: Legal necessity or common sense conclusion? *Journal of Business Diversity, 18* (4), 65-83.

National Association of Social Workers. (2020). *Social Justice*. www.socialworkers.org /Advocacy/Social-Justice.

Neff, M. A., & McMinn, M. R. (2020). *Embodying integration: A fresh look at Christianity in the therapy room*. InterVarsity.

Paradise, B. (2014). How critical race theory marginalizes the African American Christian tradition. *Michigan Journal of Law and Race, 20*, 117-211.

Pennock, R. T., & O'Rourke, M. O. (2017). Developing a scientific virtue-based approach to science ethics training. *Science and Engineering Ethics, 23*, 242-63.

Schaeffer, F. A. (1976). *How should we then live? The rise and decline of Western thought and culture*. Crossway Books.

Smith, J. K. A. (2009). *Desiring the kingdom: Worship, worldview, and cultural formation*. Baker Books.

Statement on Social Justice and the Gospel. (2018, September 4). Retrieved from https:// statementonsocialjustice.com/wp-content/uploads/2018/09/SSJG-FINAL.pdf.

Tan, S. Y. (2001). Integration and beyond: Principled, professional, and personal. *Journal of Psychology & Christianity, 20*(1), 18-28.

Tan, S. Y. (2011). *Counseling and psychotherapy: A Christian perspective*. Baker Books.

Thomas, G. (2000). *Sacred pathways: Discover your soul's path to God*. Zondervan.

Volf, M. (2019). *Exclusion and embrace, revised and updated: A theological exploration of identity, otherness, and reconciliation*. Abingdon.

White, R. E. O. (2017). Sanctification. In D. J. Treier & W. E. Elwell (Eds.), *Evangelical dictionary of theology*, (2nd ed.), (pp. 770-72). Baker.

Willard, D. (1988). *The Spirit of the disciplines: Understanding how God changes lives*. Harper Collins Books.

Willard, D. (2002). *Renovation of the heart: Putting on the character of Christ*. NavPress.

Willard, D. (2021). *Spiritual formation: What it is and how it is done*. https://dwillard.org /articles/spiritual-formation-what-it-is-and-how-it-is-done

Wolterstorff, N. (2008). *Justice: Rights and wrongs*. Princeton University.

Wolterstorff, N. (2013). *Journey toward justice: Personal encounters in the Global South*. Baker Books.

Yarhouse, M. A. (2015). *Understanding gender dysphoria: Navigating transgender issues in a changing culture*. IVP Academic.

Yarhouse, M. A. (2019). *Sexual identity and faith: Helping clients achieve congruence*. The Templeton Foundation.

Yarhouse, M. A., & Sells, J. (2017). *Family therapies: A comprehensive Christian appraisal* (2nd ed.). IVP Academic.

Yarhouse, M. A., & Tan, E. S. N. (2014). *Sexuality & sex therapy: A comprehensive Christian appraisal.* IVP Academic.

Zagzebski, L. (1999). *Phronesis* and Christian belief. In G. Brüntrup, R. K. Tacelli (Eds.), *The rationality of theism: Studies in philosophy and religion, 19.* Springer.

Zagzebski, L. (2017). *Exemplarist moral theory.* Oxford University Press.

GLOSSARY

a priori **limiting principle.** An interpretative belief or practice that assumes, independent of or prior to review of the Scripture on some topic, that the scope of inspired biblical truth does not make assertions about the area of reality represented by the topic. Proponents of such a view will not look to the Bible to find knowledge about those areas they believe are outside of the biblical scope.

adjunctive intervention. A treatment approach or activity that is formally separate from the treatment activities conducted in the treatment session but is intended to enhance treatment outcome. In integrative practice, this may involve things such as having a socially isolated depressed religious patient attend an intentionally selected home group at their church.

against model. A model of the relationship between psychology and theology described by Carter and Narramore in which either psychology or theology is rejected as offering anything of value. The sacred against model rejects psychology and views theology as sufficient for understanding of persons. The secular against model rejects theology as unscientific and inferior to the understanding offered by psychology.

alien meaning. A linguistic meaning that is outside of what would occur to a reader based on their prior personal, social, and cultural uses of language.

applied integration. The attempt to either culturally adapt or accommodate secular interventions or helping approaches for use with a Christian population or to develop explicitly Christian interventions and helping approaches derived from Christian thought and practice.

assimilation. In Hathaway's interpretative-process model of integration, assimilation refers to a process in which one understands a theological or psychological concept entirely in terms of ideas from one of the disciplines. In Piagetian terms, one of the disciplines provides schema, and the concepts from the other discipline are understood as fitting entirely within that schema. Such integration does not expand one's basic understandings but rather treats the integrative insights as further instances of prior concepts. For instance, if a psychologist sees religious discussion of sin or evil merely as instances of egoistic or antisocial behavior, they would be assimilating theology into psychological understandings.

attending to distance. A hermeneutical strategy that requires the person to focus on what does not fit well into one's prior understanding of something one is trying to understand.

By focusing on those often-subtle areas of ambiguity and resisting the urge to jump to a comfortable conclusion that fits one's preconceptions, the probability of achieving new interpretative insights is enhanced.

biblical counseling. An approach to counseling that is aimed at providing counseling derived or constructed from teachings of Scripture. The biblical counseling movement has a range of views on how exclusively such counseling derives from Scripture or whether it is open to insights from the contemporary mental health professions, but it commonly has little use for counseling techniques or approaches emerging from the latter.

biblical theology. An area of theology that attempts to understand all of Scripture in light of unfolding and unifying themes present within and across Scripture itself. Biblical theologies of the kingdom of God or of the plan of redemption are two common examples.

Christian organizational consulting. Applications of organizational-business consulting psychology or industrial-organizational psychology to Christian organizations, such as with missionary selection, congregation climate assessment, or Christian leadership coaching.

Christian psychology. (1) A term sometimes used to refer in general to explicitly integrative approaches to psychology utilized by psychologists who are Christians. (2) A worldview-based approach to psychology that is critical of mainstream psychology because of its basis in a secular worldview that results in some significant distortions. It seeks to reinterpret the good of mainstream psychology according to a Christian worldview and, where possible, to develop distinctly Christian psychological theory, research, and clinical practice, beginning with the psychological resources of the Bible and the Christian traditions. This approach is sometimes called the *Christian psychology movement* and includes transdisciplinary contributions by Christians with psychological, philosophical, and theological training.

Christian theism. A worldview broadly shared among all major historical Christian traditions. Some of its key features include trinitarian theism with the corollary that personhood and relationality are objective and eternal parts of being, the idea that humans are made in the image of God and all possess human dignity and worth as a result, the notion of sin implying that there is something foundationally defective in the current human state, the idea that defect due to sin has consequences that can be overcome only by the work of Christ on the cross, and the notion that all of history is directed toward an eternal outcome in which all humans have a part and purpose.

clinical integration. Applied integration in the clinical context. This frequently takes the form of Christian accommodations of standard treatments or the formulation of treatments derived from Christian thought and practice.

compatibility. According to Farnsworth, compatibility is a process that attempts to integrate by identifying and relating findings from each discipline that are convergent to provide an enriched understanding of a common area of interest.

complementarianism. An approach to integration that assumes psychological and theological understandings provide discrete understandings in which the explanatory power of both accounts cannot be preserved by eliminating either one or replacing them with some single other account. This integration approach is also often called a *level-of-analysis* model of integration.

complementarity. In Farnsworth's model, an integration process is complementary if it attempts to correlate findings on similar topics without any expectation that theological and psychological claims will always be about the same things or even focus on similar aspects of the same topics they may both embrace. Thus, no unified single account may result but rather a complex account with simultaneously valid psychological and theological perspectives.

concordism. A theological perspective that argues that the truths revealed by God both in Scripture (Word) and in nature (world) offer overlapping accounts of creation and are ultimately consistent (i.e., concordant). Hard concordism holds that there are many truth statements in Scripture about the natural world and therefore the Bible provides substantial knowledge pertaining to things such as natural history or human psychological functioning. On this view, it is possible that scientific claims about human origins or functions could run into frequent conflicts with those derived from the Bible. Soft concordism holds that there is overlap between what can be known from Scripture and from the world but that God did not intend to give us extensive scientific knowledge through Scripture. Consequently, the opportunity for conflict is smaller for soft than for hard concordism.

conformability. As described by Farnsworth, conformability is an integrative process in which psychological findings or theories are transformed or reworked from a Christian perspective. This approach is broader than *credibility* because the standard is not merely whether the psychological concept is in accord with a biblical teaching but whether it can conform to Christian concepts drawn from the broader domain of Christian theology.

congruence. A coherence or fit between one's phenomenal experience and one's self-concept. Rogerian thought has typically emphasized the functional importance of organismic congruence, a coherence between one's bodily impulses/desires and one's self-understanding. The notion of *telic* congruence focuses on the fit between one's ideals and one's self-understanding.

constructivism. A theory that holds that humans create or "construct" knowledge by actively employing what they bring with them to the learning task. A strong version of constructivism views all knowledge claims as *merely* human creations; thus they cannot be objectively assessed in terms of their correspondence to any external reality.

convertibility. In Farnsworth's model, convertibility is an integrative process in which theological concepts can be accepted, but only when "converted" or reconceptualized on purely psychological terms.

credibility. An integrative process described by Farnsworth in which psychological findings are accepted only if they are consistent with what is taught from Scripture.

cultural humility. An interpersonal stance in which one appreciates and is respectful toward the cultural differences of others. In order to effectively adopt this stance one must also cultivate an abiding self-awareness of the imprint of one's own culture in order to check biases, avoid prejudicial inferences, and resist blind spots that may otherwise be present.

culture war. A concept used to explain sociological conflicts between competing groups in society who are vying for their values and perspectives to gain dominance over rival ones. Culture warring sees such conflict in grave terms and seeks victory over the rival views rather than coexistence or compromise.

dualism. Dualism argues that two irreducible types of phenomenon or substance are needed to explain human persons. Substance dualists believe that humans consist of both a material body and immaterial soul or mind. Property dualists hold that humans consist of only one type of substance, but that through emergence or another path mental properties exist that cannot be fully explained or reduced to the brain processes with which they may correlate.

embodied integration. An approach to integration that emphasizes the centrality of the body for our conceptions of human personhood and functioning. A common feature of embodiment approaches is an emphasis on holism. This view is frequently contrasted with both cognitivist and Platonic views of the person. Embodied integration models have been proposed both by those who adopt a physicalist view of the soul or mind and by those who are dualists.

emergentism. A view of reality that asserts the whole can be greater than the sum of the parts. Emergentists, such as Sperry, have argued that under sufficiently complex arrangements physical reality can display characteristics that go beyond what is evident in any of the component substances. Examples of proposed emergent properties include consciousness or free will.

exemplarist personal integration. An approach to personal integration inspired by virtue ethics. This approach seeks to develop personal virtues that instantiate integration by emulating integration exemplars. An integration exemplar is someone who has well-demonstrated faithful and effective habits of Christian integration in some aspect of their own lives.

expanded horizon. An outcome of the interpretative process in which human understanding is enhanced in its ability to grasp truth by creative extension/transformation of one's prior understandings after faithfully understanding new horizons.

explicit cognition. Cognitive processes that are conscious to the subject or others and that can be articulated through formal representations, such as being put into spoken words. Explicit cognition typically involves relatively slower cognitive activities that are intentionally regulated by higher-order cortical processes.

explicit integration. A form of applied integration in which a treatment technique declares itself to be Christian, or that utilizes a recognizable technique shaped by Christian thought or practice.

fact-value dichotomy. An intellectual perspective common since the Enlightenment that makes a sharp distinction between the knowledge status of claims about the natural world and claims about morality or beauty (i.e., value). On such an account, science deals with facts while issues of value, such as those involved in religious or moral claims, are merely statements of human preference.

grand theory. An abstract and overarching theoretical account of a large range of phenomenon. Examples of grand theories in psychology include psychoanalytic theory or behaviorism.

hermeneutical-process model. An approach to integration proposed by Hathaway that sees integration as an interpretative process. The model proposes that different approaches and integrative postures may be required for competent integration at different moments in the understanding process. On such a view, integrators should not uniformly reflect a particular type of integration but should engage in interpretation processes that are faithful to the specifics of what one is intending to integrate.

hermeneutics. The study of interpretative understanding and the process of interpretation. While originally focused on the interpretation of particular kinds of texts, such as the Bible or legal documents, philosophical hermeneutics has emerged in recent centuries as a general account of all human understanding.

horizon of understanding. A concept from hermeneutics that refers to all that can be perceived or understood from an individual's particular historical, linguistic, personal, and cultural situation.

humanizer of science. An approach to recast the social sciences to make them more compatible with a robust view of persons. Typically, such proposals argue for research methodologies that are less reductive and more informed by the humanities to allow for human meaning and phenomenal experience to be more richly studied.

implicit cognition. Cognitive processes that tend to operate based on relatively fast associational and other patterns. Such processes are sometimes described as "precognitive" because they may occur outside of conscious awareness and subjects may not even be aware of their operation.

implicit integration. A form of applied integration present when standard practice approaches are used in a way that is guided by Christian beliefs or values despite there being no explicit Christian identification.

integration. In the context of the integration project, the term *integration* has been used to summarize various attempts to interrelate the secular disciplines and Christianity. In this text, *integration* is broadly used to describe efforts at fostering faithfully Christian thinking and approaches to disciplines and professional cultures that have become distinct from theology in the contemporary era.

integration project. A set of efforts to put together Christian faith and contemporary psychology that have been increasingly explicitly pursued by Christians after professional training and academia became more secular and post-Christian in the twentieth century.

integrative domains. Different historically situated spheres of life (i.e., areas of human thought, practice, culture, experience) within which Christians must find ways to faithfully function as Christian disciples if they are to submit every area of life to the lordship of Christ.

integrative module. A discrete component to treatment or counseling that is explicitly Christian and that can be incorporated in a professionally defensible way within standard treatment approaches in the field. Examples include adding a session on extending behavioral management training to church and youth ministry contexts to a parent training program, or adding a granting of grace to one's spouse component to relationship enhancement training.

integrative process. An account of the series of actions, steps, or strategies used in a particular approach to integration to attempt to interrelate aspects of Christianity and a psychological field. Farnsworth, Eck, and others have offered descriptions of multiple integrative processes.

integrative protocols. An entire treatment approach in counseling or psychotherapy that has been developed from an explicitly Christian framework or understanding. Integrative protocols detail how the treatment is to be conducted from beginning to end and may be manualized. Some have also been researched and are to varying degrees evidence based.

integrative techniques. A specific intervention that has been either drawn from an explicitly Christian practice or understanding or modified to conform to one, which may be used at any point to augment treatment. Examples might include clinical use of prayer, a Christian meditation, a forgiveness intervention, and bibliotherapy with Christian literature.

intentional integration. An applied integration approach defined by Tan (2001) as "prayerfully depending on the Holy Spirit to lead and guide the therapeutic session, using implicit or explicit integration or both in a professionally competent, ethically responsible and clinically sensitive way for the benefit and growth of the client" (p. 21).

interdisciplinary. In the wake of the fragmentation of academic fields into specialized disciplines, interdisciplinary pursuits attempt to study phenomena that may be of joint concern to multiple disciplines by fostering shared and integrative scholarly projects spanning those different disciplines. For example, the contemporary field of cognitive science draws from the disciplines of neuroscience, linguistics, cognitive psychology, computer science, and philosophy.

levels of analysis. See complementarianism.

limiter of science. A label used by Evans to describe those who believe that science can only inform us about a subset of truths about humanity or the world. Thus, science cannot be looked to as the only source of truth, and other sources of knowledge are needed to know about that which is outside of the limits of science. Evans identifies two types of limiters of science: *territorialists* and *perspectivalists*.

linear model of science. An understanding of science that makes a sharp division between basic and applied science. In this view, knowledge is discovered in basic or *pure* science and then later used for practical applications in the applied sciences.

local theoretical integration. A model of integration that proposes theoretical integrations that are delimited to much smaller ranges of psychological functioning than is found in areas such as personality theories. So for instance, a Christian model of self-regulation theory may be offered rather than an entire Christian theory of motivation.

manipulative integrative paradigm. According to Eck's metatheoretical model of integration, the manipulative paradigm represents an approach to integration that attempts to change understandings from psychology, theology, or both to allow for a single combined account. Manipulative integrators achieve this by transforming or reconstructing aspects of each discipline to allow for a synthesis.

multidisciplinary. A scholarly engagement with a topic that simultaneously involves multiple disciplines but with no systematic attempt to generate an overarching approach that represents an interdisciplinary synthesis.

narrative theory. An approach to human thought that sees it as embedded in and regulated by the internal story generated by people to make sense of their own existence. On this view, what may count as a sufficient reason for an action or judgment depends on what fits with one's narrative.

naturalism. A worldview that asserts that all that exists are natural objects or their properties. Because of this, supernatural explanations or postulates are rejected. Humans are viewed as fully a part of nature, and all sources of value and purpose must be limited to what can be experienced within the natural world. Most commonly, naturalism adopts hedonistic ethics—the idea that the only real good is the maximizing of pleasure and the minimizing of pain. Materialistic naturalism adopts a reductive view of humanity, holding humans to be entirely determined parts of the natural order. A corollary of this view is that many aspects of human experience are viewed as illusions, including consciousness and free will. Humanistic naturalism retains the belief that human existence can be explained entirely on natural terms but attempts to argue for a more robust and less reductive humanism.

nonintegrative paradigm. In Eck's metatheoretical model of integration, a nonintegrative paradigm is present when either psychological or theological understandings or claims are rejected and only one of the two areas is accepted or seen as relevant. In such a paradigm, the nonaccepted area is *rejected* and thus there is no need for further integration.

nonmanipulative integrative paradigm. According to Eck, nonmanipulative integrative paradigms see value in both Christianity and psychology but do not attempt to alter either to fit them together. Those operating within a nonmanipulative paradigm attempt to integrate by correlating ideas from Christianity and psychology or offering an account that unifies both without distorting or changing them.

nonreductive physicalism. A version of physicalism that accepts that humans consist entirely of physical substance but that also holds that humans are so constituted that our bodies generate mental and other properties that cannot be explained entirely in terms of the substances that make them up. Typically, such views adopt a variety of emergentism, arguing that the whole is greater than the sum of the parts.

nothing buttery. A term used by Crabb to refer to reductionism.

objectivism. The regulative idea that objective reality exists and progress toward its knowledge occurs through the use of particular knowing methods. In the modern era, science was most often advanced as the best way to achieve objective knowledge.

objectivity. A strict view of objectivity understands it as a characteristic of beliefs present when those beliefs accurately reflect what is the case independent of subjective bias. Softer variants of objectivity, such as that offered by Polanyi, see objectivity as the personal commitment to conform one's beliefs to the object one is studying.

panpsychism. A view that mind or mindlike qualities are an inherent part of all substance. When substances are arranged in the form of a functioning human brain, a human mind is the result. But even the smallest, isolated particles are characterized by some form of mindedness on a panpsychist view.

pantheistic monism. A worldview that holds that all reality is one undivided divine consciousness. The common human perception of a universe consisting of separate things and selves is thought to be an illusion. Such illusions are held to arise from karmic patterns and eventually balance out to allow all seemingly separate beings to return to their shared and unified consciousness as the one transpersonal mind.

parallels model. An approach to psychology represented by Christians who consider the explicit forms of the Christian life as distinct from one's conduct as a psychologist. Such a Christian would likely act indistinguishably from non-Christian psychologists during their practice hours or in their lab.

personal integration. The personal discipleship journey of the Christian who is a psychologist (or by extension a member of any similar profession).

personalism. Any perspective that holds that persons exist as real and irreducible beings possessing qualities that cannot be explained away as illusions. The reduction-resistant qualities of persons include their innate dignity and value, agency, and some degree of authentic self-determination, and possession of an inherent point of view (i.e., something it is like to be a particular person).

perspectivalism. An approach that holds that different ways of looking at or, perhaps more accurately, *describing* the world may be equally valid at the same time. In regard to at least some phenomena, multiple accounts constructed at different, nonreducible levels may be needed to give a full account.

physicalism. A view of reality that asserts only physical substances and their properties exist. This perspective is also frequently referred to as *materialism*.

post-Christian. A concept often used in historical or sociological studies that describes a loss of Christian cultural dominance in formerly Christian societies.

postmodernism. In regard to worldviews, postmodernism refers to a group of perspectives that emerged by the late twentieth century that are defined in opposition to modern worldviews. Where modernism heralded science as a highly confident path to progress and objective knowledge, postmodern views are skeptical of any confident claims to objective knowledge, scientific or otherwise. Postmodern views also tend to be cynical about claims to progress, seeing such claims as an oppressive narrative generated by some to promote the dominance of their form of life. In place of a preference for grand theories that attempt to offer universal explanations for human life, postmodernism typically seeks to provide summaries of more local areas of life, giving particular attention to voices that have been historically underrepresented.

productive tension. An interpretative posture in which a person suspends judgment about different claims that appear in conflict without any hasty resolution through a judgment that fails to fully consider any aspect of what is being claimed. By holding on to this tension but still looking for resolution, transformative insight may result in the truth from both perspectives being integrated into an expanded understanding.

professional ethics. A code of conduct that delineates behaviors and ethical decision-making processes expected of members of a particular profession. In countries with regulated mental health professions, it is standard for people who decide to enter such professions to agree to follow a formally adopted professional code.

psychology of religion. The psychological study of religion and religion-related aspects of human functioning. The psychology of religion does not presuppose any religious point of view and has been an area of psychological investigation since the earliest decades of contemporary psychology. While psychology of religion may provide useful contributions to integration, it does not have the integration of psychology and Christianity, or any other faith, as its goal. On the other hand, religiously integrative work in psychology may result in psychology of religion work, such as studying the possible connection between early attachment patterns and perceived God attachment or God image.

qualitative research. Research strategies that primarily examine nonnumerical data, such as natural language samples, in an attempt to understand aspects of human experience and the subjective meanings people make of their experience. First-person interviews, surveys, questionnaires, participant observations, and other strategies are used to generate data-thick subject records. Multiple qualitative research models have been developed that specify the investigative methods and goals of such an inquiry and guide the analysis of the qualitative data in such records. Qualitative methodologies have traditionally been aimed at accurately describing and understanding phenomena.

quantitative research. Research strategies that primarily analyze numerical data produced by measures of various aspects of human or animal functioning that are argued to be reliable and valid. Depending on the research method employed, quantitative research may be aimed at identifying the incidence of certain phenomena in a sample or context, specifying the degree of relationship between variables, predicting psychological outcomes, or inferring causal relationships through experimentation.

Quine-Duhem thesis. A thesis in the philosophy of science that asserts the impossibility of any crucial empirical tests of scientific theories. A crucial empirical test is one that is designed to either prove or disprove a theory. According to the thesis, even if a plausible test is created, the theory proponent can always call into question some auxiliary hypothesis that the test relies on to test the theory. For instance, a test skeptic could challenge the validity of the measures or point out the possibility of confounding factors that were not controlled in the study.

realism. A view about the nature of knowledge and existence that asserts there is a human mind-independent reality and that knowledge requires accurate beliefs about that reality. *Naive realism* holds that humans are able, in at least some cases, to know the world directly as it is in itself. In these instances, humans have a mental picture of the world that accurately pictures the world. *Critical realism* asserts that there is a mind-independent reality that humans can know truly but only indirectly. What humans know directly, on this account, is the way the world appears in the mind. Human perceptions are constructed from sensory input organized by *a priori* habits of mind. Humans have true knowledge of the world when the mental pictures they construct from the sensory input adequately approximate the external aspects of the world being known. *Common-sense realism* also holds that there is a mind-independent reality that humans can know. However, common-sense realism denies that this reality is known by humans forming a mental picture that accurately resembles or represents the external reality. Rather, human minds know the world when truths about the world being known are accurately detected through human senses and inferences. The mental image is more of a readout on the world that conveys information than it is a pictorial copy. *Nonrealists* deny either that mind-independent realities exist or that we can have any knowledge of them.

reductionism. An explanatory approach that attempts to explain one level of reality in terms of an allegedly lower or more basic level of reality. Some reductions treat the higher-level reality as an illusion and thus attempt to *eliminate* any need for description or language based on the higher level through the explanation. Other reductions may find value in preserving some aspect of the higher-level discourse but only by reconceptualizing it in ways that are explained by the more basic level of reality.

reinterpreter. According to Evans, an integration approach that attempts to relate psychology and Christianity in one of two ways. The first, *capitulation*, occurs when concepts from a less preferred perspective are reconceptualized in terms of concepts from the preferred perspective. The second way is to attempt to demonstrate that both perspectives are really talking about the same sorts of things by identifying concepts that closely correlate with each other from Christianity and psychology.

relativism. A view of truth or of ethics that asserts nothing is universally true or good or bad. Relativism typically denies that objective factual or moral truths exist. Truth and goodness are usually asserted to be social conventions or customs.

religious coping. Attempts to deal with negative events and other life stressors using religious beliefs, practices, or social resources or other aspects of religion and spirituality.

religiously accommodative treatment. A modification of a standard treatment to include explicit religious elements tailored to a particular religion. An example is the use of Scripture and biblical-themed rationales for cognitive interventions in Christian cognitive-behavioral therapy.

religiously sensitive clinical practice. Standard clinical practice that is mindful and engaging about client-generated religious concerns or considerations. Such practice is often reflected in asking religious or spiritual screening questions during a clinical interview proportional to the number of probes aimed at other psychosocial domains. If probe responses or spontaneous client comments generate a clinically relevant religious content, religiously sensitive clinical practice will also continue to track the religious theme as long as it is clinically useful.

role conflict. A type of intrapersonal and sometimes interpersonal tension that arises when a person experiences opposing demands arising from simultaneous roles they hold. Role theory has further specified different forms this role conflict can take. *Role overload* may arise when too great a number of expectations are present at the same time. *Role malintegration* occurs when multiple roles do not fit well together. When individuals must engage in a sequence of malintegrated roles, then *role discontinuity* occurs.

role formation. The psychosocial process by which roles are created and maintained. When an individual enters an established profession, they are typically socialized into the profession and thus taught by example, explicit instruction, prescription, and in some cases regulatory codes to enact a predefined role. This reflects the reactive and status quo maintaining aspect of role formation in which an existing role is imprinted on an emerging professional. But in addition, professionals can sometimes proactively shape roles through processes of governance, standards, and policy formation that exist in most professions. In this latter more proactive case, a professional engages in a new role formation process for the broader profession.

role integration. The attempt to live out in integrity role expectations and patterns arising from a psychological vocation in a particular context in a way that is simultaneously faithful to one's Christian identity.

scope of Scripture. The range of reality about which Scripture offers inspired truths.

separate but equal. A label used by Crabb for an approach to Christianity and psychology that sees them as both equally valid but distinct and nonoverlapping domains that should not be mixed.

social justice. A society state present when political, economic, and social goods and opportunities are fairly distributed to all.

spiritual formation. A process of spiritual development aimed at producing Christian believers who are better shaped into the image of Christ and who have lives more consistently Spirit led and empowered. Spiritual formation practices, strategies, and approaches are diverse and have been shaped by different Christian traditions and spiritual formation streams.

spiritual practice audit. A spiritual self-assessment technique proposed by Smith (2009) aimed at helping us identify our motivational desires by reflecting on questions about the habits, time, and rituals that most characterize our lives.

spiritually oriented practice. A phrase sometimes used to identify spiritually sensitive and accommodative mental health treatment that is less explicitly connected to accommodations of aspects of organized, conventional religions. While spiritually oriented practice may include accommodations of specific religious traditions, such as Christian cognitive-behavioral therapy, it may also utilize spiritual accommodations that do not profess any specific religious connection, such as in some forms of mindfulness interventions.

spoiling the Egyptians. A metaphor used by Crabb to convey the legitimacy of mining secular domains of learning for useful truths. The metaphor alludes to the collection of bounty from the Egyptians given to the Israelites as they left the land of Egypt.

sufficiency of Scripture. In the context of biblical counseling, the notion that Scripture is sufficient for all that is needed to provide counseling. This position frequently argues that passages such as 2 Peter 1:3 or 2 Timothy 3:1-13 imply this notion. Detractors of this doctrine argue that the biblical counseling sufficiency doctrine is an eisegetical misreading of the Scriptures that also is at odds with Christian tradition.

systematic theology. A type of theology that attempts to provide a comprehensive and coherent account of Christian theological teachings.

teleology. A perspective that focuses on the purpose or the end (i.e., telos) to which something is directed rather than its causes.

territorialism. A term Evans used for the view that science is limited in the sorts of things about which it can provide knowledge. Territorialists believe there are some types of objects that science cannot study, such as with Descartes's view of the immaterial mind.

theoretical integration. The attempt to modify psychological theories, especially personality theories, to fit with a Christian theological understanding, to cultivate psychological theories from the soil of Christian thought in a way that enhances psychological theory building, or to use psychological understandings to inform theology.

theory pluralism. A perspective that abandons efforts to develop single grand theories to explain large areas of functioning but instead holds that multiple smaller, more delimited theories offer more scientific utility.

tossed salad. A metaphor used by Crabb to describe an approach to integration that mixes spiritual and secular psychological techniques together in a course of treatment but without either technique losing its distinctiveness.

transformational psychology. A model of the relationship between psychology and Christianity that reconstrues their interface as a spiritual formation project rather than as integration. The model asserts that the proper interrelationship of these two areas requires the spiritual-emotional transformation of the psychologist so that resulting psychology will be Spirit led.

transpersonal psychology. A psychological perspective consisting of an eclectic and diverse range of theoretical understandings that tend to focus on the spiritual and consciousness-altering aspects of human existence. Transpersonal psychologies have often been drawn to aspects of the worldview of pantheistic monism and to New Age spiritual practices.

unity of truth. A view that all truths fit together in a coherent and noncontradictory way. This has sometimes been asserted to be an implication of objectivism. If there is a single mind-independent reality and knowledge consists in accurately representing that reality, then all true claims about the world must fit together. A Christian basis for the unity of truth concept has frequently been summarized by the phrase *all truth is God's truth*. The idea is that all truth represents truths revealed by God either through special revelation in Scripture or through the providentially provided knowledge faculties he has given us to detect truths in the world. Since the omniscient God is author of all truths found in either source and since he does not lie, humans can expect all truths to ultimately cohere.

way of the exile. An approach to being a Christian in a non- or post-Christian context that is modeled after the way God instructed the ancient Jewish exiles in Babylon to live while in exile. Jeremiah instructed them to seek the welfare of the people in whose foreign city they were living. If their captors prospered, the Jews would prosper (Jeremiah 29:7). This strategy is often depicted as an alternative to culture warring.

worldview integration. The attempt to reposition psychology with a cognitive frame that is coherently embedded within Christian thought and premised on Christian assumptions. This typically involves the identification of the alternative worldviews informing and shaping psychology and a rethinking of how psychology is altered or informed when grounded in a biblical worldview.

worldview repositioning. An approach to worldview integration that holds there is something incomplete or biased in a psychologically related field that operates on non-Christian starting points. Worldview repositioners usually argue for a transformational repositioning of the field on explicitly Christian foundations.

GENERAL INDEX

and pursuing growth, and we felt we should heed the advice of our Christian mentors. So, I headed off to college at Taylor University.

Taylor University, a Christian school, offered a specialization in the integration of psychology and Christianity. Located in a small Midwestern town, I found it was possible to insulate oneself in a Christian subculture while there. My wife and I started a small street ministry with disaffected and largely secular youth in a neighboring community. Our experiences in that setting would later influence both of our professional careers. I developed a specialty with clinical child psychology, and my wife became a public school teacher who spent her career working in urban settings with predominantly at-risk youth. We both viewed our secular work as a continuation of the call God placed on our lives during those early years. My personal integrative journey in psychology began as a subdomain of my growth and discipleship as a Christian with a felt calling to serve those marginalized in society.

I left Taylor to complete a master's degree in philosophy at a secular college—Bowling Green State University—before eventually entering my doctoral studies in psychology. I had become convinced that philosophy was a missing link in the integration literature at that time. It was a vital tool to allow me to, as Gary Collins (1977) had put it, "rebuild" my psychology on a biblical worldview. Bowling Green's philosophy program was unique in that it focused on applied philosophy. It was a degree committed entirely to the integration of academic philosophy with contemporary praxis in other disciplines. I saw its multi- and interdisciplinary integrative training as directly relevant to my goal of integrating psychology and Christianity. I was able to complete an internship in a psychology setting as a philosophy student, and I did my thesis providing an ethical defense of resource collaboration between religious institutions and secular mental health organizations. The thesis allowed me to bring together my secular studies with a systematic review of relevant Christian literature on psychology.

I chose to stay at Bowling Green for my graduate studies to work with Dr. Ken Pargament. Dr. Pargament was one of the few psychologists at that time working in a secular setting who had an active research program in the psychology of religion. In particular, he was researching the way people engage religious faith in coping with life's demands. This work fascinated me. I thought by looking at how people of faith cope, I would be most likely to find a professionally valid way to bring the resources of faith into the practice setting. My work at Taylor had been heavy on theoretical and worldview integration. In the religion and

SCRIPTURE INDEX

An Association for Christian Psychologists,
Therapists, Counselors and Academicians

CAPS is a vibrant Christian organization with a rich tradition. Founded in 1956 by a small group of Christian mental health professionals, chaplains and pastors, CAPS has grown to more than 2,100 members in the U.S., Canada and more than 25 other countries.

CAPS encourages in-depth consideration of therapeutic, research, theoretical and theological issues. The association is a forum for creative new ideas. In fact, their publications and conferences are the birthplace for many of the formative concepts in our field today.

CAPS members represent a variety of denominations, professional groups and theoretical orientations; yet all are united in their commitment to Christ and to professional excellence.

CAPS is a non-profit, member-supported organization. It is led by a fully functioning board of directors, and the membership has a voice in the direction of CAPS.

CAPS is more than a professional association. It is a fellowship, and in addition to national and international activities, the organization strongly encourages regional, local and area activities which provide networking and fellowship opportunities as well as professional enrichment.

To learn more about CAPS, visit www.caps.net.

The joint publishing venture between IVP Academic and CAPS aims to promote the understanding of the relationship between Christianity and the behavioral sciences at both the clinical/counseling and the theoretical/research levels. These books will be of particular value for students and practitioners, teachers and researchers.

For more information about CAPS Books, visit InterVarsity Press's website at www.ivpress.com/christian-association-for-psychological-studies-books-set.